D0391622

Thirsty for God

"**Thirsty for God** *offers a needed beginning text in the history of Christian spirituality. It selects a fine assortment of figures and movements from that vast tradition and offers a brief, simple, balanced view of them with some helpful personal questions and exercises along the way.*"

> **—Tilden Edwards**
> Shalem Institute, Washington, D.C.

"**Thirsty for God** *[is] for those who are seeking to connect their interest in contemporary spirituality with the rich and diverse spiritual traditions of Christianity. . . . Holt's crisp and clear prose as well as his deeply respectful ecumenical perspective make this book a delight to read.*"

> **—Edward C. Sellner**
> College of St. Catherine, St. Paul

Thirsty for God

A Brief History of Christian Spirituality

Second Edition

BRADLEY P. HOLT

FORTRESS PRESS
Minneapolis

THIRSTY FOR GOD
A Brief History of Christian Spirituality, Second Edition

Copyright ©2005 Augsburg Fortress. All rights reserved. Except for brief quotations in critical articles or reviews, no part of this book may be reproduced in any manner without prior written permission from the publisher. Write: Permissions, Augsburg Fortress, Box 1209, Minneapolis, MN 55440.

Scripture quotations are from the New Revised Standard Version Bible, copyright ©1989 by the Division of Christian Education of the National Council of the Churches of Christ in the USA and used by permission.

Photo of Trinity of Uglic by Andrei Rublev (1360–c. 1430) from the Rubliev Museum, Moscow, Russia. ©Scala/Art Resource, NY.

Photo of Celtic Cross by Todd Jones, courtesy of stock.xchng.

Cover image: Sunlight in Pantheon ©Eric Van Den Brulle/Photonica. Used by permission.
Cover Design: Laurie Ingram
Book Design: James Korsmo

Library of Congress Cataloging-in-Publication Data

Holt, Bradley P., 1941–
 Thirsty for God : a brief history of Christian spirituality / Bradley P. Holt.— 2nd ed.
   p. cm.
 Includes bibliographical references and index.
 ISBN 0-8006-3709-7 (alk. paper)
 1. Spirituality—History. I. Title.
 BV4490.H67 2005
 248'.09—dc22

                                                            2004026101

The paper used in this publication meets the minimum requirements of American National Standard for Information Sciences — Permanence of Paper for Printed Library Materials, ANSI Z329.48-1984.

Manufactured in the U.S.A.

09   08   07   06   3   4   5   6   7   8   9   10

Contents

Dedicated to Linda Lystig Holt,
nurse-theorist, philosopher, and theologian

Preface

The book you are holding could change your life in a number of ways. It could inform you about the spiritual tradition of Christianity, if you have not studied it. Whether you count yourself a Christian or not, this will make you more knowledgeable about the spiritual life. Or it could inform you about the way Christians in other cultures walk in the Spirit in our own day. But this book is not simply about *information*. It is about *formation*. It is about the ways our spirits are shaped by the Spirit of God. It is about the discovery of new being, new relationships, and new practices.

This book attempts so much in so few pages. It gives you an accessible sampling of the spirituality of over 100 individuals and spiritual movements, in order to provide a framework for your own further research into those that compel your attention. The book's strength is its breadth: selections from all major denominations, all of history, all continents. Christianity can no longer be regarded as a "Western" religion; this book is intended to be an hors d'oeuvre to increase your hunger for more exploration. Notably it connects the intellectual side of spiritual study to the practical. Every chapter includes suggested practices that are related to the content of the chapter.

This account is designed for both individuals and classes. The first edition of this book proved its worth in many settings for individuals, church groups, college, university, and seminary classes, and programs for spiritual directors. This new Revised and Expanded Edition will serve as an even better resource. It includes new material about Celtic spirituality, medieval women mystics, J. S. Bach, the holiness movement, Oswald Chambers, Thérèse of Lisieux, C. S. Lewis, Henri Nouwen, Rosemary Radford Reuther, Pope Shenoudah III, and Desmond Tutu, among many others. For the first time, the book includes maps to locate the places discussed in the text. The most noticeable change is making the suggestions for spiritual practice more prominent and more numerous.

Thanks to many who have contributed to this revision: my students at Augsburg College, Minneapolis, especially Katelynn Strieff; my colleagues on the Augsburg faculty, especially Bev Stratton, Philip Quanbeck II, Phil Adamo, Mark Tranvik, and Lori Brandt Hale, who read and critiqued portions of the drafts; Louise Lystig Frichtie, Mark Henning, and Olaf Hall-Holt who designed the maps; the Donald and Irene Grangaard Endowment for faculty development at Augsburg College; the librarians at Augsburg's Lindell

Library and the Luther Seminary Library; my editors at Fortress Press, James Korsmo and Michael West; and most of all, my life companion, Linda Lystig Holt, who read the whole manuscript and helped to make it reader-friendly.

Maps

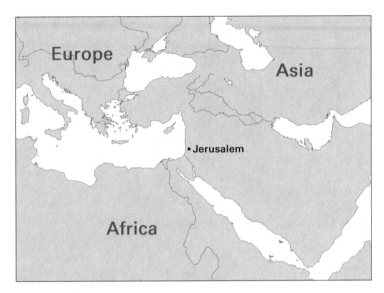

Map 1. Jerusalem in the center (ch. 1)

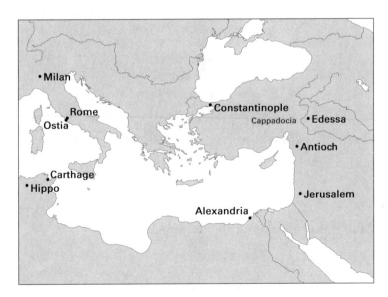

Map 2. East and West in Early Christianity (ch. 4)

Map 3. Europe in the Middle Ages (ch. 5)

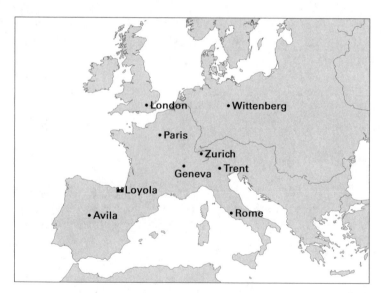

Map 4. Europe during the Reformation (ch. 6)

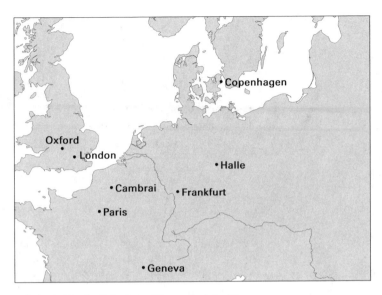

Map 5. Early Modern Europe (ch. 7)

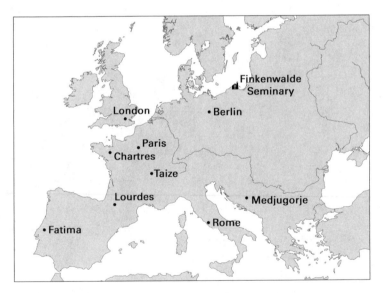

Map 6. Modern Europe (ch. 8)

Maps

Map 7. North America (ch. 8)

Map 8. Latin America (ch. 8)

Map 9. Africa (ch. 9)

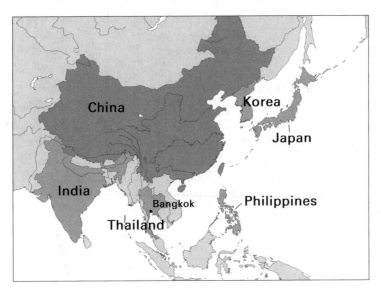

Map 10. Asia (ch. 9)

O God, you are my God;
eagerly I seek you;
my soul thirsts for you,
my flesh faints for you,
as in a barren and dry land
where there is no water.
Psalm 63:1

Ho, everyone who thirsts,
come to the waters;
and you that have no money,
come, buy and eat!
Come, buy wine and milk
without money and without price.
Isaiah 55:1

Jesus . . . cried out, "Let anyone who is thirsty come to me,
and let the one who believes in me drink. As the scripture
has said, 'Out of the believer's heart shall flow rivers
of living water.'"
John 7:37-38

Then the angel showed me the river of the water of life,
bright as crystal, flowing from the throne of God and of the
Lamb through the middle of the street of the city. On either
side of the river is the tree of life with its twelve kinds of
fruit, producing its fruit each month; and the leaves of the
tree are for the healing of the nations.
Revelation 22:1-2

Chapter 1

Spirituality and Christianity

You may be dehydrated right now but not know it. One peculiar feature of our physiology is that the signals for lack of fluid are not immediate and strong. Thus we may feel uneasy or tired when dehydrated but not recognize these symptoms as thirst. By the time we recognize thirst as such, we have already moved through the early stages of dehydration. Why does this matter? It matters because keeping our fluid levels up is vital for our bodies to function in so many important ways: for energy, for healing, for our immune systems, for electrolytes, and yes, even for sex.

So one part of our human predicament is that we do not always know what we really need or long for. Another part is that we find it difficult to act consistently on what we do know. For example, I have had a problem listening to my body. I get tired or listless during the day and take a break to eat, or I get upset or discouraged and I eat. I smile at the refrigerator motto: "If all else fails, eat!" For a long time I did not know that my body craved water, not food. I have discovered that just plain water will usually perk me up better at midmorning or late afternoon than the various combinations of caffeine, sugar, and fat that settle on my front. I have come to recognize thirst as different from hunger and to respond to my body's genuine need, at least some of the time!

One of the basic premises of any spirituality is that our nonphysical selves also thirst. We may not know what we need, and we may try to satisfy our needs with possessions, foods, or relationships that do not satisfy and that may bring dangerous side effects. Christian spirituality identifies what we really long for as the living water of God, fresh and sparkling and pure.

Another way to describe our deeper thirst is as a thirst for love. We long to be loved, to love, and to live in a universe characterized by love. Yet we discover by experience that our longings are never completely fulfilled on the human level. We need God. Paul writes of the love of God as if it were a liquid: "God's love has been poured into our hearts through the Holy Spirit that has been given to us" (Romans 5:5).

A second premise, crucial for Christians, is that God's love actively seeks the thirsty. It is as if wanderers in a dry land were trying to function in a state of dehydration, but they do not recognize the thirst or they try to fulfill their need for water by eating pretzels or potato chips! God in this parable approaches the wanderers in the form of Jesus as a servant, a water carrier, and a guide. He bears the water and points them to a beautiful fountain running over with the water of life.

> There are some things we can learn only in silence.
> —Macrina Wiederkehr, *The Song of the Seed*

Is "Christian Spirituality" an Oxymoron?

For some people, the term *Christian* and the term *spirituality* do not fit together. Many see spirituality as an alternative to Christianity, for they contrast spirituality with religion and they see Christianity as a religion. (To be consistent, this view would seem to exclude the possibility not only of Christian spirituality but of Jewish, Muslim, Hindu, or Buddhist spirituality.) According to this view, religions are restricted to doctrines, creeds, buildings, clergy, and budgets. Such institutions are interested in their own preservation and are not much interested in helping people with their problems.

Such people are eager to learn about spirituality but not about Christianity. They search for a meaningful relationship with the sacred but are put off by what they perceive as an insistence on church attendance, the meager instruction in spiritual techniques, and the impersonal nature of some church life. Other traditions may seem to have a meaningful discipline, an ancient tradition, and an openness to discovery. I ask you, seeking reader, to consider with an open mind whether Christianity may have these very same elements when considered in its wholeness.

Many people have been wounded by the church, by its indifference, its gossip, its sexism or racism. As a member of the Christian community, the church, I grieve the number of people who have experienced rejection from their church. If you are such a person, I invite you to reconsider the validity of the Christian walk on the basis of the Christian spiritualities described in this book. The treasure of the gospel of Jesus is contained in the truly clay pots of his human followers. It is the message of that gospel, and of the Healer to whom it points, that attracts people despite the faults of local and national churches.

Whereas some seekers of the spiritual may be put off by the churches, many Christians, especially pastors and theologians, may be put off by the teachings found in popular books on spirituality. It may seem to them that spirituality is nothing more than the latest fad in self-improvement.

Spirituality is a vague term that people use to include anything they want. For Protestants in particular, the term is unfamiliar; it is not part of the traditional language.

Furthermore, the term *spirituality* looks suspicious to some Christians because it sounds like "do-it-yourself" salvation. If only you do this or that, the books may suggest, you will find fulfillment or self-realization. This seems very different from finding your true self as the result of the grace of God, discovering a path through the universe by living in relationship with a revealing God who surprises the traveler with loving gifts.

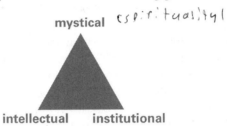

mystical *(spirituality)*

intellectual   institutional

A helpful way of relating spirituality to religion is that of Baron von Hügel, an early-twentieth-century scholar who wrote that religion has three dimensions: the intellectual, the institutional, and the mystical. All three are important for healthy religion.

Today we would call the mystical dimension "spirituality." Thus all who study religion, as I do, would be foolish to leave out the spiritual dimension, for it constitutes the very heart of religion. To put it another way, it is too restrictive to limit religion only to the institutional dimension, as some people seem to do.

So is it appropriate to speak of "Christian spirituality"? Yes, it is. In fact, the term *spirituality* was first used among Christians. One need not be Christian to practice spirituality, but Christianity offers the possibility of a vibrant personal and communal spirituality.

I believe the churches need to listen more to the groups and individuals who are seeking a spirituality. The churches have generally done little to help members or visitors grow in personal disciplines, such as prayer and meditation, or to understand the traditions concerning these central practices. Seminaries sometimes do not teach new clergy how to integrate these matters into their ministries. Adults and young people need to be introduced to a variety of approaches, since not every person functions in the same way. At the same time, support groups are important for personal guidance. Thus churches need to encourage individual exploration and experience of the faith in the context of the church's practice of communal worship.[1]

On the other hand, people in the New Age and Twelve Step groups sometimes sell Christianity short on the basis of limited experience.

Individual seekers of all types would profit from an encounter with the long history of spiritual practice in the Christian church. Like the blind man who touched one part of the elephant, one person's experience is too limited to discover reality. Previous experience through the ages serves as a guide that provides both encouragement and warning. Furthermore, churches that live up to their calling do offer individual seekers the personal community that is essential for balanced Christian spirituality.

Any spirituality depends on a view of reality for its validity. Some views of the spiritual may not be very open about their worldview. In the case of Christianity, that worldview is laid out in its theology, a simple version of which is found in the Apostles' Creed. A healthy spirituality will also be connected to ethics. Any spirituality, whether it claims to be Christian or not, that does not include responsibility toward other people is self-defeating. Seeking a spiritual thrill or high without concern for those who lack food or clothing is spiritual malpractice. Christian spirituality includes more than an introspective search for psychological health; it integrates relationships to God and creation with those to self and others.

Christian spirituality is historical and global. It spans twenty centuries of development, and it involves global connections with others whose cultures are very different from our own. I am convinced that, in teaching about spirituality, the churches and seminaries need to draw on the historic tradition and the sisters and brothers around the world. We need one another!

For example, Henri Nouwen, one of the best-known writers on spirituality in North America, remarks:

> In the free world of the United States, where most of the world's wealth is concentrated, spiritual freedom is often hard to find. Many Christians in the North are imprisoned by their fears and guilt. . . . The spiritual destiny of the people of North America is intimately connected with the spiritual destiny of the people in Latin America. I am increasingly struck by the thought that what is happening in the Christian communities of Latin America is part of God's way of calling us in the North to conversion.[2]

What Nouwen asserts here for North and South America is a specific example of what I am urging for all of us: that each of our continents has challenges—and gifts— for Christians elsewhere. We in the West do have such challenges and gifts to offer, yet it may be true that North America and Western Europe are the most in need of help. More of our churches are lethargic compared to those of Africa, Asia, and Latin America.

Our awareness often is as limited in time as it is in space. We think that the best resources must be found in the latest writer. Rather, we need to look back through the centuries to learn from people of different times as well as of different continents. We need to engage in a conversation with Christians of the past, whose mistakes as well as triumphs challenge our own assumptions and lifestyles.

What You Can Expect from This Book

I am inviting you, the reader, to an intercontinental and intergenerational conversation about spirituality. This book is an attempt to survey the varieties of Christian spirituality both in space and in time. From a twenty-first-century North American perspective, it looks back in time and around the continents to point out what is valuable for contemporary thirsty persons. It tells the multicultural story of Christian history as it relates to spirituality. Along the way, I will offer a perspective on this story while seeking to appreciate aspects of all the streams of Christianity.

After the preliminary consideration of the term *spirituality* and an overview of the Christian community on a global scale provided in this chapter, the discussion will focus on the being, relationships, and practices that constitute spirituality. Then I will describe Jesus Christ and the Bible as they relate to spirituality. The largest part of the book is a very brief description of the early centuries, the medieval age, the reformation, the "modern" period, and the twentieth century. The final chapter will draw together themes and provide suggestions for the future.

I invite you to experience what you are reading about not by simply passively reading but by experimenting with spiritual practices. I have selected and described spiritual exercises that relate to the subjects of each chapter. It is possible to use this book only for *information*, but I encourage you to use it also for *formation*. Fully understanding this particular subject requires actually doing something beyond reading about it—for example, you may experiment with new ways of living. Each person has different needs in terms of practice, and the suggestions provided may widen your span and deepen your experience. Since the proposed practices come from many traditions within Christianity, some may be unfamiliar to you. Stretch your mind, body, and soul!

The historical movements and individuals selected for this book reflect my vision of spirituality. More will be said about this later, but for now, let me indicate some criteria for choosing the subject matter that follows. I have included the most influential figures that any history of Christian spirituality must include—for example, Augustine, Teresa of Avila, John of the Cross. But I have also gone outside the older "canon" to include Protestants and Orthodox as well as Catholics, women writers and leaders, and non-Western Christians.

The Christian spiritual tradition includes some well-known names, but it also includes the ways of countless ordinary folk whose names have been forgotten. Much of this book will recount the stories and writings of the "elite," who have influenced many others by the potency of their devotion and the power of their pens. As Philip Sheldrake's *Spirituality and History* reminds us, interpreting the past is complex and has many pitfalls. One needs to have a critical eye both for the "elite," whose books are remembered, and for the interpreter of the texts, who sees value in those books for the present.[3] What is commonly called "popular piety" is also part of this book. The spirituality that is written about in a spiritual classic both reflects and influences common Christians. Some examples of popular movements in this account include charismatic Christianity, pietism, and Twelve-Step spirituality.

At times I include matters of general history or church history for background, even though these are not strictly matters of spirituality. It is essential to know the context, even if briefly, to understand the story of spirituality. A time line is included in appendix A. I have also included a glossary of specialized terms as well as an index and maps.

"Spirituality" for Christians

> The greatest religious challenge of our age is to hold together social action and spiritual disciplines. This is not just a theological necessity, dictated by the need to integrate all of life around the reality of the living God. It is a matter of sheer survival.
> —Walter Wink
>
> We might define Christian spirituality as that particular actualization of the capacity for self-transcendence that is constituted by the substantial gift of the Holy Spirit establishing a life-giving relationship with God in Christ within the believing community.
> —Sandra Schneiders, "Theology and Spirituality"

Spirituality . . . this ambiguous, six-syllable term is new to many and objectionable to some. Although it is a clumsy word, it is used so much because it seems to perform a task that no other word does. *Spirituality* is a transreligious word—that is, it is not tied to one single faith. Thus one can speak of Hindu or Muslim spirituality, or even of spirituality not rooted in a particular religion. In earlier centuries, many Christians used the words *devotion* or *piety*. But, unfortunately, these older terms have developed a flavor of otherworldly sentimentality. The term *spirituality* does not have this connotation and is more clearly inclusive of daily life in the world.

Spirituality actually refers to three distinct realities: a capacity, a style, and an academic discipline. First, it is a capacity that all people have. For example, when some people say, " I am so happy to discover my spirituality," they are referring to a dimension of the human being that makes it possible to integrate spiritual meanings with physical activities, to integrate intellectual work with ethical action. Human beings do relate to the unseen world; we call this "spirituality."

Second, we use the word to refer to *a* spirituality as a type or style of relating to God and the world. Thus one might speak, for example, of postmodern spirituality, family spirituality, Methodist spirituality, or liturgical spirituality. In each case, the adjective describes one style among others. Furthermore, I prefer to speak of "spiritual formation" rather than simply of "spirituality." The word *formation* here suggests development and shape, not just an abstract dimension of life.

Third, spirituality is a newly emerging academic discipline, the study of the first two meanings of the word. This is an interdisciplinary field that enjoys contributions not only from theologians but also from historians, sociologists, psychologists, philosophers, and so forth.[4] The book you are holding is an example of one kind of study in the field of spirituality.

From a Christian perspective, the word "spirituality" calls us to recognize the importance of its root term, *spirit*, an important biblical word. In both Hebrew and Greek, the same word (*ruach* and *pneuma*, respectively) is used to mean "breath," "wind," and "spirit." The Bible refers both to human spirit and to divine Spirit. How one understands spirit will determine how one understands spirituality. For example, if "spirit" is separated from physical reality, in a realm of its own, apart from the daily life of human experience, the resulting spirituality will become an escape into another world. But if God created the world as good and later became flesh, as the Gospel of John asserts, then "spirit" is a dimension of reality, compatible with physical existence. In this case, humans are not divided but rather are unities of body, mind, and spirit. The result is that spirituality has a much more wholistic and down-to-earth meaning. It encompasses the whole of human life and will develop in a variety of styles, depending on cultures, denominations, personalities, and gifts.

Catholic theology first used the term *spirituality* in something like the present-day usage. For most of the centuries of the church, theologians included the practice of Christianity in their discussions of doctrine. But in the eighteenth and nineteenth centuries, "mystical theology" and "ascetical theology" became specialized fields. The first described the teachings of the mystics, the extraordinary Christians of the tradition; the other discussed the path of ordinary Christian disciplines. In the twentieth century, these two subdisciplines combined into one: "spiritual theology," or "spirituality."

Various schools of spirituality were recognized, which corresponded to the better known religious orders. Thus Catholics began to write about Jesuit spirituality, Franciscan spirituality, Carmelite spirituality, and so forth.

It has only been since about 1960 that Protestants have used the term *spirituality.* The delay is partly because of basic disagreements with Roman Catholic assumptions. But Roman Catholicism's ecumenical advance in the years since Vatican II has increased the conversation between the two traditions. Now there are studies describing the distinctive types of spirituality in the Protestant denominations, just as in the Catholic orders. Here are two recent Protestant descriptions of "spirituality" from *The Westminster Dictionary of Christian Spirituality:*

> Prayer in Christian theology and experience is more than pleading or petition; it is our whole relation to God. And spirituality concerns the way in which prayer influences conduct, our behavior and manner of life, our attitudes to other people. It is often best studied in biographies, but clearly it shapes dogmas, inspires movements and builds institutions.[5]

> SPIRITUALITY. This is a word which has come much into vogue to describe those attitudes, beliefs, practices which animate people's lives and help them to reach out towards super-sensible realities. . . . This means that Christian spirituality is not simply for "the interior life" or the inward person, but as much for the body as for the soul, and is directed to the implementation of both the commandments of Christ, to love God and our neighbor. Indeed, our love, like God's, should extend to the whole of creation. Christian spirituality at its most authentic includes in its scope both humanity and nature.[6]

Spirituality begins with lived experience; "If we live by the Spirit, let us also walk by the Spirit," Paul writes (Galatians 5:25). The starting point is the Spirit of Christ living in the person, but the person is always considered in the context of a community, the body of Christ. Christian spiritualities are particular *styles* of discipleship. For example, Jesuits or Lutherans or feminists each have a particular combination of themes and practices that make them distinctive. Note that each member of these groups has distinctive gifts and traits as well. Each group or person has its own flavor. This book will give you a small taste of many flavors.

I have come to describe spirituality as experience, relationships, and practices. The experience may be undramatic, but it points to the sacred in everyday life. The relationships are the very core of our humanity. The practices incorporate intentional living with the "habits of the heart." More will be said about all of these in the next chapter.

Spirituality is a subject that demands personal involvement. Just as with learning to swim or to ride a bicycle, learning spirituality requires not only reflection but action. Therefore, the suggestions for practice included in the chapters are integral to this subject.

Analysis of Root Metaphors

Several ways have been used to classify types of spirituality. One is to place the types on a graph in which kataphatic and apophatic (see glossary) are at the left and right, heart and mind at the top and bottom.[7] Such a chart can help identify psychological tendencies in persons or schools of thought. Another helpful method for people comes from Geoffrey Wainwright, who connects H. Richard Niebuhr's well-known typology from *Christ and Culture* to spirituality.[8] Here I will not attempt to classify all types of Christian spirituality; rather, I will try to illumine certain metaphors that dominate some of the writers and schools of spirituality.

In an attempt to understand our lives, we use fundamental images, or root metaphors. Each image has value, but none is adequate by itself. For example, the Bible pictures God as rock, light, and fortress; lion, bear, and eagle; king, father, and shepherd; and mother, lover, and friend. None of these groupings alone adequately describes the nature of God. The same is true of our pictures of the Christian life.

The basis of Christian life may be pictured as *rescue, redemption,* or *justification.* "Jesus saves" means most simply that Jesus rescues the sinner from the powers greater than any person: sin and death. Redemption means setting free a slave by purchase. Justification takes place in the courtroom: the guilty one is declared innocent on the basis of another's interceding. All of these metaphors have in common the initiative of God, who loves and frees us from the internal and external powers that bind us. Some might argue that these images refer only to the inception of the Christian life, but on the contrary, the most experienced and mature saints have clung to them. Whatever role our efforts play in Christian living, these metaphors imply that fundamentally we remain in need all of our lives and rely on God's love to save, redeem, liberate, and justify. The spiritualities of the Lutheran and Reformed traditions place these metaphors in the center.

Another set of images suggests the process of Christian living. *Growth, unification,* and *healing* all describe gradual changes. Biological growth in plants and animals is taken as a model of maturing in the Christian walk. A second view is that we are divided as selves and that the Christian life is a matter of being put back together again, both in terms of integrating our person and in the sense of uniting with God. Third, healing can be both metaphor and reality in Christian spirituality. As metaphor, it suggests that the Christian walk is the process of healing what is diseased or wounded in the same sense that the man on the road to Jericho was cared for by the Samaritan and the inn keeper (Luke 10:25-37). As reality, healing is an important experience for many whose prayers for physical or emotional healing bring noticeable results. Augustine's views and those of Pentacostalists use these images. Augustine uses them as metaphor; Pentacostalists, as experience.

Traveling and returning are both involved in the metaphors of *walking, journeying, climbing,* and *homing.* Living life through time has often been compared to moving through space, as in walking down a road. This is the image used by Paul when he speaks of walking in the Spirit. The journey underlies John Bunyan's classic allegory, *Pilgrim's Progress.* It suggests both that we are on the move and have not arrived yet, and that we do have a destination. The image of climbing, whether a mountain or a ladder, is an ancient one, starting in Genesis, suggesting progress toward God and being able to look back over one's path. This image does have problems, however, for those of us who see grace as the fundamental reality of the walk, from start to finish. It seems to imply an accomplishment that could be a temptation to pride in one's worthiness. Homing as an image focuses not on the travel but on the return and on settling into one's appropriate place. Some feminist writers have preferred this image, while the Roman Catholic medieval tradition has used a Neo-Platonic version of the journey: we came from God, and we are on our return journey to God.

Death and *resurrection* become metaphors for Christian falling away and restoration, sin and forgiveness, despair and hope. The death and resurrection of Jesus are seen as the type, or the powerful first instance of this pattern. Luther spoke often of daily baptism in these terms (see Romans 6:1-11). One might also consider the cycle of Israel's departure from God and return as fitting here.

We are told that a monk given thirty seconds to describe life in his monastery for a television interviewer replied, "We fall down, then we get up. We fall down, then we get up. We fall down, then we get up. We fall down, then we get up. . . ."

Another way of picturing the Christian life is as *vocation.* The model here is call and response. The call comes from God, the self, and the world to indicate who we are to be and what we are to do. The call and response are repeated throughout one's lifetime. They may be as simple as a mother standing on the back porch calling to her young son, "Brad, time to come home!" (as God also calls us to come back home). Or they may be as complex as the call to balance career, home life, and responsibilities to society and the world.

Battle has also been a recurring image in discussions of Christian spirituality. The writer of Ephesians advises Christians to put on the whole armor of God to be able to stand against the wiles of the devil. Another view of the battle is Paul's internal struggle; different parts of himself are struggling in Romans 7. Later writers expanded on the theme of fighting with spiritual powers, with the "old self," and with the powers of the world. Starting with Johann Arndt, Pietist and Evangelical writers have been accustomed to this image.

Finally, *thirst* and *hunger* suggest human need for the Divine. Human beings are not self-sufficient, however much they may seek to be. It is God who is able to supply the "bread of Life" (John 6) and "water of life" (John 7). Even the celebration (John 2) demands wine at times!

These metaphors all help to shape our experiences. They give us a handle on interpreting our lives. Each needs the others; none is adequate by itself.

Global Christian Traditions

A living tradition is a self-critical developing stream, not a moribund repetition of the past. Tradition is the shoulder of previous experience on which we stand as we reach upward for what is new. Education involves studying the various traditions that have shaped a community, pondering the problems of continuity and change, and making decisions about adopting or rejecting elements of those traditions.

Tradition is thus much wider than customs; tradition includes narratives, doctrines, and values: "Tradition is the living faith of the dead, traditionalism is the dead faith of the living."[9]

For example, some elements of American tradition are very precious and deserve honor, but others, such as racism and greed, show that the nation needs repentance just as individuals do and that new attitudes and practices are in order. Citizens of the United States, for example, have had to reevaluate the impact of Christopher Columbus, the beliefs of the "founding fathers," and the Vietnam War.

The Christian community has inherited almost two millennia of thought, action, and prayer by people seeking to live in the power of the Holy Spirit. Great saints have exemplified the courage and love of Jesus, serving as living witnesses of God's power to redeem. But the history of Christianity is also marked by continual departures from the way of its Lord, of social and personal injustice, error, and violence. Therefore, being heirs to a tradition does not mean approving of everything in it. Rather, it means sifting out what is valuable from what is not and creatively developing neglected strands of thought.

It is vitally important for Christian spirituality today that we take a wide view of that tradition and of the global family of Christians, not simply repeating the small portion that may be familiar from our home, congregation, or ethnic group. The sweep of that tradition will open our eyes to wide resources of spirituality and guide us in our own choices.

Perhaps no one has stated the need for reading books from the previous ages so pointedly as C. S. Lewis in his introduction to a fourth-century theological and spiritual work by the young Athanasius:

> Every age has its own outlook. It is specially good at seeing certain truths and specially liable to make certain mistakes. We all, therefore, need the books that will correct the characteristic mistakes of our own period. And that means the old books. . . . Nothing strikes me more when I read the controversies of past ages than the fact that both sides were usually assuming without question a good deal which we should now absolutely deny. . . . We may be sure that the characteristic blindness of the twentieth century—the blindness about which posterity will ask, "But how *could* they have thought that?"—lies where we never suspected it. . . . None of us can fully escape this blindness, but we shall certainly increase it, and weaken our guard against it, if we read only modern books. . . . The only palliative is to keep the clean sea breeze of the centuries blowing through our minds, and this can be done only by reading old books. Not, of course, that there is any magic about the past. People were no cleverer then than they are now; they made as many mistakes as we. But not the *same* mistakes. They will not flatter us in the errors we are already committing; and their own error, being now open and palpable, will not endanger us. Two heads are better than one, not because either is infallible, but because they are unlikely to go wrong in the same direction.[10]

For perspective on the assumptions of the spirituality of our own age, assumptions that need to be questioned, nothing is better than reading the spiritual classics.

The first reason to study the tradition and the present-day Christian family is to make us aware of our own narrowness, our own parochialism. Knowing a larger part of the whole tradition gives us better questions to ask of the fads of the present. We are endangered not only with ethnocentrism, judging all things by the customs of our own ethnic group, but also with "presentism," judging all previous ages as inferior to our own.

Second, study of the tradition displays a wide variety of approaches to Christian spirituality. Too often we have restricted our concept of Christian prayer and of following Christ. The tradition shows over time a great cloud of witnesses, a treasure house of approaches to living in discipleship to Jesus.

Varieties of approach include differences of emphasis on different biblical truths, such as we have in different denominations. Just as there are four Gospels, each bringing out different perspectives on the same redeemer, so our denominations crystallize around different starting points within the story of the one Christ.

Varieties of approaches to discipleship also include national cultural differences. Christianity began in a Jewish setting; very soon became Greco-Roman, Syrian, Armenian, Ethiopian, and Celtic; and today expresses itself in virtually every major cultural group in the world.

And, of course, the differences are personal. The Christian God respects the variety of personality, so that women and men of every type have followed the Way and have left markers for introverts and extroverts, and for people who mostly use their emotions and those who use their intellects to face the world. These differences can be seen, for example, in women as diverse as Teresa of Avila and Teresa of Calcutta and in men with different temperments, such as Francis of Assisi and Thomas Aquinas.

What is the effect of studying this great variety of Christian spirituality, past and present? It is to widen the options available, to loosen our grip on nonessentials. It is to increase our wonder at the community of which we are a part.

The third reason to study the Christian spiritual tradition is that it not only displays variety but also presents norms or boundaries for that variety. Although there are many ways of living a spiritual life in the power of the gospel, there is only one Lord, one baptism, one God. The norms of genuine Christian spirituality are preeminently the Scriptures but also the creeds of the early church. Theological norms are the statements of worldview, statements about the way things are, that form the skeleton on which the flesh of spirituality depends. For example, some people in early centuries thought that spirit was better than matter and began to forbid eating or having sex or bathing. It was the faith that God created the world as good that held this dualistic spirituality in check.

A very big playing field exists for Christians, but there are also boundaries outside which the game is no longer Christian. In modern times, these lines are not always as clear as they seemed to be in past centuries, and many think that this ambiguity is appropriate to give space for exploration. Nevertheless, not every spirituality is a type of Christian spirituality, and that distinction is necessary for the identity and integrity of the tradition. My view is that Christians need to have their ears and hearts open to learn from other religious and cultural traditions, while not losing the centrality of Jesus Christ and the Bible as normative for their spirituality.

An Hourglass

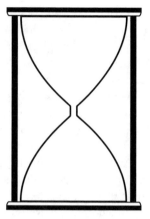

Christianity is not a European religion, although today many people view it as such. The story of its expansion shows that Christianity can as truly be claimed an Asian or an African religion as a European one. Jesus and his disciples were not Europeans, in spite of countless paintings that suggest they were. Their culture was Middle Eastern Judaism, and their biological inheritance was from the ancient Hebrews, whose roots have no contact with Europe.

Perhaps we think of Jesus as European because Jews today mostly have European roots and we assume wrongly that he must have looked like them. In fact, Jews come in all colors, and it is not clear what color Jesus' skin may have been. Some say that he was likely to have been short and dark. The point is that Jesus should be seen not as the founder of an ethnic faith for white-skinned Europeans but as a universal figure whose message can rightly be claimed by all peoples. The artistic depictions of an African Jesus, a Chinese Jesus, and a Native American Jesus all express that conviction.

We may simplify the story of Christian expansion to the peoples of the world into four main stages and picture it as an hourglass. The earliest and latest periods form the wide parts of the hourglass, while the middle period is like the narrow passage of the device.

First came a time of expansion from western Asia (Jerusalem) to three continents: eastward into Asia, southwest to Africa, and northwest to Europe (see map 1). We read in the Acts of the Apostles in the New Testament that the gospel spread from Jerusalem to Judea, to Samaria, and to the ends of the world. The narrative introduces an African into the account (Acts 8) even before Paul travels to Europe with the good news (Acts 16). During this early period, no political or economic pressure forced people to become Christians. In fact, it was quite the opposite: the intrinsic merits of the faith motivated its spread.

Because of roads and trading routes, Christianity spread rapidly in all directions. In the first century, it probably reached Roman Britain as well as Egypt, Arabia, and Syria. The Thomas Churches in India may also date from the first century, and they certainly have their roots in this very early period, even if the archeological evidence accepted by Western historians is dated two centuries later.

So, by the fourth century Christianity stretched from India in the east to Britain in the west, from the Danube in the north to Ethiopia in the south.

It is clear that, at first, Christianity was not just a Roman faith, nor even a European one, but truly a faith found in many cultures on three continents. In fact, the majority of Christians in the world may have been Asian and African until well past the end of the first millennium.

But a withdrawal marked the second period. After (1) the establishment of Christianity by Rome and Constantinople in the fourth century, (2) the doctrinal splits of the fifth century, (3) the rise of Islam in the seventh century, and (4) the turning of the Mongol Empire in the thirteenth century, most of the African and Asian churches were reduced to small minorities or were completely annihilated.

The emperors after Constantine gradually moved from recognizing Christianity as a legal religion to making it the official state religion of the empire. This Byzantine connection between the emperor and Christianity led to two unintended results. First, the rulers of other empires—Persia, for example—began to see Christianity as the state religion of their enemies and thus to persecute its followers as disloyal to their homelands. Second, it meant that complaint against the church became a complaint against the state, and vice versa. Doctrinal disputes became political matters. Some of the peoples who were ruled from Constantinople became ripe for conversion to Islam because of their unhappiness with the rule of the distant emperors.

The Council of Chalcedon in 451 defined the teaching about the person of Christ, his divine and human natures, in a way that many Africans and Asians refused to accept. These people were branded Monophysites or Nestorians, even though they did not differ fundamentally in doctrine from the powerful churches related to Constantinople and Rome, who accepted the Chalcedonian definition. The definition stated that Jesus Christ is one person with two natures, human and divine. The Monophysites rejected the idea of two natures and insisted that Jesus Christ had one divine-human nature. The dispute was mostly political and cultural, not doctrinal.

Christians who were alienated from the emperor in Constantinople by these disputes welcomed the arrival of the Arabs in the seventh century. Some centuries later, most of them adopted Islam. They did so not at the point of the sword but over time, under social, political, and economic pressure from the Muslim governments.

During this second period, Christianity was gradually indigenized in Europe, where it continued to expand. For more than a thousand years, this faith dominated southern Europe; the northern peoples of Russia and Scandinavia were won over only after kings' decisions around A.D. 1000. Christian theology and spirituality came to be shaped by Europe's various cultures—Greek, Roman, Celtic, Germanic, Slavic, Norse. For example, the celebration of Christmas on December 25 and the use of a Christmas tree or Yule log are adaptations of Christianity to previous European religions.

It came to be assumed that Christianity and European culture were one
and the same. The universal character of Christianity was in danger of being
lost. Some theologians even argued that since other peoples had not believed
the gospel at Pentecost in the first century, it was useless to give them a second chance now, for God had obviously chosen the Europeans as his own
and left the others out in the cold!

A new expansion from Europe to all the continents characterized the
third period, from the sixteenth to the mid-twentieth century. First Roman
Catholic and then Protestant missionaries took the message of the cross to
all continents. Further, the vast emigration of Europeans to the Americas,
Australasia, and South Africa made Christianity dominant in those areas.
The political background of this expansion included European imperialism—first Portuguese and Spanish, then Dutch, English, and French—and
finally the economic and cultural dominance of the United States.

Christianity spread by emigration and by mission work from the North
Atlantic, in a Europeanized form, often with little regard for the cultures and
religions it encountered. There were just enough exceptions to this general-
ization to show that the Christian gospel was never entirely imprisoned by
European political or cultural captivity. This period was fundamental to our
present situation by providing both possibility and problems: the possibility
of a world Christian community, not just a "white man's religion," and the
problems of a distorted gospel, which has suffered from European hege-
mony, racism, tribalism, and sexism.

Today, in the fourth period of development, the spread of Christianity is
not only from Europe and North America. The churches of most countries
are involved in evangelization domestically or internationally or both. The
churches of Africa and Asia are reevaluating inherited forms of the gospel
and discarding those aspects of European Christianity that do not fit in their
cultural setting. The churches of Latin America are struggling to overcome
the economic imbalances rooted in the colonial period. Christianity is weak-
ening in its old North Atlantic strongholds and is growing in the continents
of Africa, Latin America, and Asia. The twentieth century, which was predicted by intellectuals to be the one in which all religions would die out,
proved, on the contrary, to be a time of rejuvenation for all the major world
religions, including Christianity, in the non-Western world.

Thus one may view the story of Christianity as an hourglass, with wide
geographical extent in the early and most recent centuries but a narrow stem
of European isolation in the middle. It is obvious from this model that a
sound approach to the story of Christian spirituality must take into account
movements and individuals outside of Europe. My aim here is to bring
together two fields of knowledge that do not often connect: first, histories of
Christian spirituality, which often concentrate on Europeans, and second,

scholarship concerning Western missions and new indigenous movements. The early non-Western spiritualities are as important to this study as the recent ones, and I will discuss them in chapter 4.

As we look back on this story, we see that Christianity has been crossing cultural boundaries from its start on the day of Pentecost up to the present. The translations of the Bible are a witness to this, with today's consciousness of contextualization representing its climax. Contextualization is the process by which Christianity speaks to a group of people in language and symbols with which they feel at home and in which they in turn express their Christian faith within their culture. The model for this process is seen to be the Word of God, who became fully human in Jesus of Nazareth, who was incarnated in human flesh and in a particular history and culture.

The Author's Perspective

None of us is neutral about matters that are important to us. Academic subjects that aim at objectivity are still colored by the values of their researchers, professors, and sponsors. The fact that we each see things from our own perspective implies not that the world of learning is hopelessly chaotic and subjective but that we need to take into account the personal values and commitments of the speaker or writer and then seek to learn, even if our own perspective is quite different. We take what is good and leave the rest.

As a way of introducing myself, I might list some important factors that have shaped my views of the world. I am a Protestant, a Lutheran, who sees great value in the Orthodox and Catholic traditions, who sees Jesus Christ, the Gospel, and the Bible as normative for interpreting the Christian spiritual traditions. My spouse, Linda, and our three children, Olaf, Karin, and Paul, have helped me to grow up, to accept myself, and to take responsibility.

I am a North American male of Scandinavian heritage who has been changed by nearly a decade of life in Africa, teaching at the Theological College of Northern Nigeria. I believe that the study of Christian spirituality needs to include non-Western sources, people of color, and women.

Having studied for many years in institutions of higher education, my approach to religion has been very intellectual, academic, left brain. My interest in spirituality is due in part to the needs of the other side of my human nature, the experiential, emotional, spontaneous, right-brain side. On one level, this book is an attempt to bring these two sides together.

After a number of years in spiritual direction, I have completed a course for spiritual directors myself, and thus I am asking questions particularly related to this practice.

Each chapter will have a section on spiritual practice relating the content of that chapter to your own experience. Some people call this experiential learning. Take these exercises as suggestions, not demands. You are discovering new ways of being in the world, new ways of relating to those most important in your life. Do not worry too much about "doing it right." This will distract attention from your true goal: being attentive to God.

1. Learn to sit attentively in **silence**. Sit up straight, with your spine perpendicular to the floor and with both feet on the floor. (If your legs are short, you may want to put a pillow under your feet.) Close your eyes. Relax. Find a comfortable place for your arms and hands.

Become aware of the gravity pulling you down into the chair, and relax into it. Consciously relax the muscles of your body, starting with your feet and moving up to your shoulders, neck, and face. Relax your tongue, cheeks, and forehead. Soften and relax your eyes. Let your mind become disengaged from its usual chatter. Become aware of your breathing. Take two deep breaths, in through the nose, out through the mouth. (These are like deliberate sighs, a natural way of relaxing.)

Now you are relaxed but alert, ready to listen to yourself and to God. Do not try to think but do remain in a state of relaxed alertness. If you find your thoughts turning to upcoming activities, sexual fantasies, worries, or any other "static," take the distraction as a sign of something coming to the surface but return to your silence without becoming perturbed or blaming yourself. As you repeatedly do this exercise, you will be able to calm yourself more quickly and appreciate the silence for longer periods of time. This focusing in silence is a fundamental preparation for many other practices that require focusing or paying attention. One may think of this silence as giving "loving attention" to God and to oneself: "The ground of your being is holy; relax in it! Breathe deeply. Quieten your soul. Wait patiently."[11]

Determine to spend some time each day in quietness. Choose a place, either inside (for example, in a favorite chair) or outside (in a quiet place).

2. Take a **walk**. Deliberately become aware of your body's rhythms, of your breathing, heartbeat, and muscle tension. Notice how good it feels to be out of a box (what we call a room). Look up at the sky and take some deep breaths. Think of yourself as taking a walk with God or within God. If you wish, sing a song to yourself and to God.

3. **Pray**. You probably pray already, as most people do. Think about the ways you are satisfied with your prayer life and the ways in which you would like to grow. Most of us think of prayer as talking to God, and most often we

do so when we need something, so our prayers become requests. This is an authentic form of prayer, but it is a very narrow type. Throughout this book, you will find many suggestions for different types of prayer. Not everyone prays the same or ought to pray the same. You can find the styles of prayer that most help you.[12]

For now, consider broadening your understanding of prayer along the lines suggested in the definition of spirituality presented earlier in this chapter: "Prayer in Christian theology and experience is more than pleading or petition; it is our whole relation to God" (p. 8). Our whole relation to God includes gratitude, praise, wonder, confession, complaint, and all the other ways that we also relate to other people. So a simple way of expanding our styles of prayer is to use one of the following acronyms to remind ourselves of this variety:

Adoration	**P**raise
Confession	**R**epent
Thanksgiving	**A**sk
Supplication	**Y**ield

An even wider variety is explained in Marjorie Thompson's *Soul Feast*. Prayer is not only *communication* with God, of all the types mentioned above, and using writing, dance, song, and so forth. Prayer is also *communion*, simply being in the presence of God. Our relationship with God can be a wordless listening in a loving presence.

Consider broadening your relationship with God by broadening your practice of prayer.

4. **Write** about your life. Draw a line the width of your paper, and put your date of birth on the left end of the line and today's date at the right end. Mark off the decades of time. Then mark the turning points of your life—for example, when you entered a different school, moved, or changed in other ways. Give simple titles to the spaces between the marks, making them the chapters of your life.

Or make a life map. View your life not as a line but as a curving path, with important choices or moves noted.

Then consider each of these periods from the point of view of spiritual formation. Who was God for you during that time? Did you have spiritual experiences then? How did you think of your life? Who were the most important people to you? Did they serve as spiritual mentors or supports? What wounds or griefs did you suffer during each period? How do you look at them now?

5. **Write** about your future. What are your aims? Write a mission statement. (This can be a quick sentence or two written in five minutes or a carefully considered essay that may take months.) Can you formulate this
statement so briefly that you can remember it each morning? Where is God
in this statement?

Describe where you hope to be and what your relationships will be in
five, ten, or twenty years.

Suppose your life is over. What is it you would like people to remember
about you? Write your own eulogy, a speech that expresses the essence of you
in a life that you aim to live.

Aids for the Exercises

Bass, Dorothy C., ed. *Practicing Our Faith: A Way of Life for a Searching People.*
San Francisco: Jossey-Bass, 1997.

Foster, Richard J. *Celebration of Discipline: The Path to Spiritual Growth.* 2nd
ed. San Francisco: Harper, 1988.

Spiritus. The Journal of the Society for the Study of Christian Spirituality.
Johns Hopkins University Press.

Thompson, Marjorie J. *Soul Feast: An Invitation to the Christian Spiritual Life.*
Louisville: Westminster John Knox, 1995.

Suggested Reading

Original Texts

The most comprehensive set of primary sources is found in the Paulist Press
series Classics of Western Spirituality. The translations are recent, with
introductory essays to set the context for these writings. The set will include
more than fifty volumes when it is complete.

Comprehensive Surveys

Jones, Cheslyn, Geoffrey Wainwright, and Edward Yarnold, eds. *The Study
of Spirituality.* New York: Oxford Univ. Press, 1986.

McGinn, Bernard, and John Meyendorff, eds., *Christian Spirituality: Origins
to the Twelfth Century;* Jill Raitt, ed., *Christian Spirituality: High Middle
Ages and Reformation;* Louis Dupre and Don E. Saliers, eds., *Christian
Spirituality: Post Reformation and Modern.* Volumes 16–18 of World
Spirituality. New York: Crossroad, 1987–89.

Other Approaches to Introducing Christian Spirituality

Collins, Kenneth J., ed. *Exploring Christian Spirituality: An Ecumenical Reader.*
Grand Rapids: Baker, 2000.

Downey, Michael. *Understanding Christian Spirituality.* New York: Paulist, 1997.

Jones, Tony. *Soul Shaper: Exploring Spirituality and Contemplative Practices in Youth Ministry.* Grand Rapids: Zondervan, 2003.

McGrath, Alister E. *Christian Spirituality.* Oxford: Blackwell, 1999.

Other Historical Accounts and Anthologies

Christensen, Bernhard M. *The Inward Pilgrimage: An Introduction to Christian Spiritual Classics.* Minneapolis: Augsburg Books, 1996.

Madigan, Shawn, ed. *Mystics, Visionaries and Prophets: A Historical Anthology of Women's Spiritual Writings.* Minneapolis: Fortress Press, 1998.

Foster, Richard J. and James Bryan Smith, eds. *Devotional Classics : Selected Readings for Individuals and Groups.* San Francisco: HarperSanFrancisco, 1993.

Discussion guides with anthology

Mursell, Gordon, ed. *The Story of Christian Spirituality: Two Thousand Years, from East to West.* Minneapolis: Fortress Press, 2001.

The most beautiful account, with lavish illustrations and timetables.

Tyson, John R. *Invitation to Christian Spirituality: An Ecumenical Anthology.* New York: Oxford, 1999.

Waller, Ralph and Benedicta Ward. *An Introduction to Christian Spirituality.* London: SPCK, 1999.

About the "Hourglass"

Jenkins, Philip. *The Next Christendom: The Coming of Global Christianity.* New York: Oxford Univ. Press, 2002.

Walls, Andrew. *The Missionary Movement in Christian History: Studies in the Transmission of Faith.* Maryknoll, N.Y.: Orbis, 1996.

———. *The Cross-Cultural Process in Christian History.* Maryknoll, N.Y.: Orbis, 2002.

About the Academic Study of Spirituality

Hanson, Bradley C., ed. *Modern Christian Spirituality: Methodological and Historical Essays.* American Academy of Religion Studies in Religion, no. 62. Atlanta: Scholars, 1990.

Chapter 2

Spiritual Formation:
Being, Relating, and Doing

S pirituality is, in the first instance, about experience, not theory. Spirituality consists of the existential forms of life that we adopt in order to live in this universe. It is walking in the spirit. For Christians, this means walking in the Holy Spirit of the risen Jesus. In this walking, we may distinguish our being, our relationships, and our practices, for these three constitute our humanity. Our being means our place in the universe. Our four basic relationships are to God, to self, to people, and to creation. Ideally, these will be relationships of love, as explained in this chapter. To develop all four relationships, we develop habitual patterns of behavior called spiritual practices.

Being and Becoming

Spirituality is about being, because we are small yet significant persons in a big universe. The way we picture that universe and its creator will determine how we see the meaning of our own existence. We have reached a high level of spiritual life when we are able to view all of our doing as secondary and to exist simply before God: "For 'in him we live and move and have our being'" (Acts 17:28). This is a view that Paul, as a Christian, shared with Greek philosophers.

Fundamental to Christian views of spirituality are convictions about God as creator who loves and values the result of God's work. This God has made mortal human beings to share the joy of being.

> Joyful, joyful we adore thee,
> God of glory, Lord of love!
> Hearts unfold like flow'rs before thee,
> Praising thee their sun above. . . .
> Thou art giving and forgiving,
> Ever blessing, ever blest,
> Wellspring of the joy of living,

Ocean-depth of happy rest! . . .
Teach us how to love each other,
Lift us to the joy divine![1]

Become what you are! This was Karl Barth's way of speaking about development and growth in the Christian life as a way of reaching a status God has already given us in Christ. In Christ, we are chosen, righteous, holy, given eternal life, glorified. When we live toward that destination, we are becoming, growing, maturing into our true selves. The being and the becoming are gifts of God, yet paradoxically they involve human participation. This participation is the meat of spirituality.

> Remember, it is no longer you who live; it is Christ who lives in you. Christ will do just fine living in you. Your task is just to be there. You are a vessel of emptiness for Christ to abide in.
> —Macrina Wiederkehr, *The Song of the Seed*

Relating Love from and to God

When Jesus is asked to name the greatest commandment, he quotes Deuteronomy and then Leviticus (see Mark 12:28-31; Deuteronomy 6:4-5; Leviticus 19:18). The first great commandment is to "love the LORD your God with all your heart, soul, mind, and strength." Whatever else the Bible says about God that is relevant for spirituality, this is fundamental. God is to be loved with the whole self, physical, social, emotional, intellectual, and volitional.

But who is this God? It is the God whose blazing love first created and then redeemed us. This God tenderly, jealously, sometimes wrathfully, and sometimes joyously loved ancient Israel. This God took on human flesh, was mocked, and was killed to set free all peoples from sin, evil, and death. The simplest description of this one is "God is love." Spirituality means welcoming this love into our lives; allowing it to change our habits, feelings, and thoughts; and thus returning the love to the God who gave it.

Fundamental to any particular spirituality is its view of God intellectually and emotionally. The intellectual side comes out in doctrines about God's nature. The emotional side comes out in prayers of celebration and mourning. Both sides are expressed in stories and metaphors, which abound in the Bible.

The relationship to God in prayer that is portrayed in the Bible also shares this tension between the known and the unknown. The Bible both teaches about prayer and illustrates it. God is one who can be addressed by humans and who addresses them. Prayers have great variety in the Bible, showing that there is no one form of address acceptable to the Almighty.

Moses and Abraham see God as a friend and sometimes argue or barter with him. Job boldly accuses God. The Psalms contain bitter laments and joyful praises. Jesus prays for healings, gives thanks, submits to the Father's will, and calls out in forsakenness on the cross. Paul is lifted to the third heaven and cannot tell what he saw. In all of these, we see God as the known and the unknown. This tension will later show itself in the history of spirituality as the *kataphatic* and *apophatic* approaches to God (see glossary and page 75).

God in the Old Testament is known as the one who led the people out of slavery, who entered into covenants with individuals and the people of Israel, who revealed the Ten Commandments, who spoke through the prophets and yet said:

> For as the heavens are higher than the earth,
> so are my ways higher than your ways
> and my thoughts than your thoughts. (Isaiah 55:9)

Insofar as God is known, God is seen as creator of the world (Genesis 1–2 and many other places), liberator of Israel (Exodus 1–15), giver of the Torah (or Law) (Deuteronomy), judge of all people (Psalm 96), savior of the faithful (Psalm 27), and Holy One (Isaiah 6). These universal metaphors are supplemented by a number of more personal ones. God is friend, father, mother, husband. Other images from creation include God as mother bear, mother eagle, lion, rock, fortress, and fire. These images of God all fall short yet are essential for human understanding. God is none of the things listed; God is not male or female. Yet God's personal, holy, living character, revealed in story and metaphor, is important for both Jews and Christians.

The New Testament builds on the Old Testament picture but with a breathtaking assertion: God became incarnate in a human being! It is not that the Old Testament God is a God of wrath while the New Testament shows a God of mercy, for both aspects of God can be seen in both testaments. But the New Testament claims that the love of God for humanity was so great that God took uniquely human form in Jesus of Nazareth. This action affirms the goodness of creation as stated in Genesis 1 and affirms the value of human beings and human culture. For oppressed by evil as people may be, God entered the human story in a particular place and time.

Jesus himself describes God as a shepherd seeking one lost sheep, as a woman seeking a lost coin, as a father welcoming home a lost son. He addresses God as *Abba*, the Aramaic word for a father addressed by a small child. The closest we may have is "Dad" or "Daddy." Thus Jesus lived out an intimate relation to God, modeling prayer and obedience to his own followers but also inviting them to share in the oneness he experienced with the Father.

Paul the apostle writes that God declares sinners righteous and that, through the Holy Spirit, he also indwells them, giving spiritual gifts and producing spiritual fruit. Paul brings us back to the issue of God's revelation and God's mystery. He is very confident of some truths—for example, when he writes:

> For I am convinced that neither death nor life, nor angels, nor rulers, nor things present, nor things to come, nor powers, nor height nor depth, nor anything else in all creation, will be able to separate us from the love of God in Christ Jesus. (Romans 8:38)

But just a short while later, after writing about the will of God for Jews and Gentiles, Paul concludes:

> O the depth of the riches and wisdom and knowledge of God! How unsearchable are his judgments and how inscrutable his ways! . . . For from him and through him and to him are all things. To him be glory forever. Amen. (Romans 11:33, 36)

Love from and to Yourself

The second great commandment according to Jesus is to "Love your neighbor as yourself." This statement is fitting and inseparable from the first, for our love to God shows itself in love to our neighbor and even to ourselves. The main point of this second commandment is love of one's neighbor but implied is love of the self.

Some recent writers have gone overboard in trying to correct a misleading teaching about the self by making this commandment say, "Look out for number one." All of my students are convinced that you cannot love your neighbor unless you love yourself first. Someone might therefore think, "I can forget about my neighbor's needs until my own psychological problems are worked out," or believe that you should give yourself all that your heart desires and do not concern yourself with the poor. Such teaching is not an interpretation of Jesus' commandment but an expression of self-centeredness.

My question back to my students is, "How then will I learn to love myself?" I believe that we learn to love by being loved. It is not a simple process of first loving myself and then loving others. How soon will I know that I love myself enough to go to the second step? Rather, our love grows, and as we learn to love, we love both ourselves and others.

I think that feminists and others have rightly pointed out the misleading rhetoric found in some Christian teaching that suggests that loving is a zero-sum game and that love to self takes away from love to others. The ideal is to be "selfless," an apt description of how some women have felt after hearing that they must not pay any attention to their own needs but must constantly think only of the others in their families. However, it is appropriate to care for one's own needs; balancing those needs with those of others is a task for careful discernment.

Jesus did not say, "Love your neighbor and hate yourself." A proper concern for the self is the standard of care for the neighbor here. A distinction must be made between love for oneself and selfishness. The former involves care, nurture, responsibility, and faithfulness; the latter is greedy, exploitative, and idolatrous. To love oneself rightly is neither to grab from others to satisfy one's desires nor to neglect the care that we all need physically, psychologically, and spiritually.

For example, loving yourself might mean getting enough sleep and exercise, wearing a seat belt, saying "no" to the next committee, protecting yourself from abuse, or going to see a counselor when you need one. But selfishness, in contrast, might mean taking someone else's share of the credit, refusing to share with the poor, denying your own friendship to your children, or thinking about life in terms of what you can accumulate. Loving yourself involves setting healthy boundaries; selfishness digs in behind narrow boundaries to build a fortress.

The Bible does not define the self but describes the relations people have with God, others, and creation. In Psalm 139, the writer meditates on the wonders of God's relation to the self in God's creative knowledge and ubiquity. Genesis describes the person in terms of a body with the breath of life from God. This breath is the same word as "spirit." The Bible generally views a person as a unity of body, soul, mind, heart, and spirit. It does not separate these elements the way some philosophers have. Thus the self in the Bible is the whole person, including the body, soul, intellect, will, emotions, conscious and unconscious, and social and private, whatever distinctions have been made. It is this whole self that is called upon to love, serve, and praise God.

The human being is seen in the Bible as someone made in the image and likeness of God as well as a lost person subject to sin and evil. The Bible describes human bondage and promises freedom. Thus the integration and healing of the self are implicit in the message of the Bible, in such explicit teachings as redemption, liberation, forgiveness, and resurrection.

Throughout the Bible, people are called to repent from evil. In the New Testament, the most common word for repentance means turning around, changing direction. By God's grace, human beings are able not only to perceive some of what alienates them from God but also to receive new life, new direction, new birth.

Love from and to People

When Jesus explained the second great commandment, he told the story of a Samaritan who helped a bleeding man on the road. The vision of Christian spirituality includes not only "my God and I" but the world of need in which Christians have always lived. Both caring for the poor and standing up for those who are being treated unjustly are central to the Christian life.

Different kinds of love are called for in different situations. Love in public may be a demand for justice; love in private may mean personal affection. Some love is tough love, whereas some is tender love. For example, Christians are called to love refugees. Some refugees we have never seen except on television, yet God calls us to help them with practical aid, perhaps by donating our money or by advocating government aid. Some refugees may live next door, and love may take the form of hospitality and friendship. Among those we know, our community of faith, our family, and our friends are special types of relationships that call for more intimate kinds of love.

Christian spirituality has a special place for other persons who share the faith. It is not only personal but communal. The Bible does not know of separating individuals from the people of Israel or from the church; our relations with God are as members of a body, not as isolated individuals. It is as a people that we celebrate the Lord's Supper and share in Christ's body and blood. It is the community that is Christ's body, not an individual. The gifts of the Spirit are given to the community, not just individuals.

Families are important groups for spiritual nurture. The compassion and trust we show one another shape the lives of our children for years to come. It is in the family that most of us learn to pray, to read the Bible devotionally, to forgive one another, to assume our responsibilities. Loving ourselves comes initially from our parents' love for us.

Spiritual mentors or directors are also important in Christian growth. Aside from the community in general, individual guides and companions can help us see ourselves in ways that we cannot on our own. When someone else has heard our sins and spoken forgiveness and acceptance, our own assurance of God's forgiveness empowers us. The word of grace is heard more credibly from another than through a self-absolution. Spiritual directors give us companionship on the way, not only for the confession of sins. They listen carefully to us and help us discern the way forward. They help to mediate the guidance of the Holy Spirit and by their very presence help us come to new conclusions without saying a word.

It is the field of Christian ethics that studies our relation to other persons most directly. The complex ethical problems facing Christians today force us to listen carefully to the specialists who remind us of the context and the specifics of the Christian tradition that undergird us in making concrete decisions. It is important not to separate ethics from spirituality, lest spirituality be a private escape from the real world, a self-fulfillment at the cost of others. Ethics and spirituality belong together.

Love from and to the Whole Creation

Both creation accounts in Genesis (1:1—2:4a and 2:4b-25) affirm the goodness of the world and of human existence. The first account of seven days repeatedly proclaims that "it was good," and the second account implies God's approval. They both urge care for the natural world. Modern society has distorted and disregarded our accountability, as we exploit the earth for only human interest. The basis for Christian understanding of the world is the assertion that creation is good but that it is not God. The beauty and power of nature have led some to worship it; the Bible reminds us to worship the creator, not the creature. The transience and cruelty of nature have caused some to despise and mistreat it; the Bible reminds us to treat it as good caretakers or stewards.

Christian spirituality has not always given proper attention to the natural world. The influence of Neo-Platonism and other ancient philosophies has been to view the world as an uncomfortable and transient prison. The ambiguity of the term *world* in the Bible has permitted this distortion. Especially in John, *world* can be used to describe humanity organized against God—for example, as 1 John has it, "all that is in the *world*, the lust of the flesh and the lust of the eyes and the pride of life, is not of the Father but is of the world" (2:16). Obviously, the writer is not talking about the same world that God loves in John 3:16: "For God so loved the *world*, that he sent his only Son, that whoever believes in him should not perish but have eternal life."

So the term *world* has at least three meanings. It can refer to the created world that God called good in Genesis 1. Second, it can refer to humanity within that good world, as in John 3:16. Third, it can refer to human social evil. It is this third usage that has sometimes led to distortions in Christian spirituality. Both Catholic monks and Protestant Pietists have sought to love God and not love the world, but sometimes they have needed a St. Francis or a C. S. Lewis to remind them of the goodness of the natural world and the joyful pang of its beauty.

Meanwhile, it is the duty of Christians today to care for the earth and to integrate this care into their spirituality. Too long has this been a neglected aspect. The Psalms praise God for the natural world—for example, Psalm 104 meditates on the ecological relationships among the earth and the sea, humans, trees, birds, and other animals:

These all look to you
　　to give them their food in due season;
when you give to them, they gather it up;
　　when you open your hand, they are filled with good things. . . .
I will sing to the LORD as long as I live;
　　I will sing praise to my God while I have being.
May my meditation be pleasing to him,
　　for I rejoice in the LORD. (verses 27-28, 33-34)

Jesus used natural parables—for example, "Look at the birds of the air.
. . . Consider the lilies of the field" (Matthew 6:26-28); "Listen! a sower
went out to sow. . . . The kingdom of heaven is like a mustard seed"
(Matthew 13:3, 31 NRSV); "I am the vine, you are the branches" (John 15:5).

Christian appreciation for the work of God needs to be matched in our
day by taking responsibility for lifestyle and economics in order to preserve
the creation from human destruction. This may mean sacrifices: limiting our
use of private cars, eating less meat, using less fertilizer and pesticides, paying attention to all the consequences of our purchases. These lifestyle
adjustments may be most difficult for us Americans who love our cars, ham-
burgers, and lawns. Spirituality is about our lives as consumers as much as it
is about our lives as pray-ers.

We read in the Bible of a new heaven and a new earth, of a resurrection
of the body, and of the earth giving birth to a redeemed creation (Romans
8:19-25). These eschatological teachings are a call not to regard the earth
with indifference but to value it as God does, to prepare for the last day. We
do not know the how of the transformation, but we do know that it will lead
us into a new existence in a renewed creation.

Spiritual Practices or Disciplines

People express their being and their relationships in actions. If I *am* a
mother, I take care of my children. If I *am* a son, I honor my mother. If I *am*
an artist, I make beautiful things or words or music. If I love my girlfriend, I
talk to her on the phone. If I respect my mentor, I observe carefully how she
or he deals with real situations in life. If I love my God, I give time and
energy to this relationship.

Over time, patterns of behavior have developed to guide us in our
choices of actions in order to grow in the spiritual life. We do not need to
reinvent the wheel. We can learn from the experiences of so many who have
gone before us in the life of the spirit. On the other hand, our time is different, and each of us is different, so the methods of the past must be applied
not woodenly but flexibly. Each person must find her or his own pattern of

habits in order to express a vision of being and to develop the four relation-ships discussed earlier.

These habits are called practices or disciplines. We do them again and again because they nourish us. Just as the rhythm of the day may include sleeping, waking, eating, and working, so it may include praying, reading, writing, and singing, for example. These are called disciplines not because they have to do with punishment but because they are like physical or men-tal training that involves saying "no" to sloth. We lift weights as a prepara-tion for team sports; we practice scales as a preparation for playing in the orchestra or band; and we engage in spiritual practices as a necessary prepa-ration for communal life in the church.

In his opening chapter of *Celebration of Discipline: The Path to Spiritual Growth*, Richard Foster writes:

> Neither should we think of the Spiritual Disciplines as some dull drudgery aimed at exterminating laughter from the face of the earth. Joy is the keynote of all the Disciplines. The purpose of the Disciplines is liberation from the stifling slavery to self-interest and fear. . . .
>
> In one important sense, the Spiritual Disciplines are not hard. . . . The primary requirement is a longing after God.
>
> Beginners are welcome. I, too, am a beginner, even and espe-cially after a number of years of practicing every Discipline dis-cussed in this book.[2]

Note that term *discipline* comes from the same word as *disciple*. As followers of Jesus, we must pay attention, act responsibly, love without limit. Our Lord expects self-discipline from all who claim to follow him.

There is no finite list of spiritual practices. Potentially, any good action can be seen as a spiritual discipline. But certain actions have been seen as par-ticularly valuable. Foster discusses twelve disciplines in his book, labeling them as Inward (meditation, prayer, fasting, study), Outward (simplicity, soli-tude, submission, service), and Corporate (confession, worship, guidance, celebration). On the other hand, Marjorie Thompson, in her book *Soul Feast: An Invitation to the Christian Spiritual Life*, discusses a different list: spiritual reading, prayer, worship, fasting, self-examination, spiritual direction, and hospitality. She concludes with a chapter encouraging the reader to choose among the disciplines a "rule of life."[3]

Both of these books give a detailed account of the practice of these habits and how to develop them. This book too will give you a number of sugges-tions about spiritual practices, this time in the context of their historical devel-opment—that is, in telling the story of Christian spirituality, I will identify some of these same practices and some others and will invite you as a reader to try them in your own experience. The story of Christian spirituality cannot be fully appreciated merely by reading. We must also feel empathy, a shared experience that allows the story of the past to live in us. We have the intellectual equipment for analysis, but we need the experience for evaluation and appropriation. Spiritual practice will become real to us insofar as we experience it.

Spiritual Practice

1. Fundamental to our practice is our relationship with God, a relationship that is often hindered by conscious or unconscious wounds. Many of us have been taught about God's love but have a difficult time really believing it. We fend off God because of misunderstandings or painful experiences. **Write** about the history of your relationship with God, considering how you thought and felt about God as a child, an adolescent, and an adult. What have been the most important events in your experience of God?

2. Consider the ways that you love or do not love yourself. **Write** about your own view of your body, your practices concerning nutrition and sleep, and your sustaining friendships. Your life can be seriously affected by your use of seat belts, drugs (caffeine, alcohol, prescriptions, and illegal drugs), and exercise. These are all spiritual matters.

Aids for the Exercises
Hughes, Gerard W. *God of Surprises.* Cambridge, Mass.: Cowley, 1993.
Melander, Rochelle, and Harold Eppley. *The Spiritual Leader's Guide to Self-Care.* Herndon, Va.: Alban Institute, 2000.
    Many good suggestions for action on a wide variety of topics.

Suggested Reading

Bondi, Roberta C. *Memories of God : Theological Reflections on a Life.* Nashville: Abingdon Press, 1995.
Cummings, Charles. *Eco-Spirituality: Toward a Reverent Life.* New York: Paulist, 1991.
Trobisch, Walter. "Love Yourself," in *Complete Works of Walter Trobisch,* 653–92. Downers Grove, Ill.: InterVarsity, 1987.

Chapter 3

Jesus Christ and the Bible

Christian faith centers on God who became incarnate in Jesus of Nazareth. The context for understanding the meaning of this event is the history of Israel, as described in the Hebrew Bible, or Old Testament, and the interpretations of this event found in the documents of the New Testament.

Thus the foundational documents of Christian spirituality are the Holy Scriptures. All later developments have their matrix in the divine-human dialogue described in the Bible. Though it has been interpreted in somewhat divergent ways, the canon of Scripture is recognized as the norm by all major Christian traditions.

The center of the Christian Bible is Jesus himself. He is the key to its meaning, and he stands in the center of its chronology. The Hebrew Bible, or Old Testament, was written in the tenth to second centuries before Jesus. The New Testament was written in the middle to late first century A.D., with a few late books possibly written in the early second century after the birth of Jesus. Thus Jesus of Nazareth himself stands between these two collections of documents chronologically and is their central focus theologically. Christians see the Old Testament as witnessing forward to him and the New Testament as witnessing back to him. None of the books of the Bible was written at the time of Jesus, and he is not known to have written any book. (In this way, he is like Socrates, Muhammad, and the Buddha.)

This chapter is intended to show the importance of Jesus and the Bible to Christian spirituality by unpacking some of the ideas and practices implied by them for later centuries. It aims to give the reader who is not well acquainted with the Bible some basic information about the structure of this big book as well as to provide the reader who already has studied the Bible academically a new lens for exploring what is already familiar. The new lens is the use of the Bible for spiritual practice rather than only for history, doctrine, or ethics.

Jesus Christ

As the paragraphs above indicate, Christians make very big claims for the person of Jesus. On the basis of such biblical terms as *Christ, Word of God, Son of Man, Son of God, Savior,* and *Lord,* Christians eventually came to understand Jesus as the incarnation of the second person of the Holy Trinity. Maybe you are not yet ready to accept those claims but are ready to learn from Jesus the human being about spirituality. If so, take Jesus as you honestly can, and further study of the Gospels and the New Testament may lead you to conclude, with his disciples, that he is more than an ordinary mortal and even more than an extraordinary human being. The Christian theological tradition has always affirmed the full humanity of Jesus and has rejected the view that he was not human as a serious error. Thus, for the perspective of spirituality, one important teaching is that we can identify with Jesus and he with us as a human being, whatever our differences from him in gender, culture, or ethnicity.

Jesus is central to Christian spiritual formation. In short, Jesus is the *basis*, the *example*, and the *promise* of Christian spiritual formation. First, Jesus is the *basis* for Christian practice because he is, according to John's Gospel, the way, the truth, and the life. He is the light of the world, the door, the good shepherd, the vine (John 14:6; 9:5; 10:7, 11; 15:1). Jesus is the *Logos* of God, meaning the structure of reality, the creative speech, the "conversation" of God, the wisdom of God (John 1:1-5). According to the Nicene Creed (A.D. 325), Jesus Christ is "God from God, Light from Light, . . . one Being with God."

To take one of these images, Jesus is the way. Our lives, envisioned as journeys, seek the way to God, who is our source. This way is hidden from us by our stubborn refusal to let God be God—that is, by our sin. But our God is tenderhearted and compassionate. Jesus is the action of God in the world to make possible the way to God. None of our spiritual practices by themselves can get us to God. We are inevitably hobbled by our self-interest, by our desire to be the center of the universe, or by our sloth in denying our responsibility and dignity. The assertion that Jesus is the way is thus much more than the claim that he is our example. It is the claim that he is the very offering of God that makes the spiritual practices possible. It is the grace of God that initiates our relationship to God, and it is the grace of God that energizes us to activity, not to create the relationship but to exercise it, to give the relationship the attention that gives the possibility of growth. Christian spiritual practices occur in the context of the kingdom or reign of God. They are the appropriate response of the disciples of Jesus to the present and future rule of God in our own hearts and in all of the universe. We do not see this future rule yet, but the promise is, to use Julian of Norwich's famous phrase, that "all shall be well, and all shall be well, and every manner of thing shall be well."[1] Second, Jesus provides an *example* of spiritual practice by integrating his inner and outer life. He was, as a human being, on intimate terms with God. He rose early in the morning to commune with God. He referred to God as his "Abba," his dad or father. In the Garden of Gethsemane, he wrestled with God, first telling the truth about his feelings and then submitting to the Father's will. His outward life demonstrated compassion for all, especially the marginalized—women, the poor, the sick. Ultimately, his life showed compassion unto death, even for those who berated him. Jesus showed fierce opposition to those who distorted the ways of God. He used his intellect to confound his enemies. He attended temple and discussed theology with the learned. He healed all sorts of people, showing the importance of the bodies of people, not just their souls. He is the only founder of a major religion who took this time to heal people's bodies as well as their minds and spirits. A spiritual practice that looks to the example of Jesus will integrate prayer with action, will seek intimacy with God while taking a healing approach to people, and will confront the powers of evil while comforting the oppressed.

Third, Jesus is the *promise* of Christian spiritual formation because he is the resurrected Lord and he is the baptizer with the Holy Spirit. Jesus is able to be that promise because he is alive today and will bring the world to its consummation.

All four Gospels assert that John the Baptizer predicted that the one coming after him would baptize not only with water but with the Holy Spirit (Matthew 3:11; Mark 1:8; Luke 3:16; John 1:33). In John the resurrected Jesus sends "another Advocate" (John 14:16), the Spirit of truth, upon his followers. It is clear that the Acts of the Apostles sees this promise start to be fulfilled in the event of Pentecost, when the Spirit fell upon 120 of Jesus' followers (Acts 1:5; 2:1-4). Peter extended the same promise to anyone who repented, believed in Jesus, and was baptized (Acts 2:38-39). The implication of the whole book of Acts is that it is this Spirit who motivates and empowers the believers to share, evangelize, and heal. Their spirituality is centered on the Spirit given them by Jesus.

The power of the resurrection is a promise both for now and for the future. For now, Martin Luther describes the Christian life as a daily death and resurrection because of this power. For the future, the promise is that we and all creation (Romans 8:18-23) will overcome the power of death and that we will drink from the river of living water both now and in the New Jerusalem (Revelation 21:6; 22:1-2). Our spiritual practice is "tuning our instruments at the door" (John Donne) before we enter the great choir in the New Jerusalem.[2]

Jesus offers the spiritual person a new basis for spiritual practice by being the way, by giving an example, and by offering a promise for the present and the future. These three models can be summarized by saying that Jesus is the basis for our faith, love, and hope.

Spiritual Teachings in the Bible

The Bible is not simply one book but a whole library, written and collected over centuries by many writers in different situations. Thus it must be interpreted with care, considering the purpose of the writer and the cultural situation in which it was written. Generally, it is not a sound method of interpretation to take one verse as the "answer" to a present-day issue; rather, one must look for the main themes of the whole. In a book of this size, it is impossible to note the spiritual teachings of the whole Bible. Thus I have chosen a few examples that seem important, and I hope that you, the reader, will find your own way by reading both the Bible itself and other books about it, including commentaries, dictionaries, and devotional readings.

The Old Testament
Different genres or types of writing are spiritually fruitful in the Hebrew Bible, or Old Testament. Among these are various kinds of narratives, prayers, songs, prophetic oracles, and law codes. The *narratives* of the Torah, or Pentateuch, provide a basic and profound understanding of the relations among God, humanity, and the natural world. The covenant between Israel and its God is the focus of much of the five books. The *historical* books, the second main part of the canon, describe the colorful adventures of such major figures as Joshua, Deborah, Hannah, Samuel, David, Solomon, Hulda, and Josiah. The books named the *prophets* speak a living word from God to the people, not usually about the future but about their current practices. The prophets condemn spiritual practices without heartfelt obedience to God and care for other people. Finally, come the *writings*, a miscellaneous group of wisdom books, which includes Proverbs; of songs, including Psalms and Song of Solomon; and an apocalyptic book, Daniel.

Much of Genesis tells the story of the family of Jacob, also known as "Israel" (Genesis 27–50). In the final chapters of the book, we see Jacob's favorite son, Joseph, providing food for the whole family and forgiving his brothers after their attempt at murder led to selling him into slavery. As Joseph says, their plans were not God's plans. The whole story may lead to someone today who is in a difficult relationship taking comfort in the thought that a wider picture than is evident exists, that God is at work in the world with plans bigger than the individual can see.

The narrative of Naaman the Syrian general can serve as an example from the historical books (2 Kings 5). It tells how the great and mighty general must humble himself in order to be healed. His healing would not be possible but for the words of a little girl, who knows that the prophet Elijah can heal.

It is important to note that not all of the narratives of the Bible provide positive role models for spirituality. The saints of the Bible are shown "warts and all." A great deal of the Old Testament is not appropriate for children in Sunday School. This especially applies to the stories of violence and sex that demonstrate the low status of women in Israelite society. But it is not only the "nice" stories that can be spiritually fruitful for the adult reader. We may be jerked clean out of our presuppositions by the angular turns of a shocking story.

The prophets of the Old Testament speak in poetry, using striking metaphors that may burn our hearts with conviction of wrong:

> Ah, you who are wise in your own eyes,
>   and shrewd in your own sight!
> Ah, you who are heroes in drinking wine
>   and valiant at mixing drink,
> who acquit the guilty for a bribe,
>   and deprive the innocent of their rights!
> Therefore, as the tongue of fire devours the stubble,
>   and as dry grass sinks down in the flame,
> so their root will become rotten,
>   and their blossom go up like dust;
> for they have rejected the instruction of the LORD of hosts,
>   and have despised the word of the Holy One of Israel. (Isaiah
>   5:21-24)

On the other hand, the prophets speak in consoling tones when the people have become disheartened. This happened when Judah was taken into exile in Babylon. A prophet now commonly called Second Isaiah is called to give the people courage for the day when they will return home:

> Comfort, O comfort my people,
>   says your God.
> Speak tenderly to Jerusalem,
>   and cry to her
> that she has served her term,
>   that her penalty is paid,
> that she has received from the LORD's hand
>   double for all her sins. (Isaiah 40:1-2)

The Psalms have a special place in Christian spirituality as model prayers from all emotional levels. Their general character makes them appropriate for individuals with specific, contemporary problems. The Psalms are chanted by Catholic monks, included in the *Book of Common Prayer* by Anglicans, sung metrically by Presbyterians and the Church of Scotland, and used by members of all denominations in public worship and private devotion.

Poetry as well as narrative gives spiritual food to the thoughtful reader. The poetry of the Hebrew Bible includes psalms of praise that can lift the spirit to worship:

> Come, bless the LORD, all you servants of the LORD,
>   who stand by night in the house of the LORD!
> Lift up your hands to the holy place,
>   and bless the LORD. (Psalm 134:1-2)

But much of human life consists of grief and sorrow. Some Christians seem to think that they must be happy all the time, immune from the darker emotions that plague others. Getting through the denial to face honestly the hurts in one's heart is a step that may be facilitated by the Psalms. Many people are not aware of how rich the psalms of lament can be, expressing the pain of human existence and the silence of God in a frank manner:

> Be gracious to me O LORD, for I am languishing;
>   O LORD heal me, for my bones are shaking with terror.
> My soul also is struck with terror
>   while you, O LORD — how long? (Psalm 6:2-3)

Finally, the Song of Solomon, or Song of Songs, offers something completely different: erotic poems expressing the love of a man and a woman. It is a very egalitarian collection in terms of gender: the woman is just as important as the man and, in fact, speaks more. This book can be taken on the literal level to indicate the goodness of sex, as implied in chapter 1 of Genesis, where God declares the creation (including sex) to be very good. Or it can be read allegorically, as many Jews and Christians have done, seeing the partners as representatives of God and human beings in a relationship of loving longing.

The New Testament
The New Testament witnesses back to the life of Jesus. To the surprise of many Christians, it was not the Gospels that were written first but, rather, the letters of Paul. The New Testament canon is not organized in the order the books were composed! Very likely the oldest book in the New Testament is either Galatians or 1 Thessalonians. If we divide the first century into thirds for the sake of study, we find that the first third contains the life of Jesus, the middle third contains the writings of Paul, and the last third is the

period when the four Gospels were written, along with the Acts of the
Apostles and most of the other books of the collection. I like to call this last
group the "writings" of the New Testament.

Paul the theologian, missionary, and letter writer is immensely important to Christian spirituality. He sees Jesus as a world-changing event by
which God reconciled the world to himself. Although he does not report
very much about the life of Jesus in his letters, he does focus on the death and
resurrection, along with the importance of the Holy Spirit for Christian living. He addresses the practical problems of living as a Christian in the first
century, starting with the relation of Jews and Gentiles. Paul is the first of
many in Christian history who serves as the midwife of a new Christian culture. Under his leadership, the Jewish sect who followed the Nazarene was
gradually transformed into a Jewish-Gentile church community that spread
widely beyond Palestine. So began the first of many cultural translations of
the gospel message. Paul wrote in Greek and addressed Greek ways of
thought, a dialogue that led to new questions and new answers about the
faith and spiritual practice of what was called "the Way."

Among Paul's many contributions to Christian spirituality, we will mention only six. He focused attention not on human activity but on the event of
reconciliation with God through the good news about the death and resurrection of Jesus (Romans 3-8; 1 Corinthians 15). He explained spiritual life
as life in the Spirit (Romans 8). He delineated both gifts of the Holy Spirit
(1 Corinthians 12–14) and fruit of the Spirit (Galatians 5:16-26). He identified faith, love, and hope as the primary characteristics of a Christian person
(1 Corinthians 13). He described spiritual life as a life of freedom, specifically
of freedom from the law (Galatians 3-5). Paul's life became a personal example of strenuous devotion, of ecstatic visions, and of love for others while living at peace because of his confidence in Jesus Christ (2 Corinthians 4:7-18;
11–12; Acts 9–28).

What might these themes mean for us today? An exhaustive answer cannot be attempted here, but let us look at one example, the theme of freedom
from the law. Paul writes: "For freedom Christ has set us free. Stand firm,
therefore, and do submit again to a yoke of slavery" (Galatians 5:1). Spiritual
disciplines can become like the Old Testament law: helpful and life giving, or
destructive and death dealing. They become harmful when they become a kind
of legalism, a cage of rules that imprisons our spirits. For Paul, the imposition
of circumcision on gentile Christians was an enslaving rite because it made the
new covenant in Christ meaningless. Today the issues are different, but any
person can get caught up in nit-picking scrupulosity and lose the freedom
given by a secure relationship with God. If Paul is right, the grace of God in
Christ has, by securing us to him, made us free to explore the world, boldly
risking offense to the rules if done for the sake of God's glory.

In the four Gospels, we have a balanced, selective retelling of the life, death, and resurrection of Jesus. None of the noncanonical gospels, such as the Gospel of Thomas, describe all three of these essential elements. They tend to focus on Jesus' teaching alone, and often in Gnostic fashion. Gnosticism was the earliest of the heresies combated in the Christian tradition, starting in the New Testament but continuing, some would say, until the present day. Early Gnosticism asserted that the creation was not good, that Jesus could not have had a body, and that we are saved from this wretched world by esoteric knowledge given to a few. It was very "spiritual," in the sense that it denied the goodness of the physical.

A healthy Christian spirituality will engage the whole story of Jesus' life, which includes the incarnation (meaning the Word of God becoming flesh); the ministry (including healing and exorcism, teaching about the kingdom or reign of God, debating with his opponents, teaching and practicing prayer and sacrament); the Passion (Jesus' last week in Jerusalem, including his arrest, trials, suffering, and death); the resurrection (his empty tomb and appearances to the disciples concluding with his ascension); and Jesus' pouring out the Holy Spirit to empower his followers (Pentecost).

Indeed, it may be appropriate to focus on one element of this story for a week or even for a stage of one's life, but only in the context of the whole. It is possible to take only one element out of the context of Jesus' whole life—for example, the incarnation, or the healing, or the suffering. To do so distorts the meaning of Jesus for the spiritual life. For example, some today treat Jesus only as a purveyor of good advice rather than a creator of good news, reducing him to a human prophet alone. Others have such a fix on Jesus' divinity and on the cross that they seem not to listen to him at all as a prophet.

We have four canonical witnesses to Jesus' teachings about spiritual practice. It is helpful to consider each one separately, for each has a distinctive point of view about Jesus. This difference does not reduce but only enhances the credibility of their witness as a whole. Getting a four-dimensional view of Jesus is much better than having a single, homogenized view.

Matthew structures his Gospel around five major discourses, or speeches, of Jesus. The first of these is Jesus' best known: the Sermon on the Mount. Among many other subjects, this discourse touches specifically on three spiritual practices: giving to charity, praying, and fasting. In each case, Jesus warns about doing the practice to gain a good reputation among others. Rather, he says, we should do them in secret, where God sees them, so the intrinsic value is also our motive (Matthew 6:1-18). Jesus offers in this section a model prayer that many Christians today still recite from memory and that forms in its structure an example of many of the elements of a balanced prayer life. Jesus warns against the seduction of wealth, insisting that we can have but one master (Matthew 6:19-21, 24). He invites the weary to come to him, to bear his "easy" yoke (Matthew 11:28-30). He especially warns against thinking oneself righteous before God because of spiritual practices and warns against judging other people (Matthew 7:1-5; compare Luke 6:39-42; 18:9-14). In his fifth discourse, Jesus says that his genuine disciples will feed the hungry, give drink to the thirsty, welcome the stranger, clothe the naked, and visit the sick and imprisoned (Matthew 25:31-36). Finally, in his "famous last words," Jesus sends out the disciples to make other disciples, to teach, and to baptize (Matthew 28:16-20).

In the Synoptic Gospels—Matthew, Mark, and Luke—the main theme of Jesus' preaching is the kingdom or reign of God. It is widely agreed that Mark is the oldest of these three Gospels. Mark's spirituality focuses on the urgency of Jesus' message. Mark frequently uses the word *immediately* to press on from one story of Jesus to the next. In this Gospel, Jesus goes out to pray early in the morning. By healing people, he demonstrates that the reign of God is at hand. He tells parables to teach the nature of that reign.[3] He casts out demons, leaving people whole and healthy again. His identity is a secret, even to his own disciples. He repeats three times that he must go and die in Jerusalem, but his disciples don't get it. He tells them that to follow him means denying themselves and bearing the cross. Jesus' resurrection story leaves the women distressed and afraid. Mark is the favorite Gospel for some people because it is the least refined and makes Jesus most human.

Luke decides that he needs two volumes to tell the story, first a volume based on Mark, which ends after the resurrection, and a second volume to continue to tell the actions of Jesus through his followers for the next twenty-five years or so, showing how the teachings and healings of Peter and Paul mirror their master's. This second volume, which we call the Acts of the Apostles, emphasizes the role of the Holy Spirit in Christian spirituality and ministry. In Luke's first volume, he tells the story of Jesus' birth in such a way that the songs of praise he includes help to raise the reader's heart in praise as well. Luke makes clear that Jesus is from humble stock, was born in a lowly place, and was first worshiped by people of little account in their society.

Jesus reads from Isaiah at the beginning of his ministry to define his vocation, and perhaps the vocation of all who follow him: "The Spirit of the Lord is upon me" (Luke 4:18). At every important juncture, before every important decision in Luke, Jesus prays. He models compassion for all who suffer or are at the margins of society (Luke 7:1-23). Luke points us to the two greatest commandments—love to God and love to neighbor—and redefines the neighbor in the parable of the good Samaritan (Luke 10:25-37). Going against custom, Jesus, a rabbi, teaches women (Luke 10:38-42). He heals people, allowing them to stand up straight and free from oppressive demons (Luke 13:10-17). He teaches by the parables of the lost sheep, the lost coin, and the lost son (or prodigal son) that God cares for sinners, not just for those who think themselves righteous (Luke 15). Luke warns seriously about the dangers of wealth (Luke 18). His Jesus is compassionate right to his death on the cross, forgiving his persecutors and the thief beside him. He finishes his life with a prayer.

John presents us with a different vision of the importance of Jesus for spirituality: Jesus as the one who unites people with God. Rather than emphasize the reign of God, John's Gospel focuses on eternal life, light, and love. Jesus is the Word of God made flesh, who through seven carefully chosen signs clearly reveals his divine status and power. Yet only in John do we read of Jesus taking off his clothes to wash the feet of his disciples, teaching that spiritual leaders are those who serve, not dominate. In his closing discourse (John 14–17), Jesus makes clear that he is one with the Father and that his followers are one with him and with the Father. This theme of union with God will be very influential in later spiritual writings.

The third and final part of the New Testament is the writings, those books at the end of the canon beginning with Hebrews and concluding with Revelation. Here we read the concerns of the second and third generations after Paul. Defending against false teachings and organizing the flock are important here. Because of limited space, I will mention only a few themes from this varied collection that are relevant to spirituality.

In 1 John, a letter from an elder, the author elaborates on similar themes to those in the Gospel of John. The letter is especially clear about the importance of love in the Christian life. A challenging theme of this letter is the concept of "perfection" (2:5; 4:12, 17, 18), a concept also used by Matthew (Matthew 5:48; 19:21). The term *perfection* is important in later spirituality and can be misleading. The first Egyptian monks, the Roman Catholic religious orders, and the early Methodists have pondered and employed this word a great deal. The early Methodists also saw a concept of perfection as their main contribution to Christian theology and spirituality. None of these identifies perfection with the common use of the term today, and certainly not with psychological perfectionism, an affliction that many of us suffer! The word refers not to the absence of any flaws but, rather, to a fullness of development. A better translation might be "whole," "complete," "fully developed."

The Book of Revelation, or Apocalypse, presents an apocalyptic spirituality—that is, a life lived in the promise that the evil oppressor will soon be overthrown and that those who have died under his rule will be vindicated. At present, the *Left Behind* series is gaining a great deal of attention, with its dispensationalist, premillennial, posttribulation reading of Revelation. The series dramatizes a very controversial interpretation, rooted in the writings of John Nelson Darby from the 1830s. It is important, in my opinion, that this particular reading of the text should not become the standard reading, lest the spiritual message of the Book of Revelation be lost.[4]

That spiritual message includes at least two prominent themes. The first is the beauty of worship as depicted in the visions of the throne and the lamb. The concept of all the peoples of the world joining in worship is so full of wonder!

> After this I looked, and there was a great multitude that no one could count, from every nation, from all tribes and peoples and languages, standing before the throne and before the Lamb, robed in white, with palm branches in their hands. They cried out in a loud voice, saying,
>
> "Salvation belongs to our God who is seated on the throne, and to the Lamb!"
>
> And all the angels stood around the throne and around the elders and the four living creatures, and they fell on their faces before the throne and worshiped God, singing,
>
> "Amen! Blessing and glory and wisdom
> and thanksgiving and honor
> and power and might
> be to our God forever and ever! Amen." (Revelation 7:9-12)

The second theme is ultimate justice. The whole book of Revelation must be read in the context of the persecution of Christians during the time it was written. Like the Old Testament prophets, this apocalyptic book promises justice to the oppressed. But, unlike the prophets of old, it uses strange, otherworldly imagery that is very difficult to understand. The point is that the suffering ones will not suffer forever, that God is both powerful and loving enough to set things to right in the end.

The Old Testament, Jesus, and the New Testament are fundamental to Christian spirituality. Though this chapter has provided only a brief introduction, its themes will be elaborated through the story of the twenty centuries that follow it. All of the figures and movements in the rest of this book are somehow outgrowths of this chapter, for better or for worse, in different cultural situations.

The Bible in Spiritual Practice

Preparation

Both stories and poetry originally written long ago in a different culture can still be meaningful to readers today. Such writings become meaningful through the work of the Spirit of God, who uses them to address the person disposed to listen. Being "disposed" is not our usual state, however. It takes time and concentration to listen, to study, to quiet our hearts and become attentive. If we believe that God can speak to us through the text of the Bible, prayer is an essential preparation for hearing God's voice. Prayer can open our ears to hear by directing our thoughts to God and by helping us be willing to hear, sometimes when we are too distracted or too self-centered to want to hear. Willingness and attentiveness are the attitudes we want to develop as we approach the Word.

Communal Practice and Personal Practice

In the history of the Bible, communal reading comes before private reading. Remember that before the invention of printing with moveable type, around 1500, the Bible was available only in monasteries and churches, with each copy worth more than a year's wages. Even earlier than that, remember that the original biblical texts were shared in the community by reading aloud. Think of Moses (Exodus 19) and later Ezra (Nehemiah 8:1-8) reading the Torah to the people. Recall Jesus himself reading Isaiah to the congregation in Nazareth (Luke 4:16-20). Imagine the letters of Paul being read aloud, first to the addressed congregation, then later in groups of letters shared with many congregations. The four Gospels have a similar oral background.

Today, reading the Bible at home and hearing the Bible in the assembly are two of the basic Christian spiritual disciplines. In the assembly, we may encounter the Bible in liturgical responses, hymns, or prayers, depending on the particular tradition of that church. But reading the Scriptures and preaching on the Scriptures are two elements of almost all Christian worship. So if you are serious about hearing the Word of God, prepare yourself by pondering the texts in advance, if possible. Prepare by having an attitude of expectation. Expect to catch a hint from the reading, not only from the preaching.

Ideally, preaching will bring the message of one part of the Bible home to the hearer in a vivid, creative way that causes a response of faith, love, and hope in the hearer. The ideal sermon will bring the hearer a new insight into the life situation of the congregation and will proclaim the good news of God's grace in Jesus. But preaching often has a bad reputation, sometimes well deserved. Sometimes the sermon does not relate to the Bible; other times it does not relate to the hearers. But there are plenty of good preachers out there if you look for them. The main point for me as a listener is not simply to condemn or give up, but to look hard for some thought or inspiration that can be helpful in my life. If the sermon is totally unhelpful, I will look elsewhere in the service for elements that are encouraging to my spiritual life.

The general point is that it is still valuable to *hear* the Scriptures read and preached. Hearing and looking are different experiences, and looking can sometimes leave us cold while hearing touches the heart. Just as music can lead us to a depth of experience not possible in silence, so the sound waves created by oral reading can sometimes reach the heart when silent reading off the page will not do so. The eyes and the ears affect our souls differently.

This is not to say that private reading of Scriptures is not of great value! Since the Bible is now available in print in so many languages, it is possible to encounter these texts alone or in a family. It is a good idea to sing a hymn, if possible, to prepare one's heart for this reading. Then take a small portion and deal with it slowly. Engage it through praying it, journaling it, pondering it. These practices call for all the powers of your mind and heart, including interpreting, reasoning, empathizing, imagining, and responding.

Becoming constantly immersed in the story of Israel and of Jesus and the apostles is a way of shaping one's spiritual worldview. The stories of the Bible offer good and bad examples of behavior, some of it inspiring, some of it despicable. All of the virtues and vices of the human heart are on display there. The stories usually include activity of God, which often shows God's love for people in difficult circumstances.

Study

Although intellectual encounter with the Bible must be distinguished from the encounter of the heart (that is, the person), for some people the best spiritual practice is indeed applying the mind to the many intellectual challenges presented by the Bible. C. S. Lewis once remarked that he often found studying a difficult matter in theology, pipe clenched between his teeth, more helpful than reading devotional guides. The point is that although spiritual reading is different from academic reading, it does not replace study but builds upon it.

Study may mean simply reading large sections of the Bible. The knowledge gained by this discipline can be very helpful when reading small sections, to give a sense of related themes from elsewhere in the Bible or, on the contrary, to show that the small text is strange to the larger context and must be evaluated in the wider context.

Study can also mean an encounter with historical and literary methods of analyzing the Bible. These can at times be challenging to the reader's faith, upsetting previous assumptions. Such methods can be harmful to one's Bible reading as a spiritual practice if they produce such skepticism that the Bible no longer seems a divinely inspired book written by human beings but, rather, a totally human product. But such a conclusion is not necessary! These methods can serve the spiritual purpose of the Bible by showing new ways in which the texts have and will be applied.

Imaginative Meditation

One of the most important spiritual practices is empathizing with characters in these stories. For example, Henri Nouwen has written a whole book about placing oneself in the shoes of the three main characters of the prodigal son parable: younger son, elder son, and father.[5] Different moments of our spiritual lives parallel the experiences of each character. Like the younger son, we too know rebellion, escape, pleasure seeking, disillusionment, self-knowledge, and return. Like the elder son, we too know loyalty, hard work, resentment, envy, self-pity, and self-righteousness. Like the father, we too know reckless love, longing, discouragement, forgiving love, and joyful celebration.

There are two ways to use the imagination. One is to place ourselves in the ancient setting right along with the sons and the father, with Mary and Martha, with Jesus and Mary. The other is to bring the ancient persons forward to our own day, to see how they might respond to the challenges of today. In either case, as Ignatius of Loyola teaches us, we use all our senses to experience the events and persons in a living way. They will then have a deep impact on our personalities at conscious and unconscious levels.

Lectio Divina

An important method, used for centuries, is called *lectio divina* (LEX-see-o de-VEE-nah), or sacred reading. Unlike the more intellectual ways of reading the Bible that some readers may know well from university and seminary classes, this method does not so much focus on factual knowledge or theories of reconstructing the text, all of which may be useful, as it focuses on personal knowledge, knowing yourself in relation to God. It attends to the Scriptures in small pieces, slowly, orally, repeatedly. A typical procedure for a group would include silence for the group to become really present; the audible reading of the text three times, with silence between the readings; and personal reflection on what stood out in the text and why. The group may then share insights by writing, drawing, or speaking. Each may gain not only from personal attention to the text but also by what others have heard.

Macrina Wiederkehr suggests six stages for *lectio divina*. As a Benedictine sister, she has practiced this meditative reading enough to suggest some minor changes in the classic order of the four steps: reading, meditation, prayer, and contemplation. Wiederkehr suggests the name "Romancing the Word" for this process, for it may involve seeking the hidden and exposing pain as well as finding the lover! She compares the process to the familiar parable of Jesus about the sower and the seed (Luke 8:4-15). Wiederkehr begins with the fallow season: quieting the soul. This is a silent time for becoming receptive. Then comes the actual sowing of the seed: reflective reading. The text is first encountered here, taking one's time. She then inserts resting in the soil: contemplative sitting, to let the Word speak, before moving on to the reaping: meditation. This silence is more active than the previous step, as the person wrestles with the text. Next is the song of the seed: prayer. We address God with our feelings and thoughts from encountering the text. Finally, she suggests gleanings: journaling as a way to end the day, reflecting on how the text has influenced our day.[6]

Aids for the Exercises

Paulsell, William O. *Let my Prayer Rise to God.* St. Louis: Chalice, 2002.

Pennington, M. Basil. *Lectio Divina: Renewing the Ancient Practice of Praying the Scriptures.* New York: Crossroad, 1998.

Dumm, Demetrius. *Praying the Scriptures.* Collegeville, Minn.: Liturgical Press, 2003.

Magrassi, Mariano. *Praying the Bible: An Introduction to Lection Divina.* Tr. Edward Hagman. Collegeville, Minn.: Liturgical Press, 1998.

Suggested Reading

Introducing the Bible

Aaseng, Rolf E. *A Beginner's Guide to Studying the Bible.* Minneapolis: Augsburg, 1991.

Barclay, William. *Introducing the Bible.* Nashville: Abingdon, 1972.

Ferlo, Roger. *Opening the Bible.* Cambridge, Mass.: Cowley, 1997.

Koester, Craig R. *A Beginner's Guide to Reading the Bible.* Minneapolis: Augsburg, 1991.

Rhodes, Arnold B. and W. Eugene March. *The Mighty Acts of God.* Revised Edition. Louisville, Ky.: Geneva Press, 2000.

Spiritual Reading

Fitzmyer, Joseph A. *Spiritual Exercises Based on Paul's Epistle to the Romans.* Grand Rapids: Eerdmans, 2004.

Kater, John L., Jr. *Jesus, My Mentor: A Spirituality for Living.* St. Louis: Chalice, 2004.

Mulholland, M. Robert, Jr. *Shaped by the Word: The Power of Scripture in Spiritual Formation.* Rev. ed. Nashville: Upper Room, 2000.

Wiederkehr, Macrina, O.S.B. *The Song of the Seed: A Monastic Way of Tending the Soul.* San Francisco: Harper, 1995.

Chapter 4

The Beginnings of a Global Community

The first followers of Jesus were Jews, and they became one sect among others, the Nazareans (from Nazareth). They saw Jesus as the Promised One, not only as Messiah (anointed king) but as suffering servant, crucified for all, and as Lord, raised from the dead. The other Jews rejected this group, especially after the destruction of the Jerusalem temple in A.D. 70. Nazareans had largely escaped from Jerusalem, so they did not share the suffering of other Jews; they also attributed the destruction of the temple to the rejection of Jesus the Messiah (or Christ). The other Jews excluded the Nazareans from synagogue worship by inserting a curse on Christians in the liturgy of worship.

Thereafter, Judaism and Christianity separated, siblings created in the first century from the common stock of the people of Israel. The Judaism of today is the offspring of the rabbinical movement that emerged about the same time as Christianity. Each group came to interpret the Hebrew Bible (the Old Testament) by means of a later collection of their own literature. The Jews used the Talmud; the Christians, the New Testament.

The good news about Jesus came to be preached to Gentiles, especially those called "God-fearers," who were attracted to local Jewish synagogues but did not choose to be circumcised in order to become Jews. According to Acts, Paul preached to such people in his travels. Because of the Jewish rejection, the percentage of Jewish Christians dwindled, but the Gentiles gladly heard this message, which included the monotheism and high ethical standards of Judaism without the requirement of circumcision.

What happened here was that Christianity emerged from being a sect within an ethnic group into a religion accessible to all peoples. Its roots were in Hebrew and Jewish culture, but now it became, in principle, transcultural, capable of expressing itself in a variety of cultures. In practice, the believers within the Roman Empire were from various ethnic cultures, largely overlaid by late Hellenistic (Greek) culture in the East and by an emerging Latin culture in the West. Those outside Roman rule had other cultures, including

Coptic, Ethiopian, Celtic, and Persian. The long-range implication was that Christianity was potentially a world religion, a faith that could interact with all human cultures. This interaction would later involve adaptations of both the practice of Christianity and the cultures it confronted, as the gospel message produced religious traditions of various types.

Gentile Christianity in the Roman Empire began as a minor sect that was frequently misunderstood and persecuted. In its first three centuries, its members were accused of atheism (not believing in any of the gods), cannibalism (eating the body and blood of Jesus in secret ceremonies), and superstition (believing what others did not believe because of an obscure Galilean preacher). Sometimes they were thrown to the lions or simply beheaded. By the time of Constantine, the first Roman emperor who claimed this faith, about 10 percent of the people in his empire had adopted Christianity as their personal faith.

In A.D. 313, Constantine declared Christianity a licit (lawful) religion. Constantine later founded a new city in the East modestly named after himself (Constantinople) to rule the Roman Empire. The eastern part was thereafter commonly called the Byzantine Empire (see map 2). We know the city today as Istanbul, perched on the dividing line between Europe and Asia in Turkey. After Constantine, the emperors came to embrace a church-state connection that was to be of great consequence for the history of Christianity in Europe and elsewhere. They made Christianity not only licit but required of all citizens. By the fifth century, Christianity was no longer a persecuted sect but a reigning majority, with wealth, status, and power.

That position of power was to prove a stumbling block to the growth of Christianity among non-European peoples, especially the Persians, who associated it with the oppression of Byzantium. Within Europe itself, Christianity gained an imperial status it had not known during its first three hundred years of widespread growth. Now, it expanded more frequently by royal edict than out of personal conviction. Then, it had been dangerous to be a Christian; now, it was the socially accepted, even the required, thing to do. This transition meant that the hardy Christians of the first three centuries, especially the martyrs, were held in high regard by the privileged ones of the next three.

We see in the first six centuries the beginning and development of certain themes in Christian spirituality that retain their significance to the present day: worship and sacraments, charisms, witness unto death, spiritual disciplines, monasticism, and mysticism. These themes were important in both Roman and non-Roman contexts. We will now explore each of these themes.

Worship and Sacraments

> In public worship . . . we use the familiar elements of every-
> day life—food, water, oil, embrace, word—to proclaim and
> celebrate what God is doing in the world and in our lives.
> Worship distills the Christian meaning of the practices and
> holds them up for the whole community to see. . . . A
> Christian community at worship is a community gathered
> for rehearsal. It is "practicing" the practices.
> —Craig Dykstra and Dorothy C. Bass,
> "Times of Yearning, Practices of Faith"

The individualistic assumptions that we now bring to spirituality did not apply in the first century. As Judaism developed a congregational form of worship in the synagogues of the diaspora, so Christians, the first of whom were Jews, assumed that public, communal worship was basic to spirituality. Those first Jewish Christians in Jerusalem, we are told in Acts, attended prayers in the impressive temple built by Herod the Great. But Christians in other places worshiped in the local house of prayer or synagogue.

Most of the basic elements of Christian worship were inherited from the synagogue: prayer, psalms, scripture reading, sermon, singing. What was added was the weekly meal of bread and wine, which seems to be an adaptation of either the annual Jewish Passover or of a rabbi's meal with his disciples, a *kiddush*. Partaking of this common meal or Lord's Supper was a celebration of the resurrection of the Master, who had said, "Do this in remembrance of me." But it was also seen as participating in the "body of Christ" and receiving this "bread of heaven" in a very realistic manner. This Eucharist ("thanksgiving") became the center of Christian worship.

First as small groups, later as immense congregations in cathedrals, Christians gathered on the first day of the week for prayer, preaching, and the Eucharist. Worship became more elaborate as time passed, but its importance for Christian spirituality was not questioned. Private prayer no doubt had its place, but the social character of the "body of Christ" meant that common prayer was central.

Baptism as initiation into the community was seen as the end of the old life and the beginning of the new. Some took this to mean that baptism meant the forgiveness of previous sins in the old life but that the new life was to be perfect, without sin. This understanding led some to postpone baptism because they feared there would be no forgiveness afterward! Deathbed baptisms were not unknown, including the famous case of Constantine himself. A Roman preacher whom we know as Hermas had tried in the second century to dissolve this anxiety about baptism by writing in his book *The*

Shepherd that there was indeed forgiveness for the baptized. It was not until ritual confession before the assembly was seen as a medicine for the post-baptismal sinner that people began once again to be baptized upon conversion or as infants.

Christian spirituality in the early centuries was communal spirituality, originating in baptism, rooted in the worship of the congregation, and nourished by weekly celebrations of the Supper instituted by Jesus.

Charisms

The charismatic element in Christianity refers to the spiritual gifts given to individual Christians for the common good. The Greek word for such a gracious, free gift, is *charisma*. These gifts may include very ordinary acts, such as washing someone's feet or sharing one's food, and extraordinary powers, such as instantly healing a sick person or conveying a specific message from God for a given situation. Charisms are traceable to the earliest days of the church and are highlighted in both Acts and 1 Corinthians. The twentieth-century Pentecostal and charismatic movements look back to these roots as expressing essential elements of Christianity.

The book of Acts, probably written in the A.D. 80s, describes the earliest years of the church from the 30s to the 60s, from the departure of Jesus to Paul's arrival in Rome. This account emphasizes the role of the Holy Spirit in the development of the earliest church by describing the Pentecost event in chapter 2 and by referring continually to the power of God's Spirit. The following verse is often chosen as a summary of the book:

> But you will receive power when the Holy Spirit has come upon you; and you will be my witnesses in Jerusalem, in all Judea and Samaria, and to the ends of the earth. (Acts 1:8)

It can be said that living the Christian life and developing the community are not within ordinary human ability. Only when the Spirit, later described as the third person of the Trinity, empowers the disciples does the community grow.

In its first honeymoon after Pentecost, the Jerusalem church lived a communal life, sharing goods. Later the church had more difficulty overcoming cultural and ethnic differences in this sharing, so it appointed some members of the *deprived* group (the Hellenists) who were "full of the Spirit and wisdom" to oversee the distribution (Acts 6).

Here are a few more examples of the work of the Spirit in Acts. In Acts 2, Peter promises the Spirit to those who repent and are baptized. In chapter 4, the Spirit empowers Peter and the whole community to speak "the word of

God with boldness." Chapters 7 and 8 describe how the Spirit guides Stephen and Philip. Paul, like all other major figures in the early community, is "filled with the Holy Spirit" in chapter 9.

The rather glowing picture of charisms, signs, and wonders in Acts must be compared with the more troubled picture that emerges from 1 Corinthians, written in the 50s. In the latter, Paul writes to a church that is splitting apart, partly because of the spiritual pride of some who exercise charisms. He lists nine charisms in chapter 12 without saying that this is a complete list (compare Romans 12 and Ephesians 4):

> To each is given the manifestation of the Spirit for the common good. To one is given through the Spirit the utterance of wisdom, and to another the utterance of knowledge according to the same Spirit, to another faith by the same Spirit, to another gifts of healing by the one Spirit, to another the working of miracles, to another prophecy, to another the discernment of spirits, to another various kinds of tongues, to another the interpretation of tongues. All these are activated by one and the same Spirit, who allots to each one individually just as the Spirit chooses. (I Corinthians 12:7-11)

It is clear that the church members in Corinth were misusing their gifts and thus tearing the community apart. In chapter 13, Paul inserts into his discussion of gifts the beautiful and profound hymn to love: "Though I speak in the tongues of men and of angels, but have not love . . ." This chapter is much better known than his discussion of the charisms in chapters 12 and 14, but the context provided in the surrounding chapters helps us realize that he is talking about the gift of tongues.

Paul suggests love not as an alternative gift to the others but as "a more excellent way" in which the gifts are to be evaluated and exercised. He underlines that the gifts are temporary, while faith, hope and love are eternal. He emphasizes that love means patience, kindness, and humility in the exercise of the gifts.

It seems likely that many churches in the first and early second centuries practiced a spirituality that encouraged charismatic expression. For example, the remarkable *Odes of Solomon*, which are believed to come from Edessa or Antioch about the year 100, express a Syriac spirituality full of praise and love for God.[1] The author or authors are unknown, but the odes may be a hymnbook (comparable to the Psalms) that expresses a charismatic spirituality full of praise:

> As the work of the ploughman is the ploughshare,
> and the work of the helmsman is the steering of the ship,

so also my work is the psalm of the Lord in his praises.
My art and my service are in his praises,
because his love has nourished my heart,
and His fruits He poured unto my lips. (16:1-5)[2]

Syriac Christianity used feminine symbols more frequently than did
Greek or Latin. The use of female images for God is not just a recent fad
in Christianity but goes back to the early centuries. The Holy Spirit was
long identified as female in Syriac spirituality, just as the Hebrew word for
spirit is feminine. In addition, a strong devotion to the Virgin Mary developed early, including the legend that Mary bore Jesus without pain. This
view seems to romanticize the birth of Jesus instead of accepting the down-
to-earth character of Mary and the incarnation. Feminine images for God
included the breasts of God flowing with milk, a symbol of nourishment
and delight. All of these themes can be seen in the remarkable *Odes of
Solomon*.

Following hints from the Old Testament, God is seen as female. Later
several medieval mystics, men and women, would refer to God as "Mother"
but retain the masculine pronoun. It should be clear that an expression of the
feminine is not only a recent concern in Christian spirituality.

The charismatic phenomena of the first century seem largely to disap-
pear in the following centuries. We have evidence concerning this change
from a document, the *Didache*, or *Teaching of the Twelve Apostles*, commonly
dated early in the second century. It is an anonymous writing, probably from
Syria, which shows the structuring of the church out of the more fluid spon-
taneity of the charismatic period. Just as Paul dealt with problems concerning the use of tongues, this document warns about misuse of prophecy.
Specifically, it warns that traveling prophets should not be allowed to stay in
a church for more than three days lest they falsely fleece the flock.

Thus the sociological demands of better organization made it necessary
for the leadership of the churches to become more learned and less spontaneous. Further, it seems from comments by later church fathers that they did
not even know what speaking in tongues was, for they had never heard or
experienced it.

The Montanists, who were condemned as heretics, had a role to play in
the growing disfavor of charismatic phenomena. Followers of **Montanus** (ca.
157) emerged in Asia Minor in the mid-second century with a "new
prophecy," an expectation of the parousia, or return of Christ, and a rigorous set of ethical norms. Montanus himself and two female assistants,
Maximilla and Priscilla, led the group. It was charged against them that they
allowed women to speak and that Montanus claimed to be the Paraclete, or
counselor, promised by Jesus in the Gospel of John.

It seems likely that their teachings were deliberately misunderstood. We have today almost no original writings that would explain their own spirituality; we have mainly the charges of their enemies. Much of what they taught was characteristic of the church in general a century earlier. They were not in step with the later replacement of the charisms by offices, easier rules of conduct, and waning of the imminent expectation of the parousia. But the group itself moved in this direction by the third century. Tertullian, whom we will meet later in this chapter, became a Montanist late in life, but it was moral rigor that attracted him, not the exercise of charisms.

At any rate, these gifts continued to be practiced on the margins of the church until the twentieth century, when they were rediscovered by Pentecostal and charismatic groups on all continents. (See chapters 8 and 9.)

Martyrs

In Christian tradition, the martyr, man or woman, was honored for holding the faith as being of higher value than life itself, for showing what one ancient writer called "contempt" for the horrors of death. The root meaning of the word *martyr* is "witness," implying that death at the hands of Romans or others was the ultimate testimony of faith.

Today the word *martyr* has acquired a negative connotation because of radical Muslims who engage in suicide bombings, killing innocent people while thinking themselves worthy of paradise. No early Christian martyr was honored for killing others; rather, they offered themselves—as Jesus did—to an innocent death, a death of conscience. Another denigration of the word in our day is due to the concept of a "martyr complex," which suggests that the person who dies must be mentally unsound and that any healthy person would value his or her own life above all else. Others, more thoughtful, view the readiness to give one's life as the ultimate gift of the truly healthy person.

Persecution of Christians began in the New Testament period, and it did not end until Constantine's legitimizing of the faith in 313. Jesus himself had said, "Take up your cross and follow me." During the sporadic persecutions by various Roman officials in different parts of the empire, the strength of the Christians' conviction was severely tested.

The theme of martyrdom appears among the earliest group of writings after the New Testament, by the so-called Apostolic Fathers. Among them, Bishop **Ignatius of Antioch** (see map 2) (160?–220?) writes on the way to Rome, addressing letters to six churches and one bishop (Polycarp) along the way. Clearly his model is Paul, who was probably martyred in Rome about A.D. 64. Ignatius's letters have the freshness and personal character of Paul's writing and often even the phrases of 1 Corinthians and other letters.

There is a clear gap, however, between the apostle and his imitator. Ignatius's images, theology, and tone do not equal the depth of his mentor.

Ignatius describes his eagerness to die for his faith, asking readers to pray for his steadfastness. At the same time, he urges them to be unified and obedient to their own bishops and to avoid heresy, especially the teaching that Jesus did not really experience birth and death on a cross (Docetism).

"We have not only to be called Christians, but to *be* Christians," he writes to the Magnesians (4:1). For Ignatius, that calling clearly implies willingness to die for the sake of the faith: "If we do not willingly die in union with his Passion, we do not have his life in us" (5:1). It is in the letter to Rome that Ignatius most fervently expresses his desire for martyrdom, imploring them not to intercede and thus prevent his death. For Ignatius, death in the coliseum means that he will "get to God." This is his passionate desire, as the climax of his life on earth.

The world is mostly an enemy according to such a perspective. There is no time for meditating on the beauties of creation in these documents. Rather, Ignatius exhorts his readers to fight the good fight, to be faithful to their bishops, and to avoid false teaching.

Another martyr in the early centuries was **Perpetua**, who met her death about A.D. 200 in Carthage. Much of the account of her martyrdom is first-person. As the young mother of an infant, she gave up her baby to others' care as she went to the stadium to meet wild beasts and eventually the sword. She defied the authority of Rome, not only to determine her religious practice but even to choose the clothes in which she would meet her death. Her account of her last days, with a conclusion written perhaps by Tertullian, is one of the rare documents describing martyrdom as it really was rather than in rhapsodic and legendary exaggerations.

Martyrdom stands as the ultimate test of any spirituality; it is the feature of discipleship that symbolizes the world's opposition to Christian devotion as well as the utmost extent of Christian commitment. It indicates a testimony to one's faith that will not deny itself no matter what human society may do to enforce conformity. Martyrdom might be thought of as a passive act, allowing oneself to be killed. But it is clear that both Ignatius and Perpetua, though they are yielded to God's will, assertively refuse to evade holy execution. In these cases, martyrdom is action in the world based on the example of Jesus himself.

Asceticism: Money, Sex, and Power

Certain disciplines have long characterized the Christian life. These spiritual practices are characterized by self-denial for the sake of the true self. All involve saying no to a good thing for the sake of saying yes to a better one.

Together these disciplines constitute *ascesis*, or asceticism. The later vows of poverty, celibacy, and obedience constitute ways of approaching three extremely important features of human life: money, sex, and power. For most Christians, the challenge is to find a middle way between libertinism and denial of these gifts, a way to use them responsibly.

Asceticism is a word not often used favorably in our own age. The basic idea is that of athletic training in preparation for a contest, for example, a race. Paul writes:

> Do you not know that in a race the runners all compete, but only one receives the prize? Run in such a way that you may win it. Athletes exercise self-control in all things; they do it to receive a perishable wreath, but we an imperishable one. (I Corinthians 9:24-25)

The Old Testament records not only a moral code, such as the Ten Commandments, but also special ascetic rules for certain situations, such as abstaining from food, alcohol, haircuts, or sex. In the New Testament, Jesus seems to assume that his followers will fast, pray, and give alms, as was common in his own day (Matthew 6:1-4, 16-18). He speaks in dramatic metaphors about the seriousness of sexual lust (Matthew 5:27-30). He calls on followers to deny themselves and take up the cross (Matthew 16:24).

In the Hellenistic context, asceticism took on forms that seldom appeared within Judaism. The exaltation of virginity and the life of celibacy, for example, were sometimes motivated by views of the world that replaced the doctrine of creation with a world-weary, late Roman despair.

Especially from the late-twentieth-century perspective, the early practice of identifying women with sex and sin must be seen as very damaging to women, to men, and to Christian spirituality. For most young people today, the discipline most relevant is not a lifelong vow of celibacy but a practice of celibacy before marriage and faithfulness in marriage. Asceticism has a basic role in any spirituality, but ascetic practices, in my opinion, can be healthy or unhealthy.

Suppose, for example, I am considering fasting from food or from television. I use two criteria for deciding on the wholesomeness of my fast. First, does the discipline of saying no still affirm the goodness of creation? Is my motivation to gain more freedom for better service, to give up something good for something better? Second, am I expressing God's love for me or seeking to achieve it? Is my human effort replacing the grace of God? Is this effort made in order to earn the love of God? Or is this discipline a response to God's forgiving grace in Christ? Does the practice lead to the freedom of the athlete who runs in the knowledge of God's love or to the bondage of a desperate attempt to earn what cannot be earned?

Or am I punishing myself to atone for sins that Christ has already forgiven? Fasting from food or from television can be very healthy disciplines if they meet the criteria.

Three early Christian theologians wrote in different languages but nevertheless agreed on the importance of ascetic disciplines for the Christian life. Tertullian, the lawyer, lived in North Africa and wrote in Latin. Origen, head of a famous catechetical school in Alexandria, wrote in Greek. Finally, Ephrem, lesser known in the West but profoundly beautiful, wrote in Syriac.

In **Tertullian** (160?–225) we hear the voice of the rigorist who exhorts Christians to separate from the world. As a Catholic, before he turned to the rigor of the Montanists, he wrote *To the Martyrs*, *Spectacles* (pagan entertainments), and *The Apparel of Women*. Each of these ascetical writings, from about the year 200, demands separation from the pagan world of Carthage, North Africa (see map 2).

Tertullian tells (potential) martyrs that they are better off in prison than in the world, since the world itself is a vast prison with disgusting moral rot and seductive temptations all about ("To the Martyrs," chapter 2). He argues with great dialectical skill against Christian attendance at the games and plays that are dedicated to pagan gods and exhibit no respect for human life or chaste morals ("Spectacles"). Finally, he urges women to dress modestly, not in gold and makeup; he says that God did not intend women to dress that way and that there is no rational ground for such "lust" to please others. In these three essays (sermons), Tertullian makes clear that, to him, a commitment to Christian spirituality means a sharp break from "the world, the flesh and the devil" (the gods of the pagans).

His discussion of pleasure in "Spectacles" (28, 29) (the general name for the various performances in Roman amphitheaters) is instructive. At these events, people were exposed naked for all to ogle, and blood lust was encouraged by fights to the death. Tertullian writes:

> And finally, if you think that you are to pass this span of life in delights, why are you so ungrateful as not to be satisfied with so many and so exquisite pleasures given you by God, and not to recognize them? For what is more delightful than reconciliation with God, our Father and Lord, than the revelation of truth, the recognition of past errors, and pardon for such grievous sins of the past? What greater pleasure is there than distaste of pleasure itself, than contempt of all the world can give, than true liberty, than a pure conscience, than a contented life, than freedom from fear of death? To trample under foot the gods of the heathen, to drive out demons, to effect cures, to seek revelations, to live unto God—these are the

pleasures, these are the spectacles of the Christians, holy, everlasting, and free of charge.[3]

Tertullian does have a point, that Christians may not notice or acknowledge the pleasures they experience by the practice of their faith.

But what is missing here is any sense of the small, daily pleasures of life—looking at flowers, listening to music, making love with one's spouse, writing creatively, working hard physically. To put it briefly, Tertullian has missed the joys of the created order in his description of "Christian" pleasures. Only the "spiritual" pleasures remain, as a foil to the artificial, often immoral pleasures of the spectacles that Rome provided for an increasingly callous populace.

Tertullian also laid the foundations for Latin doctrinal theology. As one of the first Latin authors who had an intellectual grasp of the Christian message, he forged new terms, such as *Old Testament, New Testament, Trinity*, and *person* (to describe each member of the Trinity). His influence on Latin writers after him was immense, and he was a major contributor to the eventual orthodox view of the Trinity.

Tertullian seemed to reject Greek philosophical influence in Christian theology. He asked: "What does Athens have to do with Jerusalem?" His point was that genuine teaching came from Christ, not from the speculations of the Gnostics, who seemed to gain their inspiration from the Greek philosophers. In this regard, he was not influential, because for centuries much of the Christian theology of the Roman Empire was a synthesis of Hebrew and Greek thought.

The Good News does need contextualization, that is, expression within a cultural context that is authentic to that culture. For example, Africans today have the right and responsibility to think through the Christian message and express its implications in words (preaching, theology, prayers) and artistic expression (sculpture, dance, music) that is thoroughly African.

Tertullian's question, however, may be taken as a warning for all later Christians. He calls for an evaluation of Christian teaching to see if it is true to its sources or has been influenced by some other way of thinking that distorts it. The tendency to ignore aspects of the message that challenge our assumptions is very strong when adapting the Christian message to one's own culture. Has the genuine Gospel message been distorted by cultural adaptation? Have North Americans, for example, so interpreted the Christian message that it does not challenge their affluence in a world of poverty? In our day, he might ask, "What does Hollywood have to do with Jerusalem?"

Tertullian eventually decided that even the Catholic Church was not rigorous enough for him. He joined the Montanists, whose standards of behavior were even stricter than those of the church. He came to believe that there was no forgiveness of sin after baptism and that widows and widowers should not remarry. Tertullian's ascesis was sincere, consistent, and within the bounds of orthodoxy for much of his life. Yet he missed some very important themes in what we would consider a balanced ascesis, or spirituality, today. He seems to miss the generosity of God in forgiveness, the wonder of the good creation, and the need for authentic contextualizing.

Origen (185–254), Tertullian's younger contemporary, was intrigued by ideas. He is known as the first Christian "systematic theologian"—that is, he sought to create a rationally satisfying system of thought that embodied Christian understandings of the world and God. Origen, like Tertullian, was eventually influential in the doctrine of the Trinity, but his approach was considerably different.

Origen worked within the context of Hellenism, that is, Greek culture as spread by Alexander the Great and his successors. Origen lived in the intellectual center of Hellenism, in Alexandria (named for Alexander the Great). His question became, given the sort of worldview first developed by Plato and later developed by Plotinus (Neo-Platonism), how could one understand the Christian Scriptures?

Origen set himself the task of examining in great detail the Hebrew and Christian Scriptures. His *Hexapla* was an immense project, listing six different texts side by side for detailed comparison. Origen also wrote commentaries and preached homilies on much of the Bible. In spite of this biblical interest, Origen seems to be controlled by his philosophical assumptions rather than by his biblical studies. In 553, long after his death, Origen was condemned as a heretic.

Yet his influence continued, especially through monks who found that his spiritual teachings outweighed any questions about his orthodoxy in doctrine. This spiritual teaching focused on martyrdom, prayer, and Scripture. It saw the spiritual life as an ascent to God, much as Plotinus, the Hellenistic philosopher, had envisioned it.

Origen postulated a fall of rational beings before the creation, which resulted in human souls living in this world—that is, each of us was thought to have a preexistence in which we somehow moved away from God. The goal of human life is to return to God, and in fact Origen believed that all humans (and even demons) would so return. These beliefs were among his most controversial, leading to his later condemnation.

The days of the martyrs were far from over in Origen's day. His own father was martyred in 203, and Origen himself wanted to offer his life to the authorities at age sixteen. Thanks be to his mother, however! She hid his clothes. Without trousers, he was too embarrassed to go out of the house, and one of the greatest Christian thinkers was saved for another day. Later

Origen did in fact die from the effects of torture inflicted because of his faith and is rightly called a martyr.

Origen set forth a three-stage schema for the Christian life, which in later forms was to become normative for centuries to come. He spoke of moral, natural, and contemplative levels. These are not totally exclusive or sequential but nevertheless refer to stages of development. The moral level has to do with behavior and is illustrated by the book of Proverbs. The natural level is related to intellectual, observational activity, which is reflected in Ecclesiastes. Finally, the contemplative level refers to the spiritual union with God, which is exemplified in the Song of Solomon (read allegorically, that is, as a love song between God and the church).

Later, the purgative, illuminative, and unitive stages of spiritual growth, influenced by Neo-Platonism, would reflect this teaching of Origen. He influenced Gregory of Nyssa, who was a later theologian, and "Dionysius" (discussed later in this chapter) as well as much of Eastern and Western monasticism.

The Latin and Greek languages used by Tertullian and Origen were not the only forms of early Christian spiritual writing. Syriac, a later development of Aramaic, the language of Jesus, was used in the Middle East, both within the Roman Empire and east of its borders. This is the language of **Ephrem** (306?–373), our third ascetic writer.

Syriac spirituality developed differently from that in cultures further west. It is more closely related to Judaism, a Semitic culture, although sometimes influenced by Hellenism. It became extremely ascetic. The anchorites (hermits) in the Syrian desert used their creativity in thinking up bizarre ways to demonstrate their contempt for comfort and the ways of the world. Most famous of these hermits was Simon Stylites, who lived on a pillar. Others found different ways, such as living in logs, not bathing, or falling on their faces. But later writers tried to moderate the extremes.

Ephrem's works were copied by Syrian monks long after his death. Ephrem expressed his teachings in a symbolic poetry that is still powerful today. He was a deacon in the town of Nisibis, on the border of the Roman Empire, today in southeastern Turkey. He lived the last decade of his life in exile, after the victorious Persians insisted that all Christians leave Nisibis. He did much of his writing in Edessa, just west of Nisibis (see map 2). One of the few events of his life that we know of is his service to victims of famine. In the last year of his life, he arranged for three hundred beds as well as food for the homeless and dying, personally serving their needs.

Ephrem advocated virginity not because he despised the flesh, as some of the Greek writers seem to have done. Rather, the grounds for his asceticism were marriage with the Bridegroom, the goal of wakefulness, and the ideals of Paradise.[4] As Sebastian Brock, an expert on Syriac spirituality, explains:

> The differences between these two approaches, Hellenic and Semitic, can be well illustrated if one visualizes a circle with a point in the center, where the point represents the object of theological inquiry; the philosophical tradition of theology will seek to define, to set horoi, "boundaries" or "definitions," to this central point, whereas St. Ephrem's Semitic approach through his poetry will provide a series of paradoxical statements situated as it were at opposite points on the circumference of the circle: the central point is left undefined, but something of its nature can be inferred by joining up the various points around the circumference. St. Ephrem is always very insistent that, since the center point representing the aspect of God's being under discussion stands outside creation, it thus lies beyond the ability of the created intellect to comprehend—and any claim to be able to do so is blasphemous. In all this St. Ephrem is obviously very much in harmony with the apophatic tradition of later Greek theology.[5]

The learned St. Basil had a great respect for Ephrem, and it is perhaps through Basil that the apophatic approach, which I will discuss later, became so influential. One point to note here is that spirituality does not always follow from theology but theology can follow from spirituality. Here is a sample of Ephrem's verse, in fuller expression of an apophatic approach to God.

> If someone concentrates his attention solely
> on the metaphors used of God's majesty,
> he abuses and misrepresents that majesty,
> and thus errs
> by means of those metaphors
> with which God had clothed Himself for his benefit,
> and he is ungrateful to that Grace
> which stooped low
> to the level of his childishness:
> although it has nothing in common with him,
> yet Grace clothed itself in his likeness
> in order to bring him to the likeness of itself.
>
> Do not let your intellect
> be disturbed by mere names,

for Paradise has simply clothed itself
    in terms that are akin to you;
it is not because it is impoverished
    that it put on your imagery;
rather, your nature is far too weak to be able
to attain to its greatness,
    and its beauties are much diminished
by being depicted in the pale colors
    with which you are familiar.[6]

Like many later theologians of the East, Ephrem saw the whole process of the Christian life as *theosis*, or divinization. This term was clearly expressed only once in the New Testament: 'that you . . . may become participants in the divine nature" (II Peter 1:4). But *theosis* was understood to underlie the New Testament message, especially in John, and became the basis for much of Eastern spirituality. Here is a sample from Ephrem followed by a comment from Sebastian Brock:

Divinity flew down and descended
to raise and draw up humanity.
The Son has made beautiful the servant's deformity,
and he has become a god, just as he desired.

It has sometimes been said that the concept of the divinization, or theosis, of humanity is something that crept into Christianity, and especially Eastern Christianity, under Hellenic influence. It is clear, however, that St. Ephrem, whom Theodoret described as "unacquainted with the language of the Greeks," and whose thought patterns are essentially Semitic and Biblical in character, is nonetheless an important witness to this teaching.[7]

I have discussed the asceticism of Tertullian, Origen, and Ephrem to show my conviction that asceticism is a valid aspect of Christian spirituality. However, it is sometimes but not always based on a rejection of the fourth relationship in the model used in this book: our relation to creation. An extreme asceticism leads to despising God's good gifts of creation: our bodies and the world around us. A legalistic asceticism leads to despising God's grace in favor of personal merit. But a biblical asceticism leads to a healthy sense of being able to say no to a good thing for the sake of a better or higher one; it gives self-confidence while enabling people to serve others.

Monasticism

Africa was the scene of experiments in spiritual life that have shaped both the Western and Eastern traditions ever since. It was in Egypt that men and women first entered the desert to live out more fully the ascetical life they longed for, but the practice quickly spread to Asia and Europe.

Among the first to leave civilization for solitude was **Antony** (ca. 250–353), whose life story was written by **Athanasius** (296?–373), bishop of Alexandria. Although Antony was a Copt, one of the people of ancient Egypt, and Athanasius was of Hellenist background, they came to know each other when Athanasius was repeatedly exiled, running for protection from the emperor's soldiers to the monks of the desert. Athanasius adhered stubbornly to the full divinity of Christ as stated in the Nicene Creed of 325. He suffered five exiles imposed by opponents of the idea that Christ was of "one being with the Father."

The Life of Antony tells the story of Antony's beginnings in the ascetical life after the death of his parents. He heard the gospel read in church: "Sell all that you have and give it to the poor." Immediately he did so and, renouncing economic power, entered into training with others who knew this path, learning something from each one. A crucial step for Antony was his dwelling in a tomb, the place of death, and overcoming everything that the powers of death could throw at him. Antony seemed to die himself after a ferocious attack of demons. His body was laid out at a wake, but when the people present had fallen asleep in the middle of the night, Antony awoke and silently returned to the desert! The description of his struggle in the tomb includes Antony's rescue by Christ, who in Antony's experience (and in Athanasius's theology) was the victorious conqueror of death and demons.

Then Antony penetrated deeper and deeper into the desert, carrying his offensive to the opponents' "home territory." It was understood at that time that the desert was the dwelling place of the devil and his minions; recall that Jesus too had confronted Satan in the desert. Antony gave his whole time and energy to the struggle. Like other monks, he labored for his living, but he also spent his time meditating on memorized Scripture. Many people came to him for advice and help.

Antony's life exhibits not only discipline but tenderness and service. He both lived the utterly simplified life of a hermit and advised, reconciled, healed, and encouraged those who sought his aid. His was not so much an escape from the world as it was an engagement with the enemy of humankind in spiritual combat. Antony went forth in the power of the cross to defeat Satan through Christ's victory. In doing so, he forged a new style of Christian spiritual life, the monastic. He was not the first monk in the world, but he was among the very first who entered the far desert with specifically Christian motivations.

The sayings of many who followed Antony's example, the desert fathers and mothers (yes, women went out into the desert too!), have been collected and translated again and again.[8] These short stories and sayings have given insight into the spare, clean, and rugged life of the desert; the sayings have been a potent challenge and encouragement to all who seek a singleness of vision in our own day.

Here are some samples of the short stories and words remembered from the Egyptian mothers:

[Amma (Mother) Theodora] also said, that neither asceticism, nor vigils nor any kind of suffering are able to save, only true humility can do that. There was an anchorite who was able to banish the demons; and he asked them, "What makes you go away? Is it fasting?" They replied, "We do not eat or drink." "Is it vigils?" They replied, "We do not sleep." "Is it separation from the world?" "We live in the deserts." "What power sends you away then?" They said, "Nothing can overcome us, but only humility." "Do you see how humility is victorious over the demons?"[9]

[Sarah] also said to the brothers, "It is I who am a man, you who are women."[10]

[Blessed Syncletica] also said, "As long as we are in the monastery, obedience is preferable to asceticism. The one teaches pride, the other humility. . . . Amma Syncletica said, "There are many who live in the mountains and behave as if they were in the town, and they are wasting their time. It is possible to be a solitary in one's mind while living in a crowd, and it is possible for one who is a solitary to live in the crowd of his own thoughts."[11]

Pachomius, also in the Egyptian desert, conducted the first experiments with communal monasticism, as opposed to the individual or anchorite type practiced by Antony. But the most influential founders of communal monasticism were Basil of Caesarea in the East—that is, the Greek-speaking half of the Mediterranean basin—and Benedict of Nursia in the West—the Latin-speaking part of the empire. They were the author of "rules," patterns of community life that proved themselves over time, even until today.

In the East, **Basil of Caesarea**(330–379), from what is today Turkey, exerted a major influence on monasticism. A strong belief in the superiority of communal monasticism led Basil to write two monastic rules. His emphases were on the whole of life as thanksgiving, on the spiritual gifts, and on the importance of obedience in attacking self-will. The whole process of growth, or sanctification, is the process of restoring the image of God, lost by the first parents. Basil defended Trinitarian doctrine, just as Athanasius had done before him. He was influential in asserting the full divinity of the Holy Spirit and promoted the final acceptance of the Nicene Creed at the Council of Constantinople in 381.

Basil was influenced by the earlier Alexandrian Origen; he selected some of Origen's writings for the original collection of spiritual writings named the *Philokalia* (the love of beauty, parallel to "philosophy," the love of wisdom). Later we will discuss another, much larger *Philokalia* collected in the eighteenth century. Basil's own spiritual teaching, unlike that of Origen, leads from light into divine darkness, rather than from darkness into divine light. This surprising reversal is more fully developed by Pseudo-Dionysius, whom we will meet at the end of this chapter.

Basil had two associates: Gregory of Nyssa (his brother) and Gregory of Nazianzus (his friend). Together the three are known as the Cappadocian Fathers, after the region of Cappadocia in Asia Minor (see map 2). All shared a commitment to the Nicene Creed, but each had different gifts. Basil was the organizer, the bishop, the abbot. Gregory of Nyssa was the most gifted intellectually. And Gregory of Nazianzus was most eloquent. Macrina, the sister of Basil and Gregory of Nyssa and a theologian in her own right, influenced them very much.[12]

Evagrius of Pontus (345?–399) is an important link between the Cappadocians and later writers, especially monks, Eastern and Western. He knew the Cappadocians personally, but he also traveled to Egypt and lived in the desert there. His teaching was influenced most strongly by Origen and to a lesser degree by Gregory of Nazianzus, and he became a Christian Platonist, following the lines of the philosophy developed by Plato. Though he was later condemned with Origen, his teachings circulated anonymously or under other names. It is striking that heretical writers were so influential in Medieval Christian spirituality.

The goal of life, according to Evagrius, is the recovery of the knowledge of God and the unity of rational spirits, lost in the primordial fall. The Christian life has "stages": the practical, the natural, and the theological. Evagrius counted eight dangers to the Christian life, including gluttony, lust, avarice, dejection, anger, despondency (*akedia*, or "accidie"), vainglory, and pride.[13] These dangers were later pared down to seven by John Cassian and became the "seven deadly sins": pride, envy, gluttony, lust, anger, greed, and sloth.

Apatheia (passionlessness or freedom from passion) was for Evagrius the healthy functioning of the soul's powers. It was the desirable state for Christians but not the only goal of Christian living. He thought that the goal of prayer was a stripping of the mind, a pure consciousness of God without images or thoughts. This would restore the lost knowledge of God.

John Cassian (ca. 360–432) took Evagrius's teachings to the West. He knew Evagrius in Egypt and then traveled to Marseilles, where he founded a monastery. He wrote a number of books, including his *Conferences*, which reflected what he had learned from the Egyptian monks, especially Evagrius. These readings were canonized by Benedict for reading by monks and thus came to be commonly accepted in the West. The ideas were basically those of Evagrius but now in the context of Gaul and in Latin language. John Cassian was a cross-cultural transmitter of the ideals of the Origenist stream of Egyptian monasticism.

In the West, in Italy, **Benedict** (ca. 480–547) founded the Benedictine Order, still one of the largest Catholic religious communities. After experiments with solitude, he came to develop a system of monastic governance that gave the abbot great authority while insisting on mutual discussion and advice. His *Rule* is relatively brief and nonlegalistic: the basic principles are set down without trying to settle all cases in advance.

One of the fundamental spiritual principles of the *Rule* is the incorporation of physical labor with prayer. The motto is *Ora et Labora*. The rhythm of prayers seven times each day interspersed with physical labor and eating and sleeping in moderation became the norm for Western monks up to the present day.

Benedict also prescribed *lectio divina*, or sacred reading, for four hours each day. Monks were to read the Scriptures and the early Christian writers and then meditate on them in silence or while working (six hours daily). Benedict praised silence as a virtue. How far we have come from his ideals today, with constant noise and little time to concentrate, think, and meditate, even in church!

The vows taken by monks and nuns in succeeding centuries are not defined in Benedict's *Rule*, but they reflect his influence. He asked for vows of conversion and stability and for promises for amendment of life and staying put on one's own monastery, rather than trying to switch from one to another. Obedience is perhaps the hardest of the disciplines, and the one most emphasized by Benedict, for it implies bending the will to another, namely, the abbot. A humble renunciation of one's own will to another human being was intended to show the submission of the Christian to God. It is clear that the abbot carried a heavy responsibility in Benedict's plan.

Among the early Christian spiritualities, perhaps none has gained so much present-day interest and devotion as the **Celtic tradition,** which was also largely monastic. The Celts, a people who had moved from central Europe to settle in Ireland, Scotland, Wales, and western France, were known to the ancient Greeks as "Keltoi." The Britons, who were later conquered by the Romans, were also Celts, and it is among them that the earliest Christians were found in Great Britain. The British Museum displays archeological evidence of Christians in England in the first few centuries.

After the Romans left in the early 400s, the Angles and Saxons pushed the Celtic peoples westward to Cornwall, Wales, and Ireland.

What is not common knowledge is that there were Christians in Britain long before St. Augustine of Canterbury arrived about 600, and even before **St. Patrick** (389?–461?), who is the national saint of Ireland. Patrick, who had come from a Christian family probably in Wales, had been captured and sent as a slave to Ireland, where he was put to work herding cattle. While herding, he had a deep experience of God and reported that he prayed a hundred times a day. Patrick found a way to escape from slavery, and following a call from God, he returned to Ireland as a missionary and convinced the leaders of Celtic society of the power of the Trinity. We have very little exact knowledge of Patrick, but many legends survive. The following *lorica* (breastplate) is attributed to him:

> I arise today
> through God's strength to pilot me:
> God's might to uphold me,
> God's wisdom to guide me,
> God's eye to look before me,
> God's ear to hear me,
> God's word to speak for me,
> God's hand to guard me,
> God's way to lie before me,
> God's shield to protect me,
> God's host to secure me
> against snares of devils,
> against temptations of vices,
> against inclinations of nature,
> against everyone who shall wish me ill,
> afar and anear,
> alone and in a crowd.[14]

From the start, monasticism was important to Celtic adherents of the new faith. There was a direct influence from the Coptic monks of Egypt, and *The Life of Anthony* was well known. Originally, the church in Ireland was headed by abbots rather than bishops, who came later as part of the Roman structure of church authority. Celtic spirituality affirmed women. "Double" monasteries, for both women and men, were founded and sometimes were headed by a woman. The most famous of the women saints of Ireland, **Brigid** (died about 523), also known as Bride, Bridget, or Braid, was such an abbess. According to legend, she was very generous, even giving away her father's sword, and was even ordained a bishop by the leading of the Spirit. An Order of St. Brigid continues to revere her today in Kildare, Ireland. St. Brigid is a major figure in Irish spirituality, one of the 'trinity' of saints (the other two are Patrick and Columba).

Irish Christians emphasized the concept of the *anamchara*, or "soul friend," in their spirituality.[15] According to this concept, one was not alone in the Christian walk; the close companion could encourage and correct one along the way. This was a relationship for counsel, confession, and support, which finds biblical precedent in many friendships and mentoring relationships: Elijah and Elisha, Samuel and Eli, David and Nathan, Ruth and Naomi, Jesus and the Twelve, Luke and Paul.

> Go forth and eat nothing until you get a soul friend, for anyone without a soul friend is like a body without a head; is like the water of a polluted lake, neither good for drinking nor for washing. That is the person without a soul friend.[16]

Later, when Irish monks converted many Germanic peoples on the Continent, this distinctive feature of Celtic spirituality was practiced on the European continent. Latin Catholicism first opposed, and later much restricted, soul friendship. In Roman Catholicism, such friendship eventually became solely a relationship of private confession of sins, was restricted to the clergy, and was required for communion. Confessional books called *penitentials* prescribed the penance to be paid for a given sin. After the Lateran Council of 1215, it became required practice in Catholic churches to confess to a priest. Later, at the Council of Trent in the mid-1500s, penance was defined as one of the seven sacraments. This sacrament was amended after Vatican II, in the 1960s, to eliminate the quantitative approach of numbering instances of sins and to give more freedom of practice. Nowadays, the renamed Sacrament of Reconciliation is somewhat closer to the original Celtic practice than was the enumerating of sins in the confessional characteristic of the period from Trent to Vatican II. But the modern expression most in the spirit of *anamchara* is spiritual direction.

Like Syriac monasticism, the religious in Ireland were extremely strict in their asceticism. The practice of reciting all 150 psalms daily was common, and some stood in icy water while praying. They spoke of white martyrdom, the daily ascetic practice; red martyrdom, the shedding of blood; and blue martyrdom, the doing of significant penance for sin. Although there was apparently no red martyrdom in the transition from pagan to Christian faith in Ireland, there certainly were Celtic martyrs in England and Wales. The first of these was **St. Alban** (died in 305? or 209?), a Briton who gave refuge to a Christian priest when Christianity was persecuted by a Roman emperor (scholars argue whether it was Diocletian [305] or Septimius Severus [209]).

Alban was converted and baptized by the priest and then offered himself to the soldiers by wearing the priest's clothing. Eventually, both he and the priest were executed.

A distinctive form of asceticism was self-exile from one's home or monastery. It became common for Irish monks to leave home, as Abraham had been called to do, and to live far from the community that had nurtured them. This traveling led indirectly to the spread of Christianity in northern Europe.

Among such travelers was **St. Columba**, who landed on the Scottish island of Iona in 632. He is said to have slaughtered five thousand men and wished to do penance by saving as many among the pagan Scots. Iona became a mission station and may have been the location of one of the most beautiful manuscripts ever created: the *Book of Kells*, an illustrated biblical masterpiece that was taken back home to Ireland for safety from Viking attack. It is a symbol not only of the artistry of the Ionian monks but of their devotion to a life of learning. Many students from the Continent came to Ireland to study with Iona's scholar-saints. Today, Iona is the home of an ecumenical Christian community founded in the 1930s that emphasizes Christian living in one's calling, including prayer, meditation, and social service. I am among the pilgrims who have traveled to Iona for retreats in the restored abbey, amid Celtic crosses that predate the Viking era.

Celtic cross from the White Monastery in Adare, County Limerick, Ireland

Celtic crosses are characterized by a large circle behind the arms and the stem, possibly symbolizing the good created world. The more elaborate ones include stone carvings of the biblical story, centered in Jesus. A famous cross at Monasterboice, in Ireland, includes carvings of Paul of Thebes and Antony of Egypt, the first monks. The many crosses that still stand in Ireland, Scotland, and Wales are the lasting artistic legacy, along with the biblical manuscripts, of Celtic spirituality.

Some people today are attracted to Celtic spirituality because they see in it a rosy view of sunshine without shadow, praise without asceticism, creation without the cross. However, they must be highly selective to sustain such a view. Celtic spirituality clearly includes darkness, pain, and severe ascetic discipline; it sees the cross of Christ as the key to understanding the victory of God over the powers of evil.

There remain good reasons for people who are not ethnically Celtic to honor the Celtic tradition and to learn from it today. It affirms the glory of God in the natural world, it honors women, and it lives in daily contact with the divine. To follow and not to romanticize is the challenge faced by today's lover of Celtic tradition.

Another example of the importance of Christian monasticism was in the area we now know as **Ethiopia**. Christianity had been declared the religion of the kingdom of Axum (or Aksum) in the fourth century, after two students traveling from Tyre to India were shipwrecked on the Red Sea coast near the capital. The king put them in charge of educating his children, and around A.D. 330 King Ezana became a Christian. One of the two students, Frumentius, was named the first bishop and was consecrated by Athanasius in Alexandria. From that time until 1951, the Abuna, or chief bishop, was named by the Coptic bishop in Alexandria.

But the evangelization of the peoples of Ethiopia was not accomplished by the king. It was the Nine Saints, each from a different country, who arrived in 480 and spread the faith through monastic houses. They set about the huge task of translating the Bible into the Ge'ez language, creating one of the oldest biblical translations. They also translated *The Life of Anthony* and the *Rule* of Pachomius. In fact, these saints had lived in Pachomius's monastery before coming to Ethiopia.

The Ethiopian church grew and developed in contact with the Byzantine churches until the Arab conquest of the seventh century. Then it was shut off from Red Sea trade, became isolated, and moved inland within present-day Ethiopia. Today members of the Ethiopian Orthodox Church are expected to fast many days in the year and to pray seven times daily. Prayer is commonly said while standing, with complete prostrations at the beginning and end. The *debteras*, or choristers, sing at joyful festivals while dancing solemnly with long sticks. Some of these practices may go all the way back to the ancient monks who founded Ethiopian Christianity.

Mysticism

Mysticism is a difficult term to define or delimit, a term much used and misused. Its edges are not sharp, and the reader must always ask in what sense the term is used in order to understand the writer's meaning. The term is elastic, used by different writers in different ways. Here we will deal with mysticism only in the Christian context.

Generally, Christian mysticism has been described as a form of spirituality that sets as its goal unity with God. Mystics often have reached a level of contemplation at which they cannot describe their experiences but instead use colorful language and poetry to convey the gist of it to those who have not experienced their ecstasy. They tend to see the whole world as charged with divine glory, and they sometimes actively change the world by their vision of justice and love.

Union with God can mean complete absorption, ultimately losing one's identity in God. Communion, on the other hand, suggests a kind of loving relationship of two persons who remain distinct in spite of a unity of purpose, feeling, or knowledge. But not all mystics use either of these terms.

Bernard McGinn's magisterial study of mysticism includes eighty pages describing the ways the term *mysticism* has been understood in modern times by theologians, philosophers, and psychologists.[17] Even McGinn chooses not to give a definition of the word but rather discusses

> three headings: mysticism as a part or element of religion; mysticism as a process or way of life; and mysticism as an attempt to express a direct consciousness of the presence of God. . . . I have come to find the term "presence" a more central and more useful category [than "union"] for grasping the unifying note in the varieties of Christian mysticism. . . . From this perspective, it comes as no surprise that union is only one of the host of models, metaphors, or symbols that mystics have employed in their accounts. Many have used it, but few have restricted themselves to it. Among the other major mystical categories are those of contemplation and the vision of God, deification, the birth of the Word in the soul, ecstasy, even perhaps radical obedience to the present divine will. All of these can be conceived of as different but complementary ways of presenting the consciousness of direct presence.[18]

Thinking of the various writers who are considered mystics, I agree with McGinn. There are many kinds of mystics, and not all of them consider union the goal of their Christian life.

Two of the most influential writers of the early period—Augustine of Hippo and "Dionysius the Areopagite"—wrote in a mystical vein. They came from opposite ends of the empire—North Africa and probably Syria, respectively—and their teachings were in very different modes.

Augustine (354–430), celebrated author of *The Confessions*, introduced a narrative character to Christian growth. His was a brand-new concept: a book that narrates one's inner life with God. Augustine addressed God throughout the book, confessing both sin and faith. He told his story in a conversation with God that led him to appreciate God's love for him every step of the way.

In reconstructing his past, Augustine was searching out the ways God had been seeking him, and he saw that what happened in his life was not entirely in his own power. This sense of being in the hands of forces greater than oneself is very strong in Augustine's book, and the narrative brings down to earth some of the principles and proverbs of the Egyptian monks. It was the story of Antony of Egypt that led to Augustine's final break with his old life and his turning to a new one.

> Great art Thou, O Lord, and greatly to be praised; great is Thy power, and of Thy wisdom there is no end. . . . Thou movest us to delight in praising thee; for Thou hast formed us for Thyself, and our hearts are restless till they find rest in Thee.
> —St. Augustine of Hippo, *Confessions* 1.1

The whole of *The Confessions* testifies to a personal longing for God that is ultimately satisfied. Tracing his early years in Carthage, Augustine tells of his mother, Monica, a devout Christian who became the most influential person in his life, and of his father, Patricius, an ambitious man who was not a Christian. He recalls his unhappiness in school as well as his attraction to Manichaeism (a religion setting the matter of the world as an evil opponent to the good spiritual God) and his departure from it. Having become a teacher of rhetoric, a stepping stone to political power, Augustine sought his fortune in Rome and Milan. He found the framework for his subsequent thought in late forms of Plato's philosophy. It was the preaching of Ambrose, bishop of Milan (see map 2), that resolved his intellectual difficulties with the Bible by showing the spiritual meaning of the texts. But it took more than the intellect to lead Augustine to conversion. He was reluctant to give up sexual pleasure, so he prayed, "Lord give me chastity, but not yet!"

According to *The Confessions*, written many years after the event, Augustine sets his conversion in a garden, where he ended his struggle and gave in to God. Hearing children nearby singing "Take up and read," he read from Romans 13:13-14:

> Let us live honorably as in the day, not in reveling and drunkenness, not in debauchery and licentiousness, not in quarreling and jealousy. Instead, put on the Lord Jesus Christ, and make no provision for the flesh, to gratify its desires.

Since Augustine had been living with a concubine, this verse seemed pointed at him. His sexual life with her had been the glue that first kept him from becoming a Christian. Now, on his conversion, sexual activity was thoroughly repudiated. We do not know what became of the concubine whom Augustine sent away, but from that time on, Augustine was never able to engage in sexual relationship. His view of women and of sexual intercourse was never very positive after conversion.

Augustine later connected sexual desire with a biological transmitter of original sin, the sin inherited after Adam and Eve's first disobedience. It was the parents' sexual lust that made every birth impure. For Augustine, the starting point of Christianity thus became the fallen nature of humanity, the grace of God restoring that fall by means of Jesus' death on the cross, mediated through the sacraments. His views came to dominate later Catholic and Protestant thought and will be contrasted below with the Eastern perspective of *theosis* (divinization) and resurrection.

After his baptism in Milan, Augustine decided to return from Italy to North Africa, his birthplace. On the way, in Ostia, the seaport of Rome, he shared a profound mystical experience of the presence of God with his mother. They ascended in conversation until they in silence "slightly touched" Wisdom.

After his mother's death, Augustine returned to Africa and, because of his intellectual superiority, was ordained a priest and later a bishop, in spite of his resistance. In Hippo he established a monastic community around the cathedral and entered a long career of writing and church administration. As a bishop, he wrote letters, sermons, and treatises to defend the faith as he understood it against perversions, or heresies.

In a conflict with **Pelagius** (his dates are unknown, but contemporary with Augustine), Augustine championed the grace of God against human effort as the means of salvation. Pelagius, a contemporary of Augustine, had experienced the weak-kneed mediocrity of Christians in Britain, his home, who gave up the moral battles of the Christian life by saying, "I can't do it. If God wanted me to, God would give me the strength." Relying on grace and not on human effort seemed a "cop-out" to Pelagius.

This issue, fundamental to Christian spirituality, was to be the prime reason for the later split in the church between Catholics and Protestants. How are we to understand the role of God as Savior and the human being as actor in the Christian life? Augustine was convinced that any good thing in his life was a gift from God, not his own achievement. He had been rescued from his old life not by his own efforts but by the love of God. If he had been able to save himself, there would have been no purpose in Jesus' death and resurrection.

In the long run, the Catholic church sided with Augustine in its synod and council decisions, but in parishes the role of the human will in "working out your salvation" was often more prominent. Later the Protestants would appeal to his writings against Pelagius to support their own teaching of "grace alone."

In conclusion, Augustine left a mixed legacy for the Latin-speaking church. He was an intellectual who bound together the Platonist philosophical tradition with the biblical faith, emphasizing the Psalms and Paul. He was a synthesizer who combined the basic insights of the Greek and Latin writers of the first four centuries into an orthodox vision of truth. He was a sojourner who gave new expression to the personal walk from carnality to a loving God with whom he sought union. He was a teacher whose bad conscience, unhealthy sexual attitudes, and emphasis on original sin left a legacy of gloom and misogyny on much of Western spirituality. But for all his faults, Augustine's final word was adoration of the grace of God.

The second figure who stands at the roots of later Christian mysticism is an anonymous writer known to later centuries as **Dionysius the Areopagite**. It seems that around the year 500, a Syrian monk wrote under the name Dionysius in order to claim the authority that comes from the apostolic age, for nothing is known of the original Dionysius except his name in Acts 17:34. Thus this writer is sometimes referred to as Pseudo-Dionysius.

Four books have come down to us under this author's name: *The Celestial Hierarchy*, *The Ecclesiastical Hierarchy*, *The Divine Names*, and *Mystical Theology*. Among Dionysius's major contributions was the naming of the three stages of spiritual development, a formulation that was later to become standard in all Western mysticism: the purgative, the illuminative, and the unitive. Previous triads had been developed by Origen and Evagrius, but Pseudo-Dionysius was the first to name them in this way. *Purgative* refers to a period of cleansing; *illuminative*, to the light of God shining on the soul; and *unitive*, to an experience of oneness with God.

Neo-Platonism, a later form of Plato's philosophy, played a prominent role in the conception of the spiritual life for Dionysius. Much of his thought was parallel to that of Proclus, a contemporary non-Christian philosopher. Yet Dionysius distinctly combined Christian understandings of God with the philosophical framework of Neo-Platonism.

Dionysius operated with a worldview that is triadic and hierarchical—in fact, he invented the word *hierarchy* in Greek. He saw everything in his universe in threes, with carefully described levels from top to bottom. He did not seem as interested in the relationship of Father, Son, and Spirit as with the notion of threeness, which he saw at all levels of the hierarchy.

One of Dionysius's most powerful and distinctive teachings was his apophatic theology—that is, a theology that reaches beyond words and images. For example, he begins his discussion in *The Divine Names* by echoing Paul's hymn of praise in Romans 11 on the inscrutable nature of God:

Indeed the inscrutable One is out of the reach of every rational process. Nor can any words come up to the inexpressible Good, this One, this Source of all unity, this supra-existent Being. Mind beyond mind, word beyond speech, it is gathered up by no discourse, by no intuition, by no name.[19]

Then, in *The Mystical Theology*, Dionysius introduces the theme of divine darkness, of the need to strip away the intellect in the knowledge of God. He begins with poetry, a genre later employed by St. John of the Cross, whom we will meet in chapter 6. Dionysius writes:

> Trinity!! Higher than any being,
>   any divinity, and goodness!
> Guide of Christians
>   in the wisdom of heaven!
> Lead us up beyond unknowing and light,
>   up to the farthest, highest peak
>   of mystic scripture,
> where the mysteries of God's Word
>   lie simple, absolute and unchangeable
>   in the brilliant darkness of a hidden silence.
> Amid the deepest shadow,
>   they pour overwhelming light
>   on what is most manifest.
> Amid the wholly unsensed and unseen,
>   they completely fill our sightless minds
>   with treasures beyond all beauty.

[Reader,] . . . leave behind you everything perceived and understood, everything perceptible and understandable, all that is not and all that is, and with your understanding laid aside, to strive upward as much as you can toward union with him who is beyond all being and knowledge. By an undivided and absolute abandonment of yourself and everything, shedding all and freed from all, you will be uplifted to the ray of the divine shadow which is above everything that is.[20]

Dionysius argued that since any human concept is inadequate for God, only denials of the likeness of God to human categories could properly apply. For example, it would limit God to say, "God is just" (the positive way). It would be better to say, "God is not unjust" (the negative way). He asserts, however, after a long list of such negations, that God is beyond denial.

Apophatic spirituality encompasses both an intellectual and an affective aspect. The process of stripping one's concepts of God of all that is unworthy is called the *via negativa*, or the negative way. It is the intellectual side of apophatic theology. One of the striking features of Dionysius's writings is the combination of a highly intellectual discussion of God with an absolute denial of the power of the intellect to know God.

The affective side of apophatic spirituality is a state of utter passivity on the part of the mystic. According to Dionysius, such passivity leads to an ecstasy of love in which the human is fused with God. This theme is evident in much of later mysticism, for example, in Meister Eckhart, whom we will meet later.

The opposite of apophatic is kataphatic, which means an active attempt to image God by the use of one's imagination and emotions. The practice of meditation by means of calling forth images from the Scriptures, for example, is kataphatic. Dionysius clearly thinks that the kataphatic way has its utility, notably for beginners on the spiritual way. But for those approaching union, the apophatic way is necessary.

We conclude by noting again that Christianity in the early centuries developed in a number of cultures and was expressed somewhat differently in each. The foundational developments occurred not only in Greek and Latin contexts but in Syriac and in others less well known. The same themes that we have discussed here—worship and sacraments, charisms, martyrdom, asceticism, monasticism, and mysticism—appeared in Ethiopia and Britain, in India and Syria. The Greco-Roman synthesis, however, eventually became the dominant form of Christian spirituality, both in number and in wealth.

Spiritual Practice

1. **Communal worship** is potentially a profound spiritual practice but is not intended to stand alone. "Going to church" may be very significant for your personal spirituality or it may be irrelevant, depending on what you make of it. The Christian walk is not ideally a private walk; it means being part of a people, an organic "body of Christ" that extends down through the centuries and over all continents. The local community of faith that you choose is an expression of that "body." It can be a place where you are known, accepted, loved, challenged, and made accountable. The worship experiences that you share will be focused on Word and Sacrament. Hearing the law and the gospel preached is important for one's growth as is receiving the Lord's Supper (sometimes called the Eucharist, Holy Communion, or Mass).

Be intentional about your attendance in the assembly. Do not simply go through the motions. If you are attending a church that does not provide a meaningful worship experience, then try to change things or perhaps find a different congregation or even a denomination that can better meet your need. One cannot simply sit back and expect a congregation to serve the individual; churches are places to give service, not simply to be "spiritually entertained." It is wise to visit several different church assemblies to see the variety of ways in which God is worshiped; even within the same denomination considerable differences exist. A balance of intellect and emotion is needed, according to different styles.

Before attending a church service, take time to meditate about your intentions. Seek the presence of God and a genuine meeting with the people. Have a prayerful attitude during the service, with an open ear. When you sing a hymn, really praise God through it. On some occasions, that praise will be more precious than any other part of the service. On other days, the bread and wine of the Eucharist will be most meaningful. On still other occasions, the preacher may speak just the word you need. But it is not often that all of these things will happen in one service, so it takes a kind of patience to be in a Christian worshiping community. Some days our hearts are cold, the sermon is boring, and no one makes contact with us. On other days, the music and the Spirit invade our hearts and we leave the assembly refreshed.

2. One of the oldest types of self-denial is **fasting**. Many healthy persons can find value in fasting, but it should be done with good guidance, and in moderation to start. Diabetics, pregnant or lactating women, and others with health issues should consult their doctors first.

It is very important to take in enough fluids. (Remember the first paragraph of this book!) Be aware that fasting may not prove immediately helpful. Try it a few times to see the pattern that best fits you. Partial fasts may work better for you than complete fasts. Fasting is not a good way to try to lose weight but, when done properly, can indeed bring into focus the real values of life, resulting in a sense of interdependence with others and dependence on God. It is also wise to devote the time normally spent eating to the practice of another spiritual discipline, such as prayer or reading. Fasting can increase one's sense of freedom and strength. One discovers, "I can *choose* to eat or not to eat." This is not the highest of the gifts of fasting, however. When one recognizes one's dependence on God through an experience of dependence on food, it is possible for the Spirit to reshape the willing heart.

Consider fasting from other parts of your daily life besides eating. It may be healthy, for example, to give up television for a while and reconsider its role in your life. Or maybe you find yourself very much attached to your favorite news or talk station or maybe you cannot relate to people well because of your excessive time on the Internet or with your Walkman. Consider any of these potentially addictive activities as possibilities for fasting.

3. Go on a **retreat**. This does not mean a weekend workshop or business meeting; rather, it means going by yourself or with others to spend time with God. Most monasteries welcome retreatants. If you have not yet visited a monastery, find one in your area and make contact. Try to learn from one of the nuns or monks what life there is like. Or find a retreat center that is not a monastery.

As Macrina Wiederkehr writes: "We may feel called to take a step back and look at the mystery of life anew. That's what the word *retreat* means—to go back. . . . A retreat is a time to step back and take a new look at our lives. It is not so much a time to learn new things as to remember and feel again some of the things we have forgotten. It is a time to be lovingly attentive to the needs of the soul."[21]

4. **Meditation** is focusing one's thoughts while at the same time being open to inspirations as they come. The object of meditation may be a natural phenomenon. For example, one can sit by a lake, a seacoast, a meadow, or a forest and quietly observe and ponder. Or, one can meditate on an event in one's own life or that of a biblical figure or saint. For Christians, meditating on Jesus and the events of his life is central.

5. Keep a journal of your **dreams**. Set your journal right next to your bed so that you can write in it the moment you awake, before the memory dissolves. Over time, with the help of an experienced spiritual director or a therapist, see if you can understand yourself better and understand what God is saying.

Aids for the Exercises

Beall, James Lee. *The Adventure of Fasting: A Practical Guide*. Old Tappan, N.J.: Revell, 1974.

Dawn, Marva J. *A Royal "Waste" of Time: The Spendour of Worshiping God and Being Church for the World*. Grand Rapids, Mich.: Eerdmans, 1999.

Foster, Richard J. "Fasting," "Confession," "Worship," "Guidance," and "Celebration." In *Celebration of Discipline*, 47–61, 125–71. Rev. ed. San Francisco: Harper, 1988.

Hanson, Bradley. *The Call of Silence: Discovering Christian Meditation*. Minneapolis: Augsburg, 1980.

Hulme, William E. *Celebrating God's Presence: A Guide to Christian Meditation*. Minneapolis: Augsburg, 1988.

Kelsey, Morton. *Dreams: A Way to Listen to God*. New York: Paulist, 1978.

———. *The Other Side of Silence: Meditation for the Twenty-First Century*. Rev. ed. New York: Paulist, 1997.

Thompson, Marjorie J. "Gathered in the Spirit: Our Common Worship" and "The Practice of Self-Emptying: Rediscovering the Fast." In *Soul Feast*, 53–68, 69–82. Louisville: Westminster John Knox, 1995.

Suggested Reading

Athanasius of Alexandria. *The Life of Antony: The Coptic Life and the Greek Life*. Trans. Tom Vivian and Apostolos N Athanassakis. Kalamazoo, Mich.: Cistercian, 2003.

Brock, Sebastian, trans. *The Syriac Fathers on Prayer and the Spiritual Life*. Kalamazoo, Mich.: Cistercian, 1987.

Burton-Christie, Douglas. *The Word in the Desert: Scripture and the Quest for Holiness in Early Christian Monasticism*. New York: Oxford University Press, 1993.

Colliander, Tito. *Way of the Ascetics: The Ancient Tradition of Discipline and Inner Growth*. San Francisco: Harper, 1982 (1960).

De Waal, Esther, ed. *The Celtic Vision: Prayers and Blessings from the Outer Hebrides*. London: Darton, Longman, and Todd, 1988.

———. *Every Earthly Blessing: Celebrating a Spirituality of Creation*. Ann Arbor, Mich.: Servant, 1992.

Ephrem the Syrian. *Hymns*. Trans. Kathleen E. McVey. New York: Paulist, 1989.

Lane, Beldon C. *The Solace of Fierce Landscapes: Exploring Desert and Mountain Spirituality*. New York: Oxford, 1998.

Lawrence, C. H. *Medieval Monasticism*. 2nd ed. New York: Longman, 1989.

O'Donoghue, Noel Dermot, O.D.C. *Aristocracy of Soul: Patrick of Ireland*. Wilmington, Del.: Michael Glazier, 1987.

Sheldrake, Philip. *Living between Worlds: Place and Journey in Celtic Spirituality*. London: Darton, Longman, and Todd, 1995.

Thomas, Patrick. *Candle in the Darkness: Celtic Spirituality from Wales*. Llandysul, Dyfed, Wales: Gomer, 1993.

Chapter 5

The European Era

In this chapter, I will briefly highlight some important persons and movements in Christian spirituality from about the seventh to the fifteenth centuries. I have called the chapter "The European Era," because during this time Christianity lost ground geographically in Asia and Africa but spread to new cultures in northern Europe, notably to the future English, Germans, Scandinavians, Ukrainians, and Russians. The development of spirituality in Europe was to be significant for world history in centuries to follow.

It was a period of gradual separation of the Greek East from the Latin West. "East" and "West" here assume the Mediterranean Sea as the center of the earth, with the East centered in Constantinople and the West in Rome. The usual date of separation of the Roman Catholic and Eastern Orthodox churches is 1054, but there were many ups and downs in this relationship from about 800 to 1200. The Fourth Crusade (1202–04) finally created bitterness beyond measure when Roman Catholics sacked the Eastern capital, Constantinople.

The East

In the early centuries, the differences between East and West were cultural, but the church had an overall unity of spirit, if no single leader or pope. The various ancient cities of the apostles—Jerusalem, Antioch, Ephesus, Alexandria, Rome, and later Constantinople—each had a patriarch. But the patriarch of Rome, the only patriarch in the West, gradually claimed unique authority over the others. The other patriarchs did not agree to be ruled by him, and tensions mounted.

Drawing on the traditions of Greek theology and the ecumenical councils up to 787, the Eastern church came to have distinctive emphases that differed from those of the West. The "ecumenical" councils were those representing the whole "inhabited world." This same word, *ecumenical*, is used today for the movement to unify the churches of different denominations.

The church was not divided into denominations at that time, so representatives from the Roman East and West participated at Nicea in 325, Constantinople in 381, Ephesus in 431, Chalcedon in 451, Constantinople (II) in 553, Constantinople (III) in 680–81, and Nicea (II) in 787. After this, the Roman Catholic Church continued to call councils, but the Eastern Orthodox Church did not recognize them.

In the areas near the Mediterranean, the Eastern church lived under Islamic rule after the seventh century and was pressured to stop any evangelism or outward Christian display. In 1453, Constantinople, the very center of Byzantine rule, fell to the Muslim Turks; the great cathedral Haggia Sophia became a mosque. The city has since been called Istanbul (see map 3).

In the areas where missionaries had taken the new faith, notably Ukraine and Russia, Christianity came to be associated with czars (or Caesars), as it had been in Byzantine days, so Moscow considered itself the "Third Rome," center of a Christian empire after the fall of both Rome and Constantinople.

Eastern theology was strongly Trinitarian, firmly based on the early councils, the Holy Tradition. It saw the spiritual development of the Christian in the schema of divinization, or *theosis*, the process of humans becoming divine. This understanding of the relationship between God and humans was carefully described in such a way that humans did not lose their identity or their humanity and God did not lose uniqueness. Two of the practices commonly connected with this theological view of human destiny were the Jesus Prayer and the veneration of icons.

The Jesus Prayer

"Lord Jesus Christ, Son of God, have mercy on me, a sinner." These words have been repeated millions of times by Orthodox believers. The roots of this prayer, the Jesus Prayer, lie in Scripture. The publican prayed, "God, be merciful to me, a sinner!" (Luke 18:13). Paul exhorted, "Pray without ceasing" (1 Thess. 5:17). And Peter preached, "This man is standing before you in good health by the name of Jesus Christ of Nazareth. . . . There is no other name under heaven given among mortals by which we must be saved" (Acts 4:10, 12).

The fundamental idea of the Jesus Prayer is to pray constantly. This requires a kind of attention to God that becomes habitual while one goes about the tasks of daily life. The prayer is a short formula that is repeated constantly, in rhythm with one's breathing or heartbeat. After a period of learning, the prayer repeats itself naturally without conscious effort. It is sometimes called "the prayer of the heart."

Today the most common form of the prayer is "Lord Jesus Christ, have mercy on me." But the emergence of the prayer was gradual. Different forms of words and different understandings of their function can be seen in the fifth to eighth centuries. Kallistos Ware, a present-day scholar and bishop of the Orthodox Church, writes that there were four elements that eventually came together in this prayer:

1. Devotion to the Holy Name *Jesus*, which is felt to act in a semisacramental way as a source of power and grace
2. The appeal for divine mercy, accompanied by a keen sense of compunction and inward grief (*penthos*)
3. The discipline of frequent repetition
4. The quest for inner silence or stillness (*hesuchia*)—that is, for imageless, nondiscursive prayer[1]

Some elements of the prayer can be found in the words of the desert fathers and mothers, but it develops distinctively later with Diadochus (fifth century), who is influenced by Evagrius in seeking "prayer without thoughts" (that is without images or words) but gives a practical method for seeking it (see item 4 above). But Diadochus was also influenced by Macarius in an affective emphasis, valuing experience and not just intellect.

It may be surprising for us today that the Jesus Prayer was further developed in Gaza and Sinai, areas of recent Middle East conflict. The Sinai writers may hint at the connection between the recitation of the prayer and the rhythm of breathing, which became explicit in the Middle Ages.

It was in the Middle Ages that the prayer became widely used among Orthodox monks. Much later, in the late nineteenth century, the anonymous *Way of a Pilgrim* took the prayer to the West from Russia. Ware says that it is used in the twentieth century by more Christians, East and West, than in any century before. He clarifies its practice by writing:

> By modern Western writers it is sometimes termed a "Christian mantra," but this could give rise to confusion. The Jesus Prayer is not simply a rhythmic incantation, but an invocation addressed directly to the person of Jesus Christ, and it presupposes conscious, active faith in him as only-begotten Son of God and unique Savior. It is not, however, a form of discursive meditation upon particular incidents in Christ's life, but has as its aim to bring us to the level of *hesuchia* or stillness—to a state of intuitive, non-discursive awareness in which we no longer form pictures in our mind's eye or analyze concepts with our reasoning brain, but feel and know the Lord's immediate presence in a direct personal encounter.[2]

Recall from chapter 4 the two terms for different approaches to the presence of God: *apophatic* and *kataphatic*. Looking at the Eastern tradition, we can say that the Jesus Prayer is a kind of apophatic practice because it leads to "a direct personal encounter" without images. From this apophatic practice, we turn to one that is also distinctively Eastern but emphatically kataphatic: the use of icons in worship. The apophatic moves beyond images; the kataphatic employs images emphatically.

Praying with Icons

The visual representation of the human form in a certain style came to be a distinctive spiritual and theological expression of Orthodox Christianity. Icons, it is claimed by the Orthodox, were present even in the time of the apostles and were an intrinsic part of the Christian message from the beginning. We might expect, however, that only after the time of Constantine, when the churches had a stable existence, large buildings, and financial resources, did the golden paintings we know today begin to emerge.

Trinity of Uglic icon by Andrei Rublev

The status of icons was clarified in the eighth and ninth centuries during the Iconoclastic Controversies. These were theological and political disputes within Eastern Orthodoxy. The major theological issue behind the conflict was the nature of the incarnation. Did the Word of God really become flesh, really enter the material world in Jesus of Nazareth? If so, as the doctrinal tradition claimed, then what were the implications for the nature of Christian worship? Was the adoration of God to be purely mental, or did images and human art have an important role to play?

Iconoclasts, those who wanted to throw the paintings out of the church, argued that it was unworthy of God to be represented and venerated in a physical object. The veneration of paintings and statues appeared to be idolatry from this point of view. Some of the emperors in Constantinople used their power to destroy icons physically.

Defenders of such representation and veneration replied that this practice was consistent with the mystery of the incarnation. It was taking seriously the human nature of Jesus, the goodness of creation, and the sacramental quality of all things, for it implied that a physical object could be the meeting place between God and human beings. The seventh ecumenical council in 787 approved the use of icons, stating, "The honor rendered to the image passes to its prototype, and the person who venerates an icon venerates the person (*hypostasis*) represented in it."[3]

Thus one of the most distinctive features of all Eastern Orthodox Christianity was preserved. Today, as then, the human figures in the icons are seen as windows on eternity, as means by which worshipers may participate in the Divine. Eastern Orthodox spirituality continues a devotion to Jesus, to his mother (the "Theotokos," or bearer of God), and to all the saints by means of lighting candles and incense before icons and kissing them. Family and private worship also includes this practice, for many Orthodox homes have a special worship center with icons.

In our time, worship with icons could be called "right-brain" prayer, using images rather than discursive language. It represents one kataphatic approach in the Eastern tradition, along with elaborate liturgical gestures and architectural symbolism in churches. The apophatic approach is also present in the East, as seen in the Jesus Prayer, for example. These approaches need not exclude each other; both can be practiced to complement each other.

Gregory Palamas

Hesychia (or *hesuchia*), stillness or silence, is the word for a primary tradition in Eastern spirituality. It refers to going apart to the desert for solitude. Its greatest theologian and defender was **Gregory Palamas** (1296–1359), a monk of the famous group of monasteries at Athos in Greece, archbishop of Thessalonica, and writer of many theological volumes.

Typical of the Eastern tradition, Gregory saw the goal of the Christian life in Athanasius's statement "God became man so that man might become God."[4] This statement implied that the major axis of the faith is not human sin and divine redemption on the cross but, rather, human mortality and divine victory in the resurrection. The incarnation of God in Jesus was the way in which God defeated the powers of death and sin through the passion, death, and resurrection of Jesus.

As a theologian, Gregory made the important distinction between the Energies of God (better translated as the Activities or Workings of God), which humans may know, and the Essence of God, which they cannot know. He defended the possibility of a vision of God in this life, even before death, though it is not perfect. He defended various extreme physical disciplines used with the Jesus Prayer. Thus Gregory disagreed with his critics about our knowledge of God; Gregory argued that the prophets knew God better than the philosophers and that the monks were doing the right thing to pray instead of study. He therefore emphasized prayer and the importance of the body and its postures in prayer.

Gregory stated that union with God is essentially by God's grace but that the vision of God in this life could not be attained without hard work and was easier for unmarried monks on Mt. Athos (see map 3) than for the married. There is a cooperation, or *synergy*, between the divine grace and human will. Whoever searches with all their hearts for unceasing prayer will be given the gift of prayer (a gift of grace). The gift of tears (a constant flow of joyful tears) will be given to those whose passion for things of the earth is being transformed into passion for things of heaven. Unlike some earlier writers, Gregory sees positive passions as well as negative ones. Thus, for him, "passionlessness" (*apatheia*), or freedom from destructive passions, refers not to a denial of the body but to the transformation of body and soul together.

For Gregory Palamas, the transfiguration of Jesus was the revelatory event that showed the present and future kingdom of God. The glory of God and of Christ was visible to the three disciples present on the mountain as a sign of the actual presence of the kingdom. According to Gregory, that kingdom is still present for those given the gift of seeing it, but it will also be perfected for those who after death see God face-to-face.

The West

As the East in this period was characterized by icons, the Jesus Prayer, and hesychasm, in the context of a monastic church spreading northward, the West also spread north, developing new forms of religious orders and mysticism. Western Europe focused on sin as the enemy of humankind and on the cross of Jesus as its solution.

Among the great Western medieval spiritual teachers is **Anselm of Canterbury** (1033–1109). Anselm was born in Italy; he traveled to Normandy in France, where he became a monk and later abbot at Bec. He did not seek power and strongly resisted his election as abbot and his choice as archbishop in England. He lived in a period of great conflict between the church and the state. Although he was resolute in his defense of the rights of the church, he was always very humble and gracious in person.

Anselm is known for his contributions to systematic theology (for his teaching of the necessity of the incarnation and of atonement by satisfaction of God's justice) and to philosophical theology (for his ontological argument for the existence of God based on the very concept of God). His life of deep piety produced these writings, which became a bridge between the early and the center Middle Ages: he is said to have been the greatest theologian between Augustine and Thomas Aquinas. Anselm is also important for church-state relations and for demanding the abolition of slavery in England.

As we consider Anselm's importance for spirituality, the first point must be his personal example. All who knew him were deeply impressed by his holiness—his integrity, humility, and devotion. He fully deserves the designation "saint." Second, we see in him another example of the use of intellect by a spiritual person. He was one of the most learned figures of his age, and yet he had a keen sense of the limitations of learning. His theme phrase came originally from Augustine: "I believe so that I may understand, and what is more I believe that unless I do believe, I shall not understand."[5] Third, Anselm's prayers are revolutionary for his time. They demonstrate a number of themes creatively joined into a new way of praying. The Oxford scholar and nun Benedicta Ward says:

> The prayers are meant to be said in solitude, and the aim is to stir the mind out of its inertia to know itself thoroughly and so come to contrition and the love of God. This is to be done by a quiet and thoughtful reading of the text of the prayers, but only as much of them as achieves this aim. . . . He is not concerned that the reader should *like* the prayers; he means [the reader's] heart to be changed by them.[6]

Anselm was a strong advocate of devotion to the Virgin Mary. He spoke of Jesus as our brother and of Mary as our mother. Many of his prayers are virtual dialogues with biblical saints written in methods appropriate to the nature of the sainted person, including Mary Magdalene, Peter, Paul, and John the Baptizer. His prayers often include a strong sense of unworthiness and falling short, of a compunction (being pierced to the heart), leading to great praise for God's love. Anselm was not afraid to express his spirituality in the world of politics. He dealt with the Norman kings, always graciously, always firmly.

Anselm sounds a great deal like his distant teacher Augustine in his *Prayers and Meditations.* Here is a sample:

> I pray you, Lord, make me taste by love what I taste by knowledge; let me know by love what I know by understanding. I owe you more than my whole self, but I have no more, and by myself I cannot render the whole of it to you. Draw me to you, Lord, in the fullness of love. I am wholly yours by creation; make me all yours, too, in love.[7]

Renewals of Monasticism

In the twelfth century in the Western tradition, no one was greater than
Bernard of Clairvaux (1090–1153). He was known for reform of the monastic tradition, returning to the simplicity of the *Rule* of St. Benedict and eventually administering a vast network of monasteries. In his public life, he
preached to recruit participants in the Second Crusade in 1146, and in his
later life he had so much power he was the virtual pope of the Western
church. Our main interest here is in Bernard's influence on spirituality.

Bernard was declared a doctor of the Roman Catholic Church by Pope
Pius XII in 1953. The encyclical declaring this honor is called *Doctor
Mellifluus* (or the doctor flowing-with-honey) because of the sweetness of
Bernard's teaching compared with the dryness or harshness of some other
medieval writers. Indeed, his teaching, focusing as it does on love, is both
positive and personal, but not sentimental, as the title may suggest.[8]

In his teaching on the spiritual life, Bernard focuses most clearly on the
relationship between the self and God. Borrowing a good deal from
Augustine, Bernard, in his treatise "On Loving God," sets forth four
degrees of this love. He sees the self first of all loving only itself, then loving the neighbor and God for its own sake. Third, the soul comes to love
God for God's sake, normally the highest plane of love. But there is a fourth
level, in which the soul loves itself for God's sake. This is found only fleet-
ingly on earth but will be the constant state of the dead after the resurrection of the body.[9]

Bernard emphasizes the importance of the human Jesus for Christian
spirituality. He refers more frequently than his immediate predecessors to
the New Testament portrait of Jesus not merely as an example of a holy life
but as the divine action of love to change the hearts of human beings.
Bernard's sermons on Advent and Christmas rise to the heights of praise for
the incarnation.

His *Sermons on the Song of Songs* are a striking example of "spiritual"
interpretation of the Bible. The eighty-six discourses cover only the first two
chapters of the Song, but the most striking feature to a modern reader is the
breathtaking reversal of the sensuous, erotic metaphors of the poems to an
appeal against the passions of the flesh and a description of the joys of spiritual intimacy with God. Here the Bridegroom is Jesus, and the Bride, the
soul of the Christian. "What a close and intimate relation this grace produces
between the Divine Word and the soul, and what confidence follows from
that intimacy, you may well imagine. I believe that a soul in such condition
may say without fear, 'My Beloved is mine.'"[10]

Modern writers have suggested that the roles be reversed and that God
or Jesus become the female partner. The passionate nature of God's love is
emphasized here, suggesting a divine *eros* for humanity, in contrast to the
dispassionate *agape* demanded by some Protestant writers.[11] *Eros* suggests the

kind of longing experienced by lovers, whereas *agape* has been portrayed as the love of the unlovable, a determination of the will to seek what is good for the one loved. I believe both words are needed to convey the richness of God's love.

New Forms of Religious Orders

The thirteenth century brought many important developments for Christian spirituality and theology. It is commonly regarded as the peak of the central Middle Ages, representing the greatest fruition and fullest development in this period of history.

Among the dramatic events was the founding of mendicant (begging) orders, a new development of religious orders growing beyond monasticism. The Dominicans, the Franciscans, the Carmelites, and the Augustinians exemplified a new understanding of the need to serve church and society. Instead of binding themselves to stay in one monastery, and there to engage in communal and private prayer, these new orders called for service in the world as a friar's first priority. To varying degrees, they retained the practices of common dwellings, common prayer, and a common rule. All required the basic vows of poverty, chastity, and obedience, and the practice of these vows was adapted to new circumstances.

Dominic Guzman (ca. 1170–1221) saw the need for better preaching in the Roman Catholic Church. Heretics in southern France were making inroads on an uneducated laity; the typical and damaging response of rulers was to put the heretics down by military might. Dominic had experienced some success in persuasion rather than force, however. He founded an Order of Preachers, commonly called Dominicans, who could speak to the people with knowledge and effectiveness. Very soon this order became one of the best-educated groups in Europe, and its spirituality focused on the piety of learning.

The Dominicans helped produce some of the greatest scholars in the history of Europe, namely Albert the Great (ca. 1200–1280) and his student **Thomas Aquinas** (1225–74). Thomas later became the most influential theologian in the Roman Catholic Church, having incorporated the philosophical perspectives of Aristotle into the theological tradition he inherited from Augustine and many others.

Thomas viewed the Christian life as a colloquy, or friendship, between humans and God, emphasizing the role of charity as the measure of all vows, practices, and steps. It is said that Thomas abandoned his great work, the *Summa Theologica*, for the sake of a life of prayer and meditation. He said that all he had written was but as straw compared with the wonders he experienced in a mystical unity with God.

It was another Dominican, Alan de La Roche, who in the late fifteenth century introduced one of the most popular and enduring features of Catholic piety: the rosary. The rosary is a physical aid to prayer and meditation that consists of 150 beads usually formed into a circle with a crucifix attached. For each bead, one prays, "Hail Mary, full of grace, the Lord is with thee; blessed art thou among women, and blessed is the fruit of thy womb, Jesus. Holy Mary, Mother of God, pray for us sinners, now and at the hour of our death. Amen." Praying the rosary is a way of both repeating familiar prayers (the Our Father, the Hail Mary, and the Doxology) and meditating on sacred "mysteries," that is, important events in the lives of Mary and Jesus. There are five Joyful Mysteries, relating to the birth of Jesus; five Sorrowful Mysteries concerning the suffering of Jesus; and five Glorious Mysteries recounting the resurrection of Jesus and the honoring of Mary. These fifteen mysteries are recalled in concert with the 150 beads.

Thus the mind operates on two levels: the repetition of the Hail Mary is a way of centering the attention, while the mysteries are imaginatively relived. This devotion depends on the belief that Mary, together with all the saints, is able to hear the prayers of the faithful and is an appropriate mediator to her son Jesus and to God. Although most Protestants do not accept these beliefs, some Protestants in our own day have called for more recognition of Mary and some advocate the use of the rosary by Protestants as a Christ-centered prayer.[12]

Roman Catholic laity made the rosary less prominent after the Second Vatican Council, especially in public worship. But Pope John Paul II has strongly promoted the use of the rosary since the beginning of his reign in 1978. In October 2002, he issued an apostolic letter, *Rosario virginis mariae* (rosary of the Virgin Mary), in which he sets forth the rosary as a contemplative prayer comparable to the Jesus Prayer of the East. For example, he says the rosary, like the Jesus Prayer, is actually focused on Christ. In his letter, the pope goes on to propose the first major change in the rosary in centuries, the addition of a new set of "mysteries" for contemplation:

> Consequently, for the Rosary to become more fully a "compendium of the Gospel," it is fitting to add, following reflection on the Incarnation and the hidden life of Christ (the joyful mysteries) and before focusing on the sufferings of his Passion (the sorrowful mysteries) and the triumph of his Resurrection (the glorious mysteries), a meditation on certain particularly significant moments in his public ministry (the mysteries of light). This addition of these new mysteries, without prejudice to any essential aspect of the prayer's traditional format, is meant to give it fresh life and to enkindle renewed interest in the Rosary's place within Christian spirituality as a true doorway to the depths of the Heart of Christ, ocean of joy and of light, of suffering and of glory.
>
> I think that the following can be fittingly singled out: (1) his Baptism in the Jordan, (2) his self-manifestation at the wedding of

Cana, (3) his proclamation of the Kingdom of God, with his call to conversion, (4) his Transfiguration, and finally, (5) his institution of the Eucharist, as the sacramental expression of the Paschal Mystery.[13]

The rosary is one of the positive contributions to Roman Catholic spirituality traced to the Dominicans. Others include the tradition of using the intellect to the glory of God and using preaching as a peaceful way of turning people's minds and hearts to God. But the Dominicans were only one of the two great orders founded in the thirteenth century.

The second great founder of a mendicant order, and surely one of the most fascinating and challenging figures of the whole medieval period, is **Francis of Assisi** (1181/2–1226; see map 3), founder of the Franciscan Order, or the Friars Minor (little brothers). His life is associated also with **Clare of Assisi** (1193–1253), the founder of the Second Order for women, or the Poor Clares. It is difficult here to write briefly about figures whose lives have attracted so much attention, so many legends, so many analyses.

Francis has been called the saint who most clearly exemplifies the life of his Savior, with whose love he was enflamed. His story began when a young, enthusiastic, worldly youth heard the call of the Gospel passage in which Jesus sent out his disciples to preach in Galilee. Francis was given love for lepers and the desire to "rebuild" the church. He fell in love with "Lady Poverty" and wandered as a mendicant, praying, preaching, helping. He found freedom from possessions so exhilarating that he determined to own nothing of his own. Soon others were attracted by his joy and simplicity, and his band of twelve was approved as the Order of Friars Minor.

Later Francis was forced to compose a rule for the rapidly expanding order. He was never known as a gifted administrator; rather, he was a free spirit. He visited the Holy Land and preached to the Muslim ruler Saladin, and in 1224 he retired to pray on Mount La Verna. There he received the answer to his prayer for identification with the Savior; the *stigmata* of Christ, the wounds of the crucified Jesus, appeared in Francis's flesh.[14]

It was after this experience, during his last two years of life, that he wrote his well-known *Canticle to the Sun*, in which he addresses all things in creation as his brothers and sisters. Even death in this poem becomes a sibling of the singer, in a sharp reversal of the attitude of Paul and others who saw death as an enemy.

Francis, writing about the sun and moon, the fire and air, as siblings, is one of the few outstanding spiritual writers to make the fourth relationship of our model—the relation to the creation—a major part of his message. The legends of Francis and the wolf and Francis preaching to the birds extend his simple theme of the fatherhood of God to all creatures, not just to humans. The humility and joy expressed in this man encompass both identification with the pains of the crucified Jesus and the happy and carefree humility that trusted the Father of birds and flowers to provide his needs.

Clare, having heard Francis preach when she was eighteen (and he about thirty), asked Francis if she could become a member of his band. She secretly ran from her house on the night of March 20, 1212, and Francis with his brothers gave her the clothes of a sister and cut her hair. She became the leader of the Second Order for women, whose lives were more traditionally monastic; the sisters did not wander from place to place as the men did. For Clare, poverty was the door to contemplation of the Jesus who was himself poor and served the poor. She firmly and repeatedly resisted pressure to loosen the rule of her order; poverty of the order as a whole, not just of individuals, was preserved.

A Third (Franciscan) Order for laypeople was added later and became a powerful stimulant to Christian life for those not called to the life of the religious orders. The desire for a lay spirituality, one not connected with monks or friars, was spreading through Europe and produced a number of spiritual experiments, one of them in the Netherlands.

In order to revive the ideals of twelfth-century monasticism, Gerard Groote founded a new movement in the late-fourteenth-century Netherlands. It came to be called the "Modern Devotion" not because it was something new but because it sought to develop a devotion to Christ that was as characteristic of life outside the cloister as within it. The movement developed into a monastic order, a subgroup of the Augustinians called the Windesheim Congregation, as well as to a group of more than one hundred houses in Holland and Germany of the Sisters of the Common Life and the Brothers of the Common Life. The members practiced poverty, celibacy, and obedience but never took formal vows.

What was distinctive in the Sisters and the Brothers was a spirituality that focused on "the imitation of Christ." This theme demanded that disciples of Jesus follow the way of the cross. *The Imitation of Christ* became the title of the best-known book of spirituality throughout Western Europe for centuries. Even Dag Hammarskjold, a twentieth-century general secretary of the United Nations, secretly studied it, as we know from his book *Markings*. Knowledge of the self and denial of the self, together with contempt for the world, are enjoined on the reader of *The Imitation of Christ*. The probable author was **Thomas à Kempis** (1380–1471), one of half a dozen major leaders in this movement. The book breathes a strong eucharistic piety as well as the practice of constant meditation, not only during quiet times but also in the midst of work.

The Modern Devotion differs from the best of twelfth-century spirituality and from Dominican spirituality by seeing little value in the intellectual life. The intricacies of scholasticism and the immoral lives of some monks who claimed to be learned had convinced its members that true knowledge comes not from books but from the identification of one's life with God, from the fusion of the knower and the known. One famous paragraph in *The Imitation of Christ* reads:

> What good does it do to speak learnedly about the Trinity if lacking humility you displease the Trinity? Indeed it is not learning that makes man holy and just, but a virtuous life makes him pleasing to God. I would rather feel contrition than know how to define it. What would it profit us to know the whole Bible by heart and the principles of all the philosophers if we live without grace and the love of God? Vanity of vanities, all is vanity except to have God and serve him alone.[15]

This view was to influence Protestant Pietism in later centuries. It is a good reminder that theology calls for an appropriate life as well as intellectual tools; spirituality is part of theology. But it can also lead to despising one of God's good gifts, the human intellect.

Medieval Mystics

Women and men who gave themselves to a life of prayer and meditation in the late Middle Ages are commonly called mystics. At times, mysticism became faddish, and there was a great deal of phony pretension and seeking after supernatural phenomena. The authentic mystics, however, always warned against seeking flashy effects instead of seeking God alone.

One can distinguish two basic kinds of mystics: those who were more affective (focused on the affections) and those who were more intellectual and philosophical. The former type included many whose writings have been called "Bride-mysticism" because of concentration on the images from Song of Songs relating to marriage to Christ the Bridegroom. Bernard of Clairvaux fits this description.

Of the latter type, the most outstanding example is **Meister Eckhart** (1260?–1328?), a Dominican who influenced John Tauler (1300?–1361) and many other influential preachers and writers. His vague expressions in his German sermons led to considerable confusion as to his exact meaning. Near the end of his life, some of his Franciscan enemies brought charges against him, and a number of his statements were condemned as heretical. He was accused of heresies related to Neo-Platonism: pantheism (the view that God is the world and the world is God), making no distinction between God and the soul in mystical union, and denying God's freedom in creation.

Eckhart was influenced by Celtic and Eastern Christianity, and he served communities of women called Beguines. These women were not wealthy enough to have the dowry required to enter a monastery, so they lived according to their own rule in the world. The Beguine movement began in 1223 in the Rhine Valley but was condemned about a century later by Pope John XXII.[16] The Beguines influenced Eckhart, as he did them, especially Mechtild of Magdeburg (1208?–1282?), a visionary who became a Cistercian nun. Her book *The Flowing Light* is characterized by flowery and emotional language, including visions of hell and purgatory that may have influenced Dante's descriptions of these places.

An important issue is how much Eckhart is to be seen as a Neo-Platonist author and how much as a biblical one. It seems that Pseudo-Dionysius was a very strong influence, especially on Eckhart's doctrine of God.

Many other women and men could be chosen for discussion in this section. Among them are Joachim of Fiore (ca. 1135–1202), who developed a distinctive apocalyptic spirituality; Henry Suso (ca. 1295–1366), a Dominican follower of Eckhart; Catherine of Siena (ca. 1347–1380), whose concern for reform of the church led to direct influence on the pope; Catherine of Genoa (1447–1510), called the "Theologian of Purgatory"; and the English mystics of the fourteenth century: Walter Hilton (d. 1396), Richard Rolle (ca. 1300–1349), and the unknown author of *The Cloud of Unknowing*.

I have chosen three mystics for closer attention: Hildegard of Bingen, Jan van Ruysbroeck, and Julian of Norwich.

One of the most remarkable revivals of interest in our time is that in **Hildegard of Bingen** (1098–1179; see map 3). Through her music first of all, and then her writing and art, Hildegard has become well known in the United States after nine hundred years of obscurity. Promoters of Creation spirituality and feminist spirituality and ecological theologians have all seen something of their causes in her, but their opponents question these interpretations.

Let us consider first Hildegard's life and then her teaching. Hildegard reports having a vision of light even at age three. Her parents placed her with an anchoress, Jutta, at age eight, and she remained in a Benedictine monastery for the rest of her life. As a young woman, she became the leader of the women living under the abbot's rule at Disibodenberg, on the Rhine River. She was troubled by migraines, and some interpreters consider this the cause of her visions. After a vision at forty-two that called her to publish her visions publicly, she began to dictate her descriptions to a friend monk, Volmar, and to describe her visions to manuscript illuminators, who painted them. She worked for ten years on her first book, *Scivias* ("Scito vias Domini," or Know the Ways of the Lord), the most widely available of her nine books.[17] She wrote not only of her visions but of medicine and the natural world. She composed a great deal of music and a remarkable play, the *Ordo Virtutum* (Order of the Virtues).

During this time, against much resistance, Hildegard moved her community some twenty-two miles downriver to Rupertsberg. She defied the male leadership of the monastery to accomplish this and in so doing gave herself much more freedom as abbess. Hildegard became known to the highest officials of the church in her day. She wrote to Bernard of Clairvaux, and part of *Scivias* was approved by him and by Pope Eugenius III. She preached in many large cathedrals and religious houses. Hildegard saw herself as a prophet and was widely accepted as such.

We might expect Hildegard, as a mystic, to be most concerned with entering the divine communion, to be united with God. What we see, however, is a practical woman who was more concerned with knowing the natural and celestial worlds and, indeed, with changing the church and politics of her day than she was in seeking simple union with God. She was a reformer who did not hesitate to tell the men of the church where they went wrong. She rejoiced in *viriditas*, greenness, as the growing color of the earth. Although she seemed to accept a lower status for women in her writings, she was a fearless leader when the men in power acted improperly or crossed her wishes. She was undeniably a forerunner of today's theological feminist and ecological movements, but it would be anachronistic to think that she would adopt all the views of twenty-first-century advocates of these perspectives.

Jan van Ruysbroeck (1293–1381), though not widely known, is highly regarded by students of mysticism because he drew together the two major strands of mysticism, the affective and the intellectual. After serving for twenty-six years as a secular priest, Jan, along with three other mystics, withdrew to a forest priory in Flanders (see map 3). He composed his major works there in the vernacular, Flemish, rather than in Latin, the language of the learned.

In *The Spiritual Espousals*, Ruysbroeck uses and modifies the traditional three-stage schema of mystical growth: the purgative, the illuminative, and the unitive. His most important change is a repeated insistence that the stages do not follow one after the other but are added on. Thus the first is included in the second, and the first and second in the third. These three stages also differ from the traditional arrangement by including true union with God already in the second stage, though intermittently. Ruysbroeck calls his stages the active life, the interior or yearning life, and the God-seeing or contemplative life. In *The Sparkling Stone*, wayfarers on these steps are named the faithful servants, the secret friends, and the hidden sons of God, respectively. These stages of union with God are accompanied by a unification of the self. Similarly, though to a lesser degree, the wayfarer is united to other people. Using one of his favorite metaphors, fluidity, Ruysbroeck explains how one is melted by the heat of the Holy Spirit and flows out to all types of persons.

For Ruysbroeck, holiness in unity means the discarding of multiplicity, or at least of all things opposed to one's union with the One. Intellectually, this means approaching God with a bare mind, aware that "desire and love go in where understanding is not admitted."[18] It means entering the divine darkness, having removed creaturely images from the mind. Volitionally, it means abandoning one's will to God's will. This involves aligning all one's affections Godward, not clinging to anything in the world. And finally it means dying to oneself, "melting" and flowing into God

Ruysbroeck usually has a light and joyful tone. He is always pointing to joy, peace, rest, enjoyment in God. Though he indicates an awareness of sin, it remains on the periphery of his vision; rather, he focuses on God and the blessings of union with God.

Ruysbroeck instructs the reader in an objective tone, never directly speaking of himself. He will speak of "man" even when it seems he is indirectly referring to his own experience. His description of "spiritual drunkenness," which must reflect some of his own experience, is one of the most memorable paragraphs in the *Spiritual Espousals*. His basic approach is to say not "this is what I have seen," as does Julian of Norwich (discussed below), but rather "this is what may be seen." He maps the terrain of the spirit, which includes highly subjective features, in an objective tone.

Julian of Norwich (1353–1416?), unknown for many centuries, came into prominence in the late twentieth century. Most of what we know about her is from a single book in two versions, a Short Text and a Long Text, commonly known as *Revelations of Divine Love*. She tells us that when she was thirty and a half years old, she not only was on the point of death but received an answer to prayer that she should share in the sufferings of Christ on the cross. In fact, she was given sixteen visions, or "showings," which far exceeded the extent of her prayer. They were recorded soon afterward in the Short Text.

Julian spent the next fifteen to twenty years pondering and praying over these showings, as the Long Text indicates. In the meantime, she had become an anchoress, a woman who lived a solitary life in a small cell, in her case attached to the church of St. Julian in Norwich. So little do we know about her life that we do not know her actual name, only the name of the church that we use to identify her.

Julian's writing was informed by knowledge of Paul's letters and the Gospel of John. She also knew the main ideas of Augustine, yet she regarded herself as unlettered. Perhaps she did not know Latin, but her *Revelations*, the first book in English written by a woman, shows remarkable learning.

It is easy to contrast Julian's writing with that of her contemporary Margery Kempe, whose autobiography tells how she went to consult Julian. Margery's spiritual life was characterized by copious tears, loud groans, and erotic images, which made most of her male acquaintances very uneasy!

Margery writes that she found her visit with Julian comforting and reassuring, which does not surprise the reader of Julian's book. Julian was not only a theologian but a gifted spiritual director.

Julian is also known for writing of Jesus as our Mother. She did not invent the image, since other spiritual writers had drawn upon it before her. But she uses it in a more theologically knowledgeable way than her predecessors. It is not just that mother love is an illustration of Jesus' love for us, she says, but that the very nature of his relation to us is explained by it.[19]

In contrast to Ruysbroeck, Julian is not interested in mapping out the mystical landscape, in discussing the stages of the way, or even in giving rules for the moral life. Rather, she is setting out carefully, intellectually, the conclusions of years of pondering her showings. She is more interested in inquiring into the mysteries of God, humanity, sin, and redemption than in charting her own spiritual progress or that of others. Thus she is recognized today as a theologian, not simply a visionary.

Julian's dominating question is how to understand the presence of sin in a world created good by a good Creator. She answers the question not in discursive theology but by pondering the images and narrative of one of her showings. In this showing, a master sends his servant on an important errand, but the servant falls into a pit. The master looks on him "with pity not with blame." This fall is taken to be both the fall of Adam into sin and the self-emptying of Christ in becoming human. In the end, Julian says, sin was "behovely," or necessary, for the fullness of God's plan to send Christ and to rouse humanity to love. She concludes with a beautiful passage showing that the underlying theme of the whole is the love of God:

> And from the time that it was revealed, I desired many times to know in what was our Lord's meaning. And fifteen years after and more, I was answered in spiritual understanding, and it was said: What, do you wish to know your Lord's meaning in this thing? Know it well, love was his meaning. Who reveals it to you? Love. What did he reveal to you? Love. Why does he reveal it to you? For love.[20]

There is an eschatological dimension in Julian's vision that is often lacking in mystical writers—that is, she looks forward to the consummation of all things. The world may be a small hazelnut in a human hand, but it is precious to God, and God will redeem it. We do not get the sense in Julian that the world is only a shell, to be thrown away like garbage for the sake of human souls, but that—just as Paul writes in Romans 8—the creation will share in the redemption of the children of God. Her statement quoted and made famous by T. S. Eliot is "All shall be well, and all manner of things shall be well." Notice that she does not gloss over the reality of sin and evil. Fourteenth-century Norwich was a place that knew war, plague, and famine.

Rather, she looks forward to a mysterious act of God that she does not attempt to explain, by which God's love will triumph over the very real sin and evil present in God's creation.

Because of her interest in the theological problems associated with evil in the world and her hope for a changed creation, Julian has among the most balanced views when considered by the four dimensions of spirituality, relating to God, self, others, and creation.

Spiritual Practice

1. Quiet yourself the way that was described in the first exercise in chapter 1. Then start repeating the **Jesus Prayer**: "Lord Jesus, have mercy on me." You may wish to think the words silently, inhaling the first phrase and exhaling the second phrase. You may wish to envision the light of Jesus entering your body while inhaling and the darkness of sin or distress leaving you while exhaling. Be careful to adapt the prayer to your normal breathing rather than trying to quicken your breathing to the rate of the prayer, which may lead you to hyperventilate.

Although the words suggest contrition, the prayer may be used in any mood, whether of joy and thanksgiving or of sorrow and grief. Consider the first phrase as words of praise and the second as a general petition.

You may wish to modify the words of the prayer. The full form of the prayer is "Lord Jesus Christ, Son of God, have mercy on me, a sinner." Often, it seems appropriate while praying for the needs of the world to make the prayer plural, using "us" instead of "me." You may wish to use other designations for Jesus and other petitions or praises.

Try praying this prayer for twenty minutes each morning and evening.

2. **Icons** provide a "right-brain" approach to prayer, providing an image instead of words. Select an icon. First spend time centering yourself in silence; then put yourself in the presence of the icon. Regard the icon not as a simple picture but as a window through which you are steadily communing with another person. Put yourself on the other side of the window, and look at yourself lovingly, with all your faults and difficulties. Contemplate the other and yourself with compassion.

3. **Study** is a discipline practiced by monks and nuns in the Middle Ages that is important for all Christians. Of course, we have already spoken of studying the Bible. But study also involves the attitude of openness to learning, the skill of interpreting what we read or encounter, and the wisdom to evaluate the worthiness of a new idea or experience. Study does include

"sweating over the books," but it also involves applying ourselves to nature, people, art, and music.

4. The **simplicity** of Francis and Clare stimulates us to consider our own dependence on things. Unfortunately, a lifestyle of simplicity is not always simple. Living simply means consuming less in order to share more. It means not rushing to jam as much activity into each hour as possible. It means not wasting energy or food or possessions, so as to live in better harmony with the earth. For most North Americans, following such a simple lifestyle would involve fundamental changes in daily life. Doing so is a matter of process, not an absolute.

Begin by identifying one aspect of your life that could be simplified. Sometimes it is in fact more complicated to recycle than to throw away, to repair than to replace, to bicycle rather than drive. Finding ways to cut your own and your household's consumption and waste is nevertheless a worthwhile project. Start with only one part of your lifestyle before taking on the whole.

"Spending" time is also a sign of what you value most. Think through the times you have spun your wheels by rushing about, and see if there is a way to go at life more calmly. Taking time for the sky, the grass, and people who are important to you is part of a simple lifestyle.

How you spend your money is also a very important part of your spirituality. Giving away a significant fraction of your income to spiritual communities and to those in need is a practical sign of your spiritual commitment. For more information, see http://www.ministryofmoney.org.

5. Consider **praying** with rosary beads. If you are comfortable with the traditional prayers, use them. If not, change the text of the prayers to something that suits your own belief. For example, change the last lines of the Hail Mary and keep the first lines that come straight from the Bible. Or change the prayers more radically. Use the Jesus Prayer instead of the Hail Mary, for example.

Aids for the Exercises

Baggley, John. *Doors of Perception: Icons and Their Spiritual Significance.* Crestwood, N.Y.: St. Vladimir's Seminary Press, 1988.

Gillet, Lev. *The Jesus Prayer.* Crestwood, N.Y.: St. Vladimir's Seminary Press, 1987.

Nouwen, Henri J. M. *Behold the Beauty of the Lord: Praying with Icons.* Notre Dame, Ind.: Ave Maria Press, 1987.

Barrington-Ward, Simon. *The Jesus Prayer.* Oxford: Bible Reading Fellowship, 1996.

Suggested Reading

The Classics of Western Spirituality Series includes many volumes, including those on *Celtic Spirituality, Meister Eckhart, Francis and Clare, Bernard of Clairvaux, Angela of Foligno, Hildegard of Bingen, Julian of Norwich*, and others. New York: Paulist.

Companions for the Journey Series from St. Mary's Press, Winona, Minn. Includes *Praying with . . . Hildegard of Bingen, Catherine of Sienna, Julian of Norwich*, and so forth.

Galli, Mark. *Francis of Assisi and His World*. Downers Grove, Ill.: InterVarsity, 2002.

Jantzen, Grace M. *Julian of Norwich: Mystic and Theologian*. New York: Paulist, 1988.

Julian of Norwich. *Showings*. Classics of Western Spirituality Series. Trans. Edmund Colledge, O.S.A., and James Walsh, S.J. New York: Paulist, 1978.

Leclerq, Jean, O.S.B. *The Love of Learning and the Desire for God: A Study of Monastic Culture*. New York: New American Library, 1961.

Meyendorff, John. *Byzantine Theology: Historical Trends and Doctrinal Themes*. New York: Fordham Univ. Press, 1987.

Ruusbroec, John. *John Ruusbroec: The Spiritual Espousals and Other Works*. Classics of Western Spirituality Series. Trans. James A. Wiseman, O.S.B. New York: Paulist, 1985. (This is simply another spelling for Jan van Ruysbroeck.)

Upjohn, Sheila. *Why Julian Now?: a Voyage of Discovery*. Grand Rapids: Eerdmans, 1997.

Van Nieuwenhove, Rik. *Jan van Ruusbroec, Mystical Theologian of the Trinity*. Notre Dame, Ind.: University of Notre Dame Press, 2003.

Chapter 6

Protestant and Catholic Reform

The sixteenth century was a time of religious turmoil even greater than that of earlier centuries. Northern Europe broke away from the South and East in a wrenching struggle that was to divide Europe for more than four hundred years. Most thoughtful Catholics of the time agreed that reform was needed, but views about what kind of reform varied widely. Those Catholics who became Protestant came to the view that not only church political structures needed reform, but theology, liturgy, sacraments, and spirituality did too. Such reform was not welcome in Rome, and the pope excommunicated and condemned these Catholics. Separation from the Roman Catholic Church became the inevitable result.

Reformers who remained Catholic, on the other hand, managed to get approval at the Council of Trent for educational reform for priests, correction of obvious abuses by bishops, and a more centralized administration of the church. The Catholics of Spain led the way in this branch of spiritual reform.

Both sides would transform Western Christendom, making a clear break from the later Middle Ages into the modern era.

Protestant Reformation

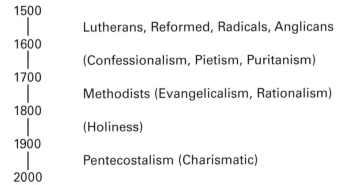

TABLE OF PROTESTANT DENOMINATIONS AND MOVEMENTS
1500
   | Lutherans, Reformed, Radicals, Anglicans
1600
   | (Confessionalism, Pietism, Puritanism)
1700
   | Methodists (Evangelicalism, Rationalism)
1800
   | (Holiness)
1900
   | Pentecostalism (Charismatic)
2000

Luther and Lutherans

> I believe that by my own understanding or strength I cannot believe in Jesus Christ my Lord or come to him, but instead the Holy Spirit has called me through the gospel, enlightened me with his gifts, and made me holy and kept me in the true faith, just as he calls, gathers, enlightens, and makes holy the whole Christian church on earth and keeps it with Jesus Christ in the one common, true faith. Daily in this Christian church the Holy Spirit abundantly forgives all sins—mine and those of all believers. On the last day the Holy Spirit will raise me and all the dead and will give to me and all believers in Christ eternal life. This is most certainly true.[1]
>
> —Martin Luther, *The Small Catechism*

It was a spiritual problem that drove **Martin Luther** (1483–1546) of Wittenberg to the extraordinary lengths of leading a reformation (see map 4). He searched for a gracious God by performing the many religious duties of late medieval piety, but those duties could not satisfy him. Only when he understood Paul's words about the gospel and the righteousness of God in Romans 1 did the gates of paradise open. He understood for the first time that God's righteousness was a free gift, not a human achievement. He felt that he had been set free from the law of penances, pilgrimages, and monasteries in order to love his neighbor in the ordinary deeds of daily life.

Unlike some other reformers, Luther did not want to abandon the Catholic heritage; rather, he wanted to reform it. His norm was his understanding of the gospel, that people are justified (made right with God) by grace through faith. By this yardstick, he decided to keep most of the Mass, vestments, calendar, and architecture of the church.

He introduced the vernacular Bible, hymn singing, and a reform of the Sacrament of Confession, but he uprooted churchly pilgrimages (visiting distant holy places), relics (supposed bones and artifacts related to biblical figures and saints), and vows of celibacy (no sex). These he saw as human attempts to merit what could never be merited but could only be received, namely, the grace of God.

Just as we look back on the tradition today to decide what is helpful and what is not, so Luther did in his time. As he looked back on the writings of the fathers and the mystics, he used the gospel as articulated by Paul as the standard by which he judged the spiritual tradition. This approach led him to approve of some writers and disapprove of others.[2]

Luther's appreciation of the mystical tradition can be seen in his publication of the *Theologica Germanica* (German Theology), which was an anonymous treatise from the previous century. Twice he shepherded this book through the press because he thought it helpful to the lay reader. His own more distinctive perspectives, however, come out in *The Freedom of a Christian*, published in 1520. The mystical image of the marriage of the soul to Christ here takes on a new significance: the exchange of Christ's righteousness for the soul's sin. The treatise begins with paradoxical statements, a feature of Luther's thought on many subjects:

> The Christian is a perfectly free lord of all, subject to none.
> The Christian is a slave of all subject to all.[3]

At the root of this paradox is Luther's view that the gospel has set us free from sin, death, and Satan, and that it also sets us free to serve our neighbors as we become Christs to them.

Luther struggled with *Anfechtungen*, or spiritual attacks, all his life. For Luther, *Anfechtung* meant deep despair, a challenge to his standing before God, falling into an abyss of guilt and the taunts of Satan. Luther viewed these experiences not as inevitable parts of the spiritual journey but as spiritual warfare with evil. The objective, sacramental side of his faith came to his rescue here, for he could answer, "I am baptized," and thus still his doubts, for he believed God had laid claim to him, however weak or sinful he might be.

In fact, Luther believed that Christians remain sinners all their lives. For all their good intentions and good works, for all their prayers and Bible reading, they remained sinners, and their pious sins were sometimes worse than those of the flesh. He claimed that Christians are simultaneously saints and sinners: both condemned under the perfect law of God and at the same time regarded by God as perfectly righteous because of the atonement of Jesus on the cross. Thus he did not expect very much external change in Christian growth; he was suspicious of claims to growth in holiness and did not count such growth as his goal. Luther simply wanted "progress" in realizing his need for God's grace.

Luther's teaching on spirituality was very pragmatic, yet suspicious of methods to attain union with God. When asked by his barber how to pray, Luther replied with a very practical letter in which he advised returning to the basics: the Ten Commandments, the Creed, and the Lord's Prayer. Make a garland, he advised, by finding in each part of these teachings something to learn, something for which to ask forgiveness, something to praise and thank God for, and something to petition for the aid of someone.[4]

This same return to the basics surely underlies Luther's *Small Catechism*, which has affected the spirituality of Lutherans ever since. It is in his *Large Catechism* that Luther sets out one of his most basic spiritual teachings—that the Christian life is a daily baptism, a daily dying and rising with Christ in repentance and forgiveness:

These two parts, being dipped under the water and emerging from it, indicate the power and effect of Baptism, which is simply the slaying of the Old Adam and the resurrection of the new man, both of which actions must continue in us our whole life long. Thus a Christian life is nothing else than a daily Baptism, once begun and ever continued.[5]

Luther is known for advocating a "theology of the cross" in contrast to a "theology of glory." Luther opposed a style of theology that stood outside the human condition to interpret everything as a great system. This is the style he thought that Aristotle the philosopher had used and that the medieval theologians were following. Luther's "theology of the cross," however, began with the suffering of Christ on the cross, an event that went against human reason and expectation. Here, on the cross, one finds God, Luther said. Here, God is crucified and reveals his loving grace to humankind.

We might extend Luther's approach to a "theology of the cross" to a "spirituality of the cross" as well, which similarly follows Jesus through suffering and pain and does not provide a triumphal thrill that elevates one to the heavens.

One of Luther's key concepts was vocation. By this he meant neither the churchly call to the monastery or the priesthood nor what we would call today a certain range of skilled occupations. Rather, his concept of vocation encompassed all of life; it was God's call to be a disciple of Jesus, to fulfill our roles as family members, to love our neighbors, and, yes, to serve our neighbors by means of our ordinary occupations. One of Luther's memorable sayings was that the shoemaker is called to show his vocation not by sewing crosses on his products but by making sturdy shoes!

In the century after Luther's death, his followers kept busy defending themselves and his teaching from Roman Catholics and from distortions within the Lutheran Church. This period, sometimes called the Orthodox or Confessional period, was a time of systematizing and defending Luther's new understanding of the gospel.

In this setting, a remarkable friendship developed between an older pastor, whose writings paradoxically became the cutting edge of a new movement, Pietism, and a young intellectual, who later was regarded as the prince of the Lutheran Orthodox theologians. **Johann Gerhard** (1582–1637), the young man, entered the ministry because of **Johann Arndt's** (1555–1621) on him at age fifteen. Gerhard himself was not deaf to the call for a Lutheran piety, as he wrote *Sacred Meditations* himself, but the spirit of the age had little time for the affections of the heart, preferring the polemical, the pedantic, and the objective.

Arndt was an innovator in the sense that his sermons and writings were not like those of his contemporaries. He was less interested in defending the "pure doctrine" of Lutheranism than in promoting genuine spiritual renewal in its followers. His four books of *True Christianity* were a wake-up call to sleepy Lutherans, a prophetic call for awareness of sin, and a challenge to renewal through daily rebirth. Arndt was accused of Roman Catholic and heretical tendencies and was saved from condemnation only by his young friend Gerhard. Arndt laid the foundations for Lutheran Pietism, which would emerge in the late seventeenth century.

Luther was a dominating personality for his followers. Even today, Lutherans revere and study him more than any other denomination does its founder. He never set out a system, but the vigor of his struggles and the forthrightness of his proclamation have marked not only those who still bear his name but many others as well. Yet the Lutheran tradition did not always follow Luther; it did not always even know him. Not until the twentieth-century "Luther Renaissance" were his works published and studied thoroughly. The tradition and the man stand in a dialogue, often in tension.

Reformed Protestantism

The Reformed branch of Protestantism began in Zurich, Switzerland under the leadership of **Ulrich Zwingli** (1484–1531), a contemporary of Luther. Zwingli went even further in his rejection of the Catholic tradition than did Luther; and at their only meeting, in 1529, the two clashed over the meaning and practice of the Lord's Supper. Zwingli died shortly thereafter in a battle against a Catholic army.

Zwingli wanted only a spirituality of the Word, with little or no emphasis on the liturgy or the sacraments. He put aside such Catholic traditions as the lectionary (Scripture readings appointed for certain days in the church year), vestments, musical instruments, and church visual art. To him, all were distractions from the central matter: the Word. If the Bible did not command a given practice, that practice was an invention of the Papists and ought to be abandoned; it is said that he even nailed shut his church organ. This contrasted with the opposite principle for Luther. For him, if a practice did not contradict Scripture, it was approved.

Characteristic of Zwingli's spirituality is an emphasis on both inwardness and scriptural knowledge. He made a sharp distinction between inward and outward discipleship and regarded only the inward as valuable. Thus the outer was identified with "the world" and was seen as having little value.

Zwingli wanted most of all to overcome human ignorance by teaching the Bible. Thus the aesthetic, sacramental, and mystical dimensions of the Catholic tradition were put aside for the sake of a Bible-based rationalism, which was to affect many parts of the Reformed tradition, including the

Puritans of New England and much of American Protestantism to the present day. This part of the Reformed tradition is in tension with a more moderate strand coming from John Calvin.

John Calvin (1509–64), a later reformer, barely escaped from France after the authorities learned of his Protestant views. He went out the back door while the police knocked on the front! Calvin wanted to be an "ivory tower" scholar, but the people of Geneva compelled him to settle there and direct the course of their experiment with a new religious and political order. In Geneva he inherited the Swiss tradition of Zwingli, who by this time was viewed as a martyr, so Calvin was not able to change Zwingli's positions. For example, Calvin wanted weekly communion services, as his piety was much more eucharistic, but Zwingli's four-times-a-year pattern had already taken hold.

Calvin's theology is commonly understood to include the teaching of predestination (the teaching of God's choice before creation of who should be saved), but the later Calvinism was often quite different from that of Calvin himself in its theological emphasis and its spirituality. Calvin's teaching grew out of a sense of God's sovereignty and love. If humans could not justify themselves and only God could do so, then it followed logically that the gift of justification was God's to give to the ones who were chosen. The point of predestination for Calvin was the comfort of knowing that one's relationship to God was secure. One did not need to worry about the final judgment; God had already made the choice. Thus the believer could live in confidence, carrying out the will of God without anxiety.

The starting point for Calvin's spirituality was not predestination but the mystical union of the believer with Christ. He taught that humans are joined to Christ in baptism, and that people grow in that union throughout life. Notice that this union is viewed quite differently from that of the mystics in the Catholic or Orthodox traditions. This mystical union is given to all Christians by faith, not as the end of a long road with progressive stages of growth. Thus every Christian is a "mystic," living in union with Christ, the way Paul speaks of being "in Christ" in the New Testament.

Calvin spoke of both justification and sanctification as divine gifts in this process. Fully agreeing with Luther that justification was by grace alone, he gave fuller emphasis to the simultaneous gift of sanctification, the theological term for the process by which people become holy. Calvin, unlike Luther, expected to see an observable growth in holiness in Christians. He asserted that we are saved not *by* works but *for* them.

Calvin places more emphasis on the spiritual disciplines, whereas Luther valued freedom from prescribed practices. Calvin's writing also shows his focus on the community, not just the individual. He doubted the ability of the intellect to know the self and had a high regard for the power of language. Much more, he was awed by the power and sovereignty of God and by God's tenderness; he discussed God both as Father and as Mother of Christians.[6]

The Reformed tradition in Europe, like the Lutheran tradition, went through a period of scholasticism, defining itself doctrinally, and then a Pietist reaction. The spirituality of Zwingli often overshadowed that of Calvin, and the theology of Calvin was misinterpreted by placing predestination in the spotlight, rather than his ideas about mystical union. The Reformed tradition has kept alive better than some others, however, the concept of Christian public responsibility. Reformed piety cannot remain indifferent to the sufferings of others in society; Christians have a responsibility for the health of the common life.

Anabaptists

Various small groups who differed from both the Catholics and the Lutheran and Reformed Churches were of great variety and were persecuted on all sides. Many of these groups affirmed "believers' baptism" and were thus called "re-baptizers," or Anabaptists, since most Europeans had already been baptized as infants. Their belief in baptism by immersion sometimes was cruelly parodied, as they were put to death by drowning.

These groups were feared and despised because their teachings not only differed radically from the Catholic-Protestant consensus but had political, social, and economic implications that threatened the rulers. They seemed to be anarchists. Luther condemned them as "Swarmers" (*Schwermer*). Some groups said that direct inspiration from God superseded the teaching of the Bible. They thus seemed to promote spiritual and political anarchy. The radical takeover of the city of Münster in 1534–35 gave the movement a bad reputation in the eyes of both Catholics and Protestants. Two men took over as "kings," demanded total conformity to their views, approved of polygamy, and claimed that the kingdom of God had come to earth. Of course, many Anabaptists did not approve of this "kingdom" either.

The common belief among such groups was that infant baptism was invalid, that—just as in the New Testament accounts—a person needed to *choose* to be baptized after coming to faith. Only then did one become a member of a select community, those persecuted by the world, being the only true disciples of Jesus, sharing the practice of the New Testament, including the rejection of public office or fighting in an army. Great variety existed among these groups, with some being pacifist and others militaristic.

Many of the radical sixteenth-century groups died out, but one that has remained to the present day is that of **Menno Simons** (1496?–1561). Menno gathered the fragments of various radical groups to form the fellowship we know as the Mennonites. He believed that a person in Christ is a new creature and assumed that those who were converted and baptized would no longer follow the ways of this world but rather live without serious sin. The community of the church needed to be protected from false teaching and immoral actions by excommunicating those who trespassed. The Amish later took this church discipline most seriously and separated from the other Mennonites.

Anabaptist spirituality, including Mennonite spirituality, developed the expectation of personal discipleship, separation from the fashions of the world, a strict moral code enforced by a close community, pacifism, simple lifestyle, and direct inspiration of the Holy Spirit. Mennonites have much to teach others about simple living in the twenty-first century.

Anglicans

The Church of England experienced stormy trials in the sixteenth century. The extremes of Roman Catholic and Reformed Protestant views produced famous martyrs and even civil war in the following century. The emphasis in Anglican spirituality became the common liturgy as the context for personal growth. As one Anglican put it: "*The Book of Common Prayer* is a rule of life. It is meant to describe, shape, and support the Anglican way of being Christian."[7]

Thomas Cranmer was the first author of the prayer book (1549), but it has gone through many revisions since then. Praying the Psalms is a significant part of Anglican worship; this practice follows the liturgy of the monastic hours. The collects, or common prayers, of this collection reveal Anglican sensibilities and exquisite literary style. Here are two examples:

> Almighty God, to whom all hearts are open, all desires known, and from whom no secrets are hid: Cleanse the thoughts of our hearts by the inspiration of your Holy Spirit, that we may perfectly love you and worthily magnify your holy name; through Jesus Christ our Lord. Amen.[8]

> O God, from whom all holy desires, all good counsels, and all just works do proceed: Give unto thy servants that peace which the world cannot give, that our hearts may be set to obey thy commandments, and also that by thee, we, being defended from the fear of all enemies, may pass our time in rest and quietness; through the merits of Jesus Christ our Savior. Amen.[9]

The story of Anglican spirituality beyond the sixteenth century includes many poets. Among the first was **George Herbert** (1593–1633), whose poetry reveals startling images and deep devotion. Herbert is often cited as an Anglican of moderate views. He was a parish priest for a short time and wrote *A Priest to the Temple; or, the Country Parson*, which was published after his death in 1652. This book is an early, profound meditation on pastoral care that has influenced clergy of many denominations in their care of souls.

Another early poet-priest was **John Donne** (1571–1631), who is known for his witty poems based on his convictions concerning the incarnation—he combined flesh and spirit in striking ways. Donne is also remembered for his meditation that "no man is an island," all of humankind being part of a continent, deeply tied to one another, and "death be not proud."

Two of the most influential of Anglican divines were **Lancelot Andrewes** (1555–1626) and **Jeremy Taylor** (1613–67). Some Anglicans in our generation see Andrewes as one who embodies the best of Anglican spirituality. He led a major part of the translation team for the King James, or Authorized, Version of the Bible in 1611. He was an influential clergyman in his own day and later influenced the twentieth-century poet T. S. Eliot. Taylor's books *Holy Living* (1650) and *Holy Dying* (1651) are practical guides to devotion, drawing on biblical and patristic sources. Taylor was one of the greatest composers of English prayers.

Early Anglicanism contained the seeds for the three main branches of emphasis that developed more clearly later in its history. The liberal, or broad church, strand (eighteenth century) emphasized the role of the human intellect in appropriating and expressing the truth of God, found in nature as well as Scripture. The evangelical, or low church, strand (eighteenth century) emphasized the teachings of the Protestant reformers in Europe, with special emphasis on lively singing and preaching for conversion. The catholic, or high church, strand (nineteenth century) emphasized the role of bishops and sacraments, the early fathers of the church, and continuity with Roman Catholicism. These three strands are not as prominent today as they were in the past, but are still discernable.

It took a long time for the variety of viewpoints to be accommodated, but eventually the Anglican Church embraced wide differences in theological perspective. What has developed out of those experiences in our own day is a view of Anglicanism as a bridge among the Catholic, Protestant, and Orthodox traditions. Many Anglicans would not classify this church as Protestant, since they see it as a separate branch of Catholicism. (In America, the Anglican Church is called Episcopal, formerly Protestant Episcopal.)

The Anglicans today want to include as many views as possible within their communion and have therefore agreed not to be exclusive about theological or ethical views but to be united in one form of worship, *The Book of Common Prayer*. Worship has priority over theology as a basis for their unity. Anglicans have thus developed a strong tradition of spirituality with many strands. Communal worship stands at the center; personal piety is practiced in that context.

These four types of Protestant churches in the sixteenth century—the Lutherans, the Reformed, the Anabaptists, and the Anglicans—were to increase in number and variety as time passed. Today their communions are found around the globe in various cultural contexts. What all had in common was an emphasis on the Bible and a strong conviction of the need for reform of Roman Catholicism, not only in various abuses but also in basic principles and common practices of spirituality.

The Catholic Reformation

At the very time that some Catholics were leaving the church in frustration, others were working to curb the abuses that most people agreed were hindering its life. There was a great need for change in the institutional life of the church and for a response to the theological challenges of the Protestants.

The **Council of Trent** attempted to deal with both. It met sporadically in northern Italy from 1545 to 1563. The council made progress in improving education for priests and outlawing abuses by bishops. The office of bishop, for example, could no longer be sold to the highest bidder nor inherited by a bishop's (illegitimate) son.

On the theological side, the council drew up doctrinal statements that defined Catholicism as distinct from Protestantism, defending what Protestants had attacked. Protestants were condemned for teaching justification by faith alone. The seven sacraments were definitively chosen at this time, in contrast to the two sacraments recognized by Protestants. The canon of Scripture was defined to include the Apocrypha or Deutero-Canonical books of the Old Testament. The conservative, defensive response of Trent is understandable in its context but is nevertheless regrettable: Catholics and Protestants rejected each other for four hundred years thereafter. It was not until Vatican II in the 1960s that the door was opened for serious conversation between these two branches of Christendom.

Ignatius Loyola and the Jesuits

About the same time that Luther was defending his teachings in Germany, **Ignatius Loyola** (1491?–1556) experienced a profound conversion from reading spiritual literature in Spain (see map 4). He was lying recuperating at home after a cannon ball wound in the Battle of Pamplona in 1521 when he read the life of Jesus and lives of the saints. He dedicated himself entirely to Jesus Christ instead of to romantic knighthood. Later, at Manresa, he began writing one of the most powerful books in the history of Christian spirituality, his *Spiritual Exercises*.

After traveling to the Holy Land to fulfill a vow of thanksgiving, Ignatius took up the study of theology in Paris. Here a group of like-minded persons gathered around him. This group eventually moved to Rome and received the pope's permission to form a new order, the Society of Jesus, in 1540. Ignatius was elected the superior general and spent the rest of his life leading the order from its headquarters in Rome.

The *Spiritual Exercises* are really a manual written for a retreat director. The instructions are simultaneously very specific and very flexible. It was intended that the retreatant would spend thirty days, passing through four "weeks," during which a number of experiences would lead to discernment of the direction of life for that person. During the retreat, the person would meet daily with a spiritual director, pray for four or five hours, participate in the Mass, and keep silence. Ignatius himself, however, encouraged the director to adapt this program to individual needs, and the retreat is now often given in several shorter periods, except that Jesuits still participate for the full thirty days.

The paradoxical feature of the *Exercises* is their appeal to the affections or emotions to accomplish their purpose, while remaining very rational. The retreatant's imagination is especially employed to reconstruct biblical scenes, in which the retreatants participate and feel the motions of their hearts. The program is designed to give individual freedom within a clear, fixed pathway, leading to a clear decision about how to follow Jesus. The daily examen (examination of conscience) is an important discipline described in the *Exercises*. It is an exercise in surrender to God and discernment of God's leading.

The Jesuit Order, which Ignatius founded, was to be a radical new form of religious community. It went another step beyond the mendicant orders (the Franciscans and the Dominicans) to individualize the commitment to a religious order. Whereas "stability," the promise to stay in one place, was part of Benedictine monastic vows, the Jesuits saw travel to wherever they were needed as their ascetic duty. Also, the ideal of "contemplative in action" meant that the Jesuit did not always live in community but was often alone; for those who were together, there was no chanting of the Divine Office. This departure from the tradition meant that service to others was a higher priority than communal worship. Yet each Jesuit was expected to find time in the day to say his own office, that is, to pray the prayers and read the Scriptures appointed for that day.

Ignatius's ideals were formed partly by Paul, who was also the basis for Luther's reformation. But Ignatius and the Jesuits were totally opposed to Lutheranism and took special vows of loyalty and obedience to the pope. They argued at the Council of Trent for strong language to condemn Luther's view of justification by grace through faith alone. What inspired Ignatius was Paul's lifestyle as a missionary, his willingness to be all things to all people in order to save some; what inspired Luther was the theological content of Paul's letters.

Spiritual direction became a Jesuit specialty, growing out of the retreats. In later history, Jesuits came to be the confessors or directors for many of the powerful rulers of Europe and were suspected of using their influence directly for the pope.

The ideal of travel for service, inspired by the apostle Paul, led many Jesuits to become missionaries to Latin America, Africa, and Asia as well as to Europe. Two of the most notable were Matteo Ricci (1552–1610) in China and Roberto de Nobili (1577–1656) in India. They developed a high regard for their host cultures and went far (the pope said too far!) in adapting Christianity to those cultures. As a result, they gained adherents from some of the most powerful and well educated of those societies, but they were not able to found lasting churches. Their approach would prove to be a sharp contrast to much later mission history, when the poor and marginal members of society would be attracted to Christianity by missionaries who did not much respect the host culture.

The early Jesuit balance between the mystical and the practical proved difficult to maintain after the death of Ignatius. Because of political activities, the order was suppressed in 1774. It was reestablished in 1814, without the political intrigue, and has become the largest single Catholic order in the world.

Teresa of Avila and John of the Cross

Mother Teresa of Jesus (1515–82), as her contemporaries called her, is one of the great mystics and reformers of Spain. She had become a Carmelite, a member of an order founded on Mount Carmel in the Holy Land in the mid-twelfth century. Teresa became the leader of a reform movement that followed the early strict rule of the Carmelites rather than a more recent, mitigated one. The Reform movement came to be called "discalced," or shoeless. Teresa was involved in founding many new houses of nuns and in defending the Reform to church authorities.

It is as a mystic, however, that Teresa has had her greatest influence. Her *Life* gave a direct view of her trials and development. She described her severe illness of 1538–39, her conversion to a deep spiritual life in 1554, and her vision of Christ sending a spear through her heart in 1559. The men around her did not know how to deal with her frequent visions and "locutions" (words from God) and told her they must come from the devil. She was deeply troubled until she obtained sounder advice from another mystic. Her story illustrates the importance of good spiritual direction.

Teresa's *Interior Castle* is a thorough analysis of spiritual development. In seven "mansions," she describes the soul's journey to God, from the purgative through the illuminative and to the unitive. She also classifies prayer, meditation, and contemplation. She writes of two kinds of passive contemplation, the prayer of quiet and the prayer of union, which were her daily practice.

Like her younger associate John of the Cross, Teresa describes severe trials near the end of this journey. Her prose, however, is much more understandable than John's, as she uses metaphors and experiences of daily life to explain her meaning. She also wrote poetry, but John is unequaled in verse.

The writings of **John of the Cross** (1542–91) reflect a life of dramatic reversals. John was invested with considerable responsibility by Teresa even as a young man, when he joined the Reform movement in the Carmelite Order. She had already founded the movement among the nuns; he was to found it among the monks. In fact, he became for a time Teresa's own spiritual director during the time she experienced what she called the "spiritual marriage."

John was later kidnapped and imprisoned in a dank cell for six months by his opponents in the order who were against the Reform movement. It was in prison that he began to compose poetry, first only mentally and then on paper. After escaping from prison, he was elected again for responsible posts in the Reform branch of the Carmelites and wrote most of his prose works during the 1580s. However, because of his willingness to be a "whistle-blower," because of stating his frank opinion in a committee meeting with the vicar general of the order, he was stripped of all his offices and sent to an obscure post, where he became ill and died at age forty-nine.

Out of this life of passion and conflict, John wrote works on spiritual theology that led to his selection as a doctor of the Roman Catholic Church. His main works are *The Ascent of Mount Carmel, The Dark Night, The Spiritual Canticle,* and *The Living Flame of Love.* These prose works do not enjoy the same esteem as his poetry for stylistic excellence; his explanation of the poetry is often dense and repetitive. Nevertheless, his poetry is among the best ever written in the Spanish language. Here is a sample in translation:

One dark night,
Fired with love's urgent longings
—Ah, the sheer grace!—
I went out unseen,
My house being now all stilled;

In darkness, and secure,
By the secret ladder, disguised,
—Ah, the sheer grace!—

In darkness and concealment,
My house being now all stilled; . . .

O guiding night!
O night more lovely than the dawn!
O night that had united
The Lover with His beloved,
Transforming the beloved in her Lover.

Upon my flowering breast
Which I kept wholly for Him alone,
There He lay sleeping,
And I caressing Him
There in a breeze from the fanning cedars.

When the breeze blew from the turret
Parting His hair,
He wounded my neck
With his gentle hand,
Suspending all my senses.

I abandoned and forgot myself,
Laying my face on my Beloved;
All things ceased; I went out from myself,
Leaving my cares
Forgotten among the lilies.[10]

The most distinctive concept for which John is known is the dark night. He uses this metaphor in at least two ways: to describe the inability of the intellect to grasp God, and to describe the experience of the soul on its journey to the mountaintop, to union with God. In the first sense, he is saying something that had become widely accepted in the Middle Ages from the influence of Pseudo-Dionysius: a negative theology that underlined the inadequacy of any concept or image to describe God. In the second, however, he was to give classic expression to the experience of lostness, confusion, drought, and panic that is often part of the spiritual path. An awareness of this dark night is necessary for all people on the spiritual journey, but especially for spiritual directors.

The Reformation period drastically changed the practice of Christian spirituality. The split between Catholics and Protestants meant that each side lost something of what the other could offer. Consider what Luther could offer to Catholics and what Ignatius could offer to Protestants: from Luther, a simple method of prayer, and from Ignatius, the practice of the daily examen. The hostility between the two meant that such sharing would not be possible for centuries afterward. But both were now going to face intellectual challenges that would change the beliefs that were integral to the practice of their spirituality.

Spiritual Practice

1. Spend some time in silence as described in the first exercise in chapter 1. Now take the **Lord's Prayer** one phrase at a time, and "make a garland" for each one as Luther suggested. For each phrase, think of something to give thanks for, something to repent of, and some guidance for daily life. Then go on to the next phrase. If one thought is especially precious, stay with it. Don't worry about finishing the whole prayer.

2. The daily **examen** may be done in a variety of ways, but here is one that I find helpful. At bedtime, briefly review the day, looking especially for grace notes from God and for problems that have arisen. Then, the next morning, examine the previous day in more detail. Use these words to guide your thinking: *insight, review, thanks, repentance,* and *renewal.* First, ask God the Holy Spirit for insight, for we do not really know ourselves very well. Seek to recognize what your own inclinations might pass over, whether gifts, strengths, or sins. Then review the events of the day. Give thanks for all the gifts of the day. Repent and ask forgiveness for wrong choices or bad attitudes; ask for healing of neurotic guilt or broken relationships. Renewal means receiving God's forgiveness and strength for a new day as well as making very practical resolutions about what will help you in this day to avoid the pitfalls you have experienced before.

It is very helpful to write down some brief points each day that arise from the examen.

3. Use the *Book of Common Prayer* as your book of **prayers**, even if you are not Anglican or Episcopalian. The book contains orders for morning and evening prayer that are rich with tradition and beautiful in expression. The whole Psalter is found within this book as well as a suggested reading guide for all the days of the year. Consider the value of prayers written by others in relation to your own spontaneous prayers. Neither, in my opinion, should exclude the other.

4. Review the suggestions at the end of chapter 3 for using the **Bible**.

5. Try the simple **"stop, look, and listen"** method developed by John Ackerman. It includes quiet, examen, and *lectio.*[11]

6. Discern your **vocation**. Ignatius perhaps paid more attention to discernment than any other writer. To discern is to see, often in a situation where seeing clearly is difficult. He asked retreatants to attend to their experiences of consolation and desolation—that is, to the times they felt connected with God and the times they felt disconnected. These observations became the basis for determining the leading of God in one's life choices, especially if one were to become a Jesuit.

Martin Luther perhaps paid more attention to vocation than most other writers. Vocation is about a calling from God, from yourself, and from the world. Luther demanded that the concept of vocation be separated from ecclesiastical denotations—that is, he insisted that vocation is for all Christians, not just the clergy or members of religious orders. He insisted that God calls all Christians.

You are called by God to trust God's love, to act with love for others. You have a calling as a parent or child. You may also be called to a particular occupation in order to reflect these prior calls. Working in the world—whether in the home, office, school, or factory—is a vocation from God. Spirituality involves the way you view your work to express the core of your values. Consider how your work experience, with all of its difficulties, can be a place where creative accomplishment and compassion give glory to God.

In most cases, this is not a once-and-for-all decision. Discerning God's vocation for me has meant many turns in the road. I sought God's leading about my choice of college, my major, my further studies, my spouse, my first employment, our children, and so forth. The quest to discern does not finish until we have completed the race.

In all these cases, consulting a spiritual director can be helpful. Writing in a journal can also help one notice the movements of God's grace in life. Both can help to find a leading of God. Parker Palmer reminds us that discernment demands knowledge of the self, not simply of God. For Parker, finding your vocation is finding your true self. The third element in vocation is the world. Knowing God and self must be complemented by knowing what the world needs. Study to see which needs stand out for you—environment, poverty, HIV/AIDS, evangelism, oppression, hunger, violence—and devote your life to addressing that need.

God

Self   World

Aids for the Exercises

Bennethum, D. Michael. *Listen! God is calling! Luther Speaks of Vocation, Faith, and Work*. Minneapolis: Augsburg Fortress, 2003.

Diehl, William E. *The Monday Connection: A Spirituality of Competence, Affirmation, and Support in the Workplace*. San Francisco: Harper, 1991.

Driskill, Joseph D. *Protestant Spiritual Exercises: Theology, History and Practice*. Harrisburg, Pa.: Morehouse, 1999.

Dreyer, Elizabeth A. *Earth Crammed with heaven: A Spirituality of Everyday Life*. New York: Paulist, 1994.

Kolden, Marc. *The Christian's Calling in the World*. St. Paul, Minn.: Centered Life, 2002.

Luther, Martin. "A Simple Way to Pray." In *Luther's Works*, vol. 43, 187–212. Philadelphia: Fortress, 1968.

Palmer, Parker. *Let Your Life Speak: Listening for the Voice of Vocation*. San Francisco: Jossey-Bass, 2000.

Schuurman, Douglas James. *Vocation: Discerning our Callings in Life*. Grand Rapids: Eerdmans, 2004.

Suggested Reading

Calvin, John. *John Calvin: Writings on Pastoral Piety*. New York: Paulist, 2001.

The Collected Works of St. John of the Cross. Trans. Kieran Kavanaugh and Otilio Rodriguez. Washington, D.C.: ICS Publications, Institute of Carmelite Studies, 1979.

Ignatius. *Spiritual Exercises*. Classics of Western Spirituality Series. New York: Paulist, 1991.

Leith, John H. *John Calvin's Doctrine of the Christian Life*. Louisville, Ky.: John Knox, 1989.

Lull, Timothy F., and William R. Russell, eds. *Martin Luther's Basic Theological Writings*. Minneapolis: Fortress, 2004.

Senn, Frank, ed. *Protestant Spiritual Traditions*. New York: Paulist, 1986.

Teresa of Avila. *Interior Castle*. New York: Doubleday, 1989 (1961).

Chapter 7

The "Modern" Era

I n the seventeenth to nineteenth centuries, Christianity faced many new challenges as it began to move from Europe to become once again a transcontinental faith. After sputtering attempts by Portuguese and Spanish missionaries in the sixteenth century, Christianity came to the North Americas in the seventeenth and following centuries by emigration, and then to Africa and Asia in the nineteenth century by a populist mission movement. Much of Christian attention in this period, however, was focused on European and American problems: new cultural developments, urbanization, the industrial revolution, and dreadful wars. The relatively young Protestant churches as well as the Catholic and Orthodox churches developed new approaches to spirituality to meet the challenges of the new cultural eras. In this period, we move from the pieties and conflicts of the 1600s, through the rise of rationalism and evangelicalism in the 1700s, to the romantic and historical consciousness of the 1800s.

"Enlightenment"

The cultural changes in Europe from the fifteenth to the nineteenth century were so dramatic that historians began to think of themselves as living in an entirely new era. They looked back on history now in three main stages: the ancient, the middle (or medieval), and the modern. With the rise of a new style of learning, sometimes called Renaissance humanism, in the fifteenth and sixteenth centuries, the theological method of scholasticism receded gradually into the background. The rise of Protestantism ended the sole dominance of the Catholic Church in European culture. The secular interests of the Renaissance separated the spiritual into a separate sphere.

The full implications of the Renaissance were not realized, however, until the 1700s, when a new movement identified with such rationalist thinkers as Newton, Voltaire, Kant, Locke, and Franklin emerged. Called the Enlightenment, this movement understood itself to be the dawn of a new day after the long night of the Middle Ages. Its theme was that the age of superstition was passing and that human beings now could use the clearheaded guide of their own reason to test every proposition claiming truth.

In the thirteenth century, Aquinas had welcomed reason as a divine gift to accompany and provide the basis for revelation. His synthesis of reason and revelation, of nature and grace, was one of the great intellectual accomplishments of the Western church. Aquinas's system was dismantled by later philosophers in such a way that revelation no longer had an independent claim to truth but had to be submitted to the judgment of what was thought reasonable. For example, miracles were not thought reasonable, but proving that a rational God existed was thought very reasonable. Yet *reason* is in fact a variable term; what is thought reasonable at one time varies greatly from other times. It was not long before the prevailing proofs of God's existence were challenged.

A theologian of our own day, Darrell Jodock, summarizes the "modern" with this list of themes: (1) autonomous reason, (2) progress and antitradition, (3) objectivity and an infatuation with science, (4) optimism, (5) individualism, and (6) mechanism.[1] The "modern" worldview saw God as a distant, intelligent designer who set the universe going like a great clockwork and then left it to run on its own. Religion was largely reduced to morality, leaving little room for an affective spirituality.

In our own time, many people believe that we are again moving into a new era and that the "modern" paradigms of science and philosophy no longer fit our experience. Thus many writers speak of the "postmodern" era, not yet giving a name to the new age but indicating that the assumptions that framed the seventeenth to nineteenth centuries are becoming obsolete. New paradigms demand new theologies and new spiritual styles.

Yet much of our European and North American way of thinking is still oriented to those modern assumptions. We are still secularists, separating spirituality from the "real world"; we still tend to think of science as the arbiter of that real world; we are still optimistic about technological progress; and we are still individualists.

It is the period of the Enlightenment, I am convinced, that separates the cultures of the Western world from the rest of the world. The assumptions and the continuing effects of the Enlightenment make a gap between Christians in Europe and North America and their brothers and sisters elsewhere. It is important to see how this period has affected Christian spirituality for good and for ill. In this chapter, we will look at spiritualities that developed before, during, and after the Enlightenment of the eighteenth century.

Protestant Spiritualities

After the period of reformation, many of the Protestant movements went through three periods of development. The first was a confessional period, when the attention of the leaders was focused on defining and defending the denomination intellectually. The second was a Pietist period, calling for more attention to the needs of ordinary people, especially in the affective dimension of the spiritual life. And finally, the rationalist period, or the Enlightenment, described above, brought the critique of an autonomous reason to bear on both the Bible and the practices of the churches. Rationalism reduced the role of religion to teaching universal ethical norms and so had little emphasis on personal relations to God or on the death and resurrection of Jesus.

It should be noted that in the English-speaking world, the periods of Pietism and rationalism overlapped; each was competing with, and to some degree influencing, the other. For example, John Wesley read John Locke and was very much interested in empirical verification. Across the Atlantic, Benjamin Franklin went to hear the evangelist George Whitefield and could not prevent himself from contributing all his coins to Whitefield's orphanage project.

Puritans, Quakers, Pietists

The Puritan movement in the Church of England began as early as the 1500s and continued into the 1700s to Jonathan Edwards, the "last Puritan." This was a movement to purify the Anglican Church along Reformed Protestant lines. Thus it took its inspiration from the teachings of Zwingli in Zurich and of Calvin in Geneva.

Many of the scholars who have studied the movement regard the popular view of Puritans as uninformed and unfair. The Puritans were more affirming of human work, play, and sexuality than they are given credit for.

The Sabbath day became the mainspring of the Puritan calendar, as the annual calendar of the Catholic Church with Advent and Lent was discarded. The Sabbath day was to be devoted to religious pursuits, with emphasis on hearing the Word preached and on receiving the sacrament of the Lord's Supper.

Puritans did experience raptures that are comparable to those of the Catholic mystics, though they might abhor the comparison. They were also free to use erotic metaphors for these intense experiences, and they frequently quoted the Song of Songs or Bernard's spiritualized version, in which the lovers are Christ and the soul.

The Puritan theology was meant to lead to an assurance that one was indeed predestined (chosen) by God for salvation. Like many other forms of

Christian spirituality, the Puritans thought that their life in God was so important that halfway measures were not possible: Christianity demanded the whole of personal and social life. One of the most eminent of the Puritans was **John Owen** (1616–83), a theologian closely connected to both Oxford University and Oliver Cromwell. He was a Calvinist whose writings, about eighty in all, included both devotional and polemical works.

It was from prison that **John Bunyan** (1628–88) wrote one of the most influential English Christian classics, *Pilgrim's Progress*. The book is an allegory of the Christian life, using a protagonist named Christian who meets trials and temptations—such as Vanity Fair, the Slough of Despond, and the Delectable Mountains—on his way to the Celestial City. The basic metaphor of life as a journey is a rich one. It is clear from this story that Bunyan and other Puritans saw Christian spirituality not as a hobby for "couch potatoes" but as a vigorously challenging struggle with the world and one's own desires. Bunyan's allegory influenced the spirituality of Protestants for centuries to come.

Contemporaries of the Puritans, and often in conflict with them, were the Quakers, the group that called itself the Society of Friends and which continues its witness for peace in the present day. The Friends in England are parallel to the radical wing of the Reformation in Germany: in both places, the new sects were persecuted and feared for undermining religious teaching and threatening the foundations of public order (see pp. 105–6).

George Fox (1624–91), founder of the Quakers, believed that the Holy Spirit spoke directly through people, to what he called "that of God in every man." This inspiration seemed to rank higher than Scripture and so was opposed by the established church. The charismatic early meetings for worship, without clergy or sacrament, depended on individuals to wait in silence for the inspiration of the Spirit and to hear what others were led to say.

Quakers in America distinguished themselves from other Christians by their witness for peace and fair dealing with all peoples. William Penn, founder of Pennsylvania, dealt more fairly with American Indians than other early colonists did. His Quaker convictions led to a respect for Native people not shown by others.

Later, the Quakers were the first Christian denomination in America to publicly oppose slavery. They were tugged in this direction by the tender conscience of **John Woolman** (1720–72). Woolman came to abhor slavery and spent much of his life personally confronting slave owners and speaking in Quaker meetings. His *Journal* is a book of inspiration that is still widely read.

The Quakers demonstrate a spirituality that is simple and wholistic: social justice activity is not separate from listening to the Spirit. Though we may smile at their refusal to take off their hats or address officials in polite English, the same principles that led to these offensive actions led the

Quakers to oppose war and stand for the rights of Native Americans and African slaves. Their spirituality led them to oppose social convention on all levels, and many early Quakers suffered prison and death for their courageous discipleship.

In Germany, Lutheran Pietism was a movement of church reform begun by **Philip Jacob Spener** (1635–1705) under the influence of Johann Arndt. Like Arndt, Spener saw the churches as passive and indifferent, not aware of the true Christianity of the Gospels. Like Arndt, he called for self-examination, repentance, and conversion. And like Arndt, he tired quickly of the polemics that seemed to dominate Lutheran sermons.

Spener went beyond Arndt by publishing a program of church reform and organizing groups to accomplish it. He wrote *Pia Desideria* ("pious hopes"), which unlike its title was very concrete in its proposals. Most of the proposals would not sound radical today. For example, he called for midweek Bible studies, lay activism in the church, sermons that built up the hearer instead of arguing with other preachers or showing off classical learning, and seminaries that taught pastoral care. But in Spener's day, these proposals seemed radical, and he faced considerable ostracism, leading even to his forced departure from his parish in Frankfurt (see map 5).

The social side of Pietist reform was developed by **August Herman Francke** (1663–1727), who was both a professor of theology at Halle and founder of institutions for social help. Francke started orphanages, schools, and a lending library, and he also trained some of the first Protestant missionaries to leave Europe. Ziegenbalg and Plotschau traveled to India under Danish sponsorship. They made a good start in studying Indian religion and culture as well as in publishing books in indigenous languages. Pietism was the motivating factor for Lutheran missions throughout the world, and its legacy is the worldwide fellowship of Lutherans, possibly the largest Protestant denomination in the world.

During this same period, one of the greatest composers and performers, **Johann Sebastian Bach** (1675–1750), produced music that still stirs the souls of the faithful. Bach was influenced by all three Lutheran movements—Confessionalism, Pietism, and Rationalism—as indicated by Jaroslav Pelikan:

> All the attempts by Orthodox Lutheran confessionalists, in his time or ours, to lay claim to Bach as a member of their theological party will shatter on the texts of the cantatas and the *passions,* many (though by no means all) of which are permeated by the spirit of Pietism. Above all, the recitatives and arias for individual voices . . . ring all the changes and sound all the themes of eighteenth-century Pietism: all the intense subjectivity, the moral earnestness, and the

rococo metaphors of Pietist homiletics, devotion, and verse. . . . Yet, it would be, if anything, an even more uncritical oversimplification to interpret Bach as a party-line Lutheran Pietist, for he repeatedly showed, by his revisions and by his musical settings of those very texts, that he was not to be confined by the categories of Pietism any more than he was by those of Rationalism and Confessional Orthodoxy.[2]

Bach scholars argue heatedly over whether Bach is to be interpreted primarily as a "sacred" or as a "secular" composer. Pelikan argues that we cannot know Bach's inner motivation but that we can know he "began his compositions by writing '*Jesu Juva* [Jesus, help]' and closed them by writing '*Soli Deo Gloria* [to God alone be glory].'"[3] Furthermore, we know from Bach's personal Bible that he wrote in the margins thoughts that indicated his personal devotion to Christ. But however pious or impious Bach may have been, his attitude toward his secular works, which represent about 25 percent of his compositions, demonstrates a worldview that is not divided by sacred or secular:

> The attitude reflected in this craftsmanship bespeaks the conviction of Luther and the reformers that the performance of any God-pleasing vocation was the service of God, even if it did not lead to the performance of chorales. The Bach of the Peasant Cantata, the partitas, and the concertos was not "too secular." There were, rather, the expression of a unitary . . . world view, in which all beauty, including "secular" beauty, was sacred because God was one, both Creator and Redeemer.[4]

Later, Pietism spread to Scandinavian Europe, led by **Hans Nielsen Hauge** (1771–1824) in Norway and by **Carl Rosenius** (1816–68) in Sweden. Hauge's life was dramatic, for after an ecstatic, mystical experience while working in farm fields on April 5, 1796, he felt God's call to preach and teach throughout Norway and Denmark. By so doing he broke the Conventicle Act of 1741, which forbade laypersons, those not ordained as pastors, from leading religious meetings. Hauge traveled throughout Norway, leading meetings, and then spent most of a decade in Danish prisons. A practical, intelligent man, Hauge stimulated his followers to economic activity that led to their prosperity. He was self-taught and opposed the Rationalism of the church of Norway, so the wrath of the clergy and the state came down on him. But his movement has been called the first nationwide folk movement in Norway. He was influential among the many Norwegians who emigrated to the United States in the nineteenth century.

Rosenius, unlike Hauge, was the son of a pastor and had higher education, though he was not ordained. He spent most of his life in Stockholm as
the editor of the *Pietist*, a periodical founded by his mentor, the English
Methodist George Scott. In addition to preaching and teaching repentance
and conversion, avoiding worldly pleasures, and trusting that God was
behind every circumstance of life, Rosenius wrote hymns. Neither of these
two Pietist leaders disagreed with the content of Orthodox theology; rather,
they disagreed with the way their pastors and their societies were responding
to it. They saw the age as "cold" and wanted to light a fire of warm faith in
the Nordic Lutherans.

Thus the Pietist movement emphasized personal conversion, with the
expectation of a renewed life, an outer change coming from inner rebirth. It
broke new ground in Bible study for the laity, social institutions, and foreign
missions. The Pietists insisted on congruence between one's profession and
one's behavior; Christianity was a life to be lived, not just a mental faith.
There was also a dark side of Pietist spirituality: a tendency to feel self-
righteous and a legalism that made all pleasure something "worldly." In the
context of the Rationalism of their day, the Pietists had a tendency toward
anti-intellectualism. The heart, and not the brain, was the locus of their
spirituality. Like the Puritans, Pietists were in danger of taking their spiritual temperature constantly and thus focusing on themselves instead of others, the world, and God.

Evangelicals and Methodists

The Pietists influenced the Evangelicals, who emerged in the following century in England and New England. The 1700s were an age in which both
Rationalism (witness the U.S. Constitution) and evangelicalism (witness the
rise of the Methodists) developed. Evangelicalism seems an obvious foil to
Rationalism, and yet it shared many of Rationalism's assumptions. It had an
inquiring practical bent; John Wesley was willing, one might say, to do scientific research in the realm of the spiritual by waiting to see which religious
experiences were valid and which led nowhere.

We can describe early evangelicals in three settings: the Anglican
church, the Methodist movement, and the Congregationalist churches of
New England. What all had in common was preaching for repentance,
expecting a changed life after conversion, and finding room for expressions
of emotion not always tolerated in the previous denominations.

No single person led the Anglican branch of this movement. Perhaps
one of the best known in North America is **John Newton** (1725–1807),
because he was the author of the beloved hymn "Amazing Grace" ("how
sweet the sound / that saved a wretch like me"). Newton had been a cap-
tain in the slave trade, was dramatically converted, and became an Anglican

priest. He loved to preach and actually died in the pulpit. Like other Evangelicals, he believed in early rising for prayer, Bible reading as an indispensable part of devotion, and the gathering of the family for group prayers.

In its second generation, Anglican evangelicalism produced one of the outstanding social reformers of the modern era, **William Wilberforce** (1759–1833), whose persistent voice in the British Parliament led to the abolition of the transatlantic slave trade in the early 1800s. His prayer life is said to have given him the perseverance over the decades necessary for the passage of this legislation. A leading member of the Clapham Sect, a fellowship of wealthy Evangelicals, he wrote *A Practical View of the Prevailing System of Professed Christians in the Higher and Middle Classes in This Country Contrasted with Real Christianity.*

In the third generation came **Henry Venn** (1796–1873), general secretary of the Church Mission Society, who advocated "self-governing, self-supporting, and self-propagating churches" instead of continued dependency on foreign missionaries in Africa and Asia.[5] Venn's concept is fundamental to the practice of indigenous Christian spirituality. Ahead of his time, Venn advanced Samuel Ajayi Crowther to be the first African bishop in the Anglican Church. When Crowther died (long after Venn), his successor was a European bishop, a step backward that was much resented by Nigerians. The reversal of Venn's policy of indigenous leadership led to the founding of some of the first African indigenous churches, whose spirituality was to be much more African (see chapter 9).

The Methodist story of the 1700s is full of drama and opposition. **John Wesley** (1703–91) and his brother Charles were uncommonly devoted, partly through the reading of the *Imitation of Christ* and British devotional writers. With a few other students, the Wesleys formed a group for regular prayer, holy communion, and prison visitation at Oxford University. The group came to be ridiculed with such names as "The Holy Club" and "Methodists." Their daily time schedules and other strict requirements led to this charge of "Method-ism." But it would be years before the Methodists emerged as a Christian denomination.

For all his zeal, John Wesley was not at peace until he attended a meeting on Aldersgate Street in London, where he was then able to come to personal faith in Christ and peace of heart. He described this experience in a famous passage for May 24, 1738, in his *Journal.* Someone was reading from Luther's preface to the Epistle to the Romans:

> About a quarter before nine, while he [Luther] was describing the change which God works in the heart through faith in Christ, I felt my heart strangely warmed. I felt I did trust in Christ, Christ alone

for salvation; and an assurance was given me that he had taken away *my* sins, even *mine,* and saved *me* from the law of sin and death.[6]

Ever since this writing, Wesleyan spirituality has been known as the spirituality of the warm heart. Wesley's new emphases gradually made him unwelcome in Anglican churches. These rejections led Wesley to begin preaching outside the church buildings in fields and in the streets. His parish, he said, was the world, and he traveled constantly, often preaching five times a day. He said he wanted to spread scriptural holiness over the land. In other words, he looked for practical changes in the lives of the converted. One such change was avoiding gin, which had been the ruin of many families. Instead of spending money on gin, Wesley encouraged saving money in "thrift clubs" and wrote pamphlets on improving one's health. These habits took hold among many poor Methodists to such a degree that English society was changed and the Methodists tended to move out of poverty.

The most contentious of Wesley's teachings concerned Christian perfection. Wesley understood the biblical passages on perfection (for example, Matthew 5:48; 1 John 3:4-10) to mean that the work of sanctification could follow justification and lead to perfect love in the intentions of the believer. Furthermore, he taught that some persons experienced this "entire sanctification" as "second blessing," an instantaneous experience. Wesley never claimed this experience for himself but reported it of several of his followers.

John Wesley's own spirituality differed from that of his followers. He was educated and committed to the Anglican Church. He liked to read the New Testament in Greek and to critically read the Eastern Orthodox and Catholic mystics. Frequent Communion was important to him. But many of the early Methodists were not highly educated and had little interest in the history of spirituality. Their practical experience was that the Anglican Church, comfortable in its upper-class culture, was not especially friendly to them. To them, reading the word was more important than attending Communion services. So after his death, the Methodists went against the wishes of John Wesley and formed a separate denomination.

Charles Wesley (1707–88) did not travel as John did. He stayed at home, raised a family, and wrote five thousand hymns. He was surely one of the greatest of English hymn writers, bringing together biblical language, emotional power, and poetic beauty. Hymns express spirituality, and Charles's collections surely had much to do with shaping not only Methodist piety but also Protestant devotion throughout the English-speaking world. Evangelical faith, whether of Luther or of the Wesleys, longs to sing the praise of its savior. Here are some of Wesley's "greatest hits":

O for a thousand tongues to sing my great Redeemer's praise,
the glories of my God and King, the triumphs of his grace!

Hark! The herald angels sing, "Glory to the new-born king;
Peace on earth, and mercy mild, God and sinners reconciled."

Rejoice, the Lord is king! Your Lord and King adore;
Rejoice, give thanks, and sing, and triumph evermore:
Life up your heart, lift up your voice; Rejoice, again I say rejoice!

You servants of God, your master proclaim,
And publish abroad his wonderful name.

Love divine, all loves excelling, Joy of heav'n, to earth come down!
Fix in us thy humble dwelling, All thy faithful mercies crown.[7]

The Wesleyan heritage was to produce many branches, not only the large Methodist churches in the United States but also the smaller holiness groups founded in the 1800s, such as the Salvation Army and the Church of the Nazarene. The former concentrated on urban evangelism among the poor; the latter, on developing the doctrine of complete sanctification.

The third strand of the evangelical revival took root on the other side of the Atlantic. In America, **Jonathan Edwards** (1703–58) and **George Whitefield** (1714–70) were two of the most prominent leaders of a spiritual movement later called the Great Awakening. Edwards was a brilliant philosopher and theologian who served as pastor to the Congregationalists in Northampton, Massachusetts. Under the influence of his startling metaphors, the formal, sleepy congregation woke with earnest repentance and faith, accompanied by controversial behavior. He reported and defended the revival in his *Faithful Narrative of the Surprising Work of God* (1737), which demonstrates his own Enlightenment concern to observe and reason from the observable facts. Edwards's later analysis of the revival is his 1746 *Treatise Concerning Religious Affections*.

John E. Smith writes of Edwards: "The whole of his thought might be viewed as one magnificent answer to the question, *What is true religion?*"[8] Edwards seeks to sift the authentic from the inauthentic expressions of spiritual fervor, not only in the Great Awakening, but in general; his analysis is relevant to all kinds of spiritual experiences. He does not regard hysteria, excess bodily effects, or enthusiasm as relevant signs of truth or falsity. He starts with the fruits of the Spirit as listed in Galatians 5:22, identifying them with affections. Then he moves to list twelve such affections that are signs of genuine religion or spirituality.[9] Perhaps no writer has investigated the authenticity of spiritual behaviors with such thoroughness, earnestness, learning, and love of beauty as Edwards did.

Whitefield, unlike Edwards, was a gifted orator who could hold people in the palm of his hand, who traveled throughout the colonies speaking in any church that would welcome him. He established the pattern of much later American religious life by calling people to conversion in the course of a traveling ministry. His ministry also had a social aspect; he established an orphanage in Georgia.

We turn now to the converse of the Evangelicals. A century later, in England, some leaders began a movement that would come to be called "high church."

The Oxford Movement

The Church of England received a new impetus toward ancient spiritualities from a movement that began in Oxford about 1830. Some Anglican leaders, deeply disturbed by the incursions of the state into church affairs and by the rationalism that had invaded the church at the time of the Enlightenment, proposed a renewal of spiritual life along new lines. Evangelical revival, with its emphasis on individual conversion, did not satisfy the needs they saw in the church.

The movement's leaders emphasized the teachings of the church fathers and the importance of the church as a divine institution, kept by apostolic succession as an organic community of faith. Thus they raised the awareness of the importance of bishops and of sacraments and liturgy. They were influenced by the Greek fathers toward views of divinization as the theology of Christian life. All these views were expressed in a series of *Tracts for the Times* (1833–41), for which the group became known as "Tractarians."

The three most important leaders of the Oxford movement were **John Keble** (1792–1866), **John Henry Newman** (1801–90), and **Edward Pusey** (1800–82). Keble is best known as the author of a book of poems, *The Christian Year* (1827). He had considerable influence on Newman as a professor of poetry at Oxford. Newman, an evangelical in his early days, became a high church proponent and then broke with the Anglican Church in 1845 to become a Roman Catholic. He was made priest and cardinal of the Catholic Church in England. A great scholar, he nevertheless was very pragmatic about the disciplines of prayer. Pusey was also a scholar, a professor of Hebrew. Like the others, he often quoted the Greek and Latin fathers but also knew the Syriac writers, such as Ephrem. He knew the spiritual writers discussed in this book very well and edited a series of translations of the fathers. He revived the practice of sacramental confession in the Anglican Church and was much sought after as a spiritual director. He also helped to found Anglican religious orders, parallel to the Roman Catholic ones, such as the Anglican Benedictines. Followers of the Oxford movement were sometimes called "Puseyites."

French Roman Catholics

There were a number of French Catholic spiritual writers in the modern period whose influence has gone beyond France and beyond the Catholic Church. The first of these were **Francis de Sales** (1567–1622) and **Jane de Chantal** (1572–1641), who shared a "Jesus-centered, affectionate friendship" and originated the Salesian tradition. Together they founded a new religious order, the Visitation of Holy Mary, of which Jane de Chantal became the superior. As Catholic bishop of Geneva, Switzerland, de Sales was very much involved both in preaching Catholic Reformation tenets from the Council of Trent and in giving spiritual direction to individuals. He corresponded with Madam de Chantal and others who became spiritual directors in their own right.[10]

De Sales came to write his *Treatise on the Love of God* and *Introduction to the Devout Life* as a means of reaching others, and his clear style and use of many illustrations showed his intent that "devotion," or holiness, was for everyone, not just the clergy or members of religious orders. His teaching is positive, even optimistic, in tone, but his underlying intent is very serious. De Sales made a clear distinction between the will and the emotions. For him, the commitment of the will to God was to be resolute, whatever the emotional distractions.

Cardinal Pierre de Berulle (1575–1629), called the founder of the French school of spirituality, was influenced by personal contact with de Sales and by reading the church fathers, Ruysbroeck, and St. Teresa of Avila. He helped to introduce St. Teresa's Discalced Carmelites (see chapter 6) into France. The most important feature of his spirituality is Christocentrism, that is, its focus on Jesus Christ. The incarnation and the eucharistic presence of Christ are central. Unlike de Sales, however, Berulle and the French school tend to be pessimistic about human nature and severe in ascetic practice.

One of the greatest influences of the French school on popular piety was devotion to the Sacred Hearts of Jesus and Mary, developed by St. John Eudes (1601–80). These were devotional movements emphasizing the humanity of these exalted figures. The theme of the heart was a reference to the love of Jesus and of Mary toward the faithful by the passion of the cross.[11]

Later developments in France led to the denunciation of both Quietism and Jansenism by the Catholic Church. The complexities of these movements make it difficult to describe them within the limits of our space here.

The roots of Quietism go back at least to Miguel de Molinos (b. 1628), who, for unclear reasons, was condemned by Pope Innocent XI. Molinos seems to have taught such an abandonment to God that all things become indifferent to the soul, including the soul's own salvation and ultimately the soul's relation to God. Thus the love of God paradoxically produces indifference to God. This is the view condemned as Quietism.

Accused of a similar teaching were **Mme. Jeanne-Marie Bouvier de la Mothe Guyon** (1648–1717) and her advisor **Francois Fenelon** (1651–1715), archbishop of Cambrai, in France (see map 5). Fenelon came to be accepted into the highest circles of French society and was put in charge of the education of King Louis XIV's grandsons. He introduced Mme. Guyon to these circles, but when her writings were condemned, he refused to join in attacks on her character and for this was exiled from the court. She spent four years in the Bastille, and he was forced into obscurity.[12] He wrote a courageous letter to Louis XIV, frankly denouncing his war policies that brought suffering to so many for the sake of the king's personal glory.

Fenelon was involved in spiritual direction by letter, like his admired predecessor Francis de Sales. Because this advice was not lost in oral speech but preserved in writing, it still speaks to twenty-first-century Christians. He is especially helpful for those of us who are continually too hard on ourselves:

> Every time you insist, against your better judgment, on undertaking these self-examinations which have been so often condemned you disturb and upset yourself, dry yourself up, make prayer impossible and so remove yourself from God. . . . You are also taken up almost exclusively with yourself. Tell me, can all this be the work of God?[13]

Fenelon had a great deal to say about abandonment to God, which he describes this way: "True abandonment simply means letting oneself fall into the arms of God as a child falls into the arms of its mother."[14]

Jeanne Guyon was theologically uneducated but very sensitive spiritually. She has been decried as "hysterical" by many writers then and since, but these judgments may contain implicit sexism. Her willingness to express all of her feelings in her writings, sometimes in excessive ways, weakened her defense; she and Fenelon were declared guilty of Quietism.

Those condemned as Quietists focused on abandonment to God's providence, on passive reception of God's grace. The Jansenists, on the other hand, who were involved in the condemnation of the Quietists, concentrated on the active working out of one's salvation. They emphasized the moral purpose in Christian living, despite a renewed teaching of Augustine's doctrine of predestination. It was predestination that ultimately led to the condemnation of the Jansenists also. The Jesuits, strong defenders of free will since

Reformation times, were vigorous opponents of Jansenism. It was from a Jansenist background that a distinctive French writer, Blaise Pascal, emerged.

Pascal and Kierkegaard

Two writers who seem to stand apart from their traditions and do not easily fit any of the groups we have spoken about are Blaise Pascal and Søren Kierkegaard. Both writers have been considered influential founders of the existentialist movement in the twentieth century, but neither shares the views of twentieth-century existentialists.

Blaise Pascal (1623–62), who lived in France, was a brilliant scientist and mathematician. Like Kierkegaard, Pascal also exercised outstanding literary ability; his *Provincial Letters* are still studied as models of French style. He gathered fragments of ideas for a rational defense of the Christian faith, which were published after his death as *Pensees* (thoughts). In these writings, his stance was that of the individual awed by the wonders of the universe, trying to decide whether or not to trust the Christian message. He wrote of the wager that every human being must make, betting one's life on the truth of the faith. He argued that it was better to live as a Christian and be disappointed after death than to live as an atheist and be wrong in the end.

Pascal is well known for his line "The heart has its reasons of which reason knows nothing" (*Pensees* 423). By saying this, he was rejecting the narrowing of evidence for the Creator and Redeemer. Pascal was a layperson not trained in theology, and he did not have wide influence in his own day, but his remarks have been treasured not only in France but throughout the Christian world.

A lonely Danish Protestant voice of the nineteenth century takes a similar but distinctive stance on Christian spirituality. **Søren Kierkegaard** (1813–55) was a loner from his youth forward. After studying theology and philosophy in Copenhagen, he came to reject both the reigning philosophy, that of Hegel, and the dominant form of Christianity, the Lutheran folk church. He could not identify with either the intellectuals or the Pietists. Rather, after breaking his engagement with Regina Olson, he wrote some forty books in fifteen years, which he later called his "authorship." On the one hand, the books attacked the reigning orthodoxies and set out his own new philosophy, and on the other, they developed "edifying discourses" for the individual believer. Kierkegaard calls on his reader to become a real self. He sees selfhood not as a given, not to be taken for granted. Rather, he says, "I" must become a self through the choices I make.

Kierkegaard was a harsh critic of the Lutheran Church of his day and was not liked. Although he was Lutheran in his understanding of justification, he scathingly charged that Lutheran free grace was being misappropriated, taken for granted, in a system where everyone assumed themselves to be Christian. Thus one's Christianity became an easy, unimportant matter. On the contrary, Kierkegaard amazed everyone by saying that he was *not* a Christian, that this title was too high for him to claim. He hoped to make people stop and think about the commitment entailed in being a Christian.

He was an intellectual, and many of his philosophical works are difficult to understand. But his edifying discourses are written simply and directly. They are instead difficult not because of terminology but because of their demands on the will and the affections.

What is missing in Kierkegaard is a sense of the communal character of Christian faith. Because of his own life experience, he drew a picture of Christian spirituality that was individualist in the extreme. Further, the issues that engaged him did not include the relationship to nonhuman creation. Thus he is mostly focused on relationships to God and self.

One of the many valuable features of Kierkegaard, however, is his ability to skewer facades of spirituality. It is a special danger for people who *study* spirituality to think they are *living* it. His disdain for preachers dressed in fine robes, preaching about the crucifixion to make money, also applies to the aesthete who dabbles in spirituality as a sort of interesting hobby. Kierkegaard distinguishes the *admirer* of Jesus from the *disciple* of Jesus and presents as an example of an admirer Judas Iscariot, who betrayed him!

Orthodoxy

Eastern Orthodox spirituality has a way of drawing upon its Holy Tradition, which renews it age after age. Under the rule of Muslim Turks, long after the death of the Byzantine Empire, the Greek church renewed itself by reading the collection assembled by **Nicodemus of the Holy Mountain** (1749–1809) and **Macarius of Corinth** (1731–1805). This collection, entitled *Philokalia* ("the love of beauty") drew upon writers in Eastern Christendom from the fourth to the fifteenth centuries. Among its themes were the Jesus Prayer, the need for personal spiritual direction, and the virtues needed not only by monks but by laypeople who seek to know union with God. The book, first published in 1782, was soon translated into Slavonic and Russian, but only recently into English. It has become perhaps the most influential book in Orthodox spirituality up to the present day. Its teachings follow Evagrius but surprisingly do not include any writings by the Cappadocians or by Pseudo-Dionysius.

At the time of its publication, this multivolume set was expensive and not readily accessible. Most people in Russia were not able to afford it. But one anonymous writer popularized its message in a much shorter work, *The Way of a Pilgrim*. This work appeared in 1884 and has remained the popular approach to the Jesus Prayer ever since.

The Way of a Pilgrim tells of a Russian pilgrim's longing to know the meaning of the constant prayer that Paul counsels in 1 Thessalonians 5:17: "Pray constantly." Since the book is a narrative, the reader's interest is focused on what will happen next as the pilgrim seeks help for over a year and finally finds what he seeks with an old man who says:

> The continuous interior prayer of Jesus is a constant uninterrupted calling upon the divine Name of Jesus with the lips, in the spirit, in the heart; while forming a mental picture of His constant presence, and imploring His grace, during every occupation, at all times, in all places, even during sleep. The appeal is couched in these terms, "Lord Jesus Christ, have mercy on me." One who accustoms himself to this appeal experiences as a result so deep a consolation and so great a need to offer the prayer always, that he can no longer live without it, and it will continue to voice itself within him of its own accord. Now do you understand what prayer without ceasing is?[15]

The pilgrim's adventures while praying constantly are more interesting than other writers' long theological discussions of the meaning of the prayer. The book has now been translated into many languages and is available in English.

The Little Flower

At the very end of the period comes one of the most beloved of Roman Catholic saints, **Thérèse of Lisieux** (1873–97). During her short life of twenty-four years, Thérèse found a simple way of spiritual life that has been influencing readers ever since, through her *Story of a Soul*, published exactly one year after her death. The later Teresa of Calcutta chose her name after this French saint (see chapter 8).

Thérèse Martin grew up in an intensely pious bourgeois family in northwestern France. Like many Catholic families of the time, it seemed necessary to turn inward in order to nourish the faith, as the culture of France had been dramatically changed by the French Revolution one hundred years earlier. Thérèse therefore did not have much to do with the outside world; it was a trauma to attend public school. By age fourteen, she had determined to enter the Carmelite convent in Lisieux, and she overcame many obstacles to join her three older sisters there. She chose the name "Thérèse of the Child Jesus and of the Holy Face." She wrote several plays about Joan of Arc, patroness of France, and letters of encouragement to people in trouble. Her prayers for a murderer seemed to result in his repentance just before his execution. At the request of her superior, who was also her blood sister, she wrote her autobiography, *The Story of a Soul*, in three drafts. Thérèse developed tuberculosis and endured great physical and spiritual pain in the last years of her life, as she was given no pain relievers until the very last moment. In the last eighteen months, she was in a dark night of the soul.

Thérèse was declared a saint in 1925. Later, in an honor given to very few saints, she was declared a doctor of the Roman Catholic Church—that is, a teacher for all the faithful—in 1997 by John Paul II. Mary Frohlich lists three factors in Thérèse's international, intercultural appeal: her childlikeness, her transformation of suffering into love, and her sisterliness.[16]

Thérèse is commonly known as the "little flower," for her attitude in life reflected what she wrote:

> Jesus deigned to teach me this mystery. He set before me the book of nature; I understood how all the flowers He has created are beautiful, how the splendor of the rose and the whiteness of the Lily do not take away the perfume of the little violet or the delightful simplicity of the daisy. I understood that if all flowers wanted to be roses, nature would lose her springtime beauty, and the fields would no longer be decked out with little wild flowers.
>
> And so it is in the world of souls, Jesus' garden. He willed to create great souls comparable to Lilies and roses, but He has created smaller ones and these must be content to be daisies or violets destined to give joy to God's glances when He looks down at his feet. Perfection consists in doing his will, in being what he wills us to be. . . . I am writing the story of the *little flower* gathered by Jesus.[17]

Thérèse is known both for her deep love and for her devotion to the Virgin Mary. We conclude her story with this short prayer, illustrating both:

> O Mary, if I were the Queen of Heaven and you were Thérèse, I would want to be Thérèse so that you could be the Queen of Heaven![18]

Mission Spirituality

The earlier Catholic missions of the sixteenth and seventeenth centuries had not planted lasting churches for a number of reasons. In spite of a few notable exceptions among the Jesuits, the mission stations were often staffed by unworthy personnel, who had no training or preparation for the work and little or no support from their orders. Further, the mission work was an ancillary arm of nationalist imperialism, so that control by Spain or Portugal, or gaining wealth by gold or slaves, was higher in priority than proclaiming the Savior. Greed for gold and inhumanity undermined the very basis of missionary work. Thus most of the sixteenth-century churches in Africa and the Americas died out.

There were a few outstanding missionaries who spoke out against the abuses of soldiers, traders, and missionaries. One such missionary was **Bartholomew de las Casas** (1484–1566), whose writings remain today as the most severe indictment of the Spanish treatment of American Indians. In his thorough discussion, Gustavo Gutiérrez demonstrates las Casas' commitment to justice for the Indians of Central and South America.[19] The unshakable conviction of those early Catholic missionaries, and the continuing basis for the missions from Europe and North America that came later, was the conviction that salvation was possible for the world's people only if they heard the word of the cross, believed its message, were baptized, and became part of the church. This led many of them to overlook the damage that was done to native cultures by Europeans.

Both missionaries and the peoples among whom they served assumed that religion and culture were fixed together in such a way that becoming European was essential to becoming Christian. This is an assumption similar to that of some early Jewish Christians who demanded that gentile converts become Jews before they could be Christian. Paul passionately disagreed. So do I. It is possible to be authentically Christian in any culture.

It is important to note that missionaries have not always been destroyers of local cultures but instead have, in the long run, stimulated local cultural expression. The translation of the Bible and other Christian materials into local languages, which are the heart of local cultures, has preserved the languages from some of the ravages of modern language imperialism. No language that has its own Bible has ever disappeared, as have many other languages of small groups.[20]

Eastern Orthodox missionaries had earlier spread the faith from the Mediterranean into the Slavic lands. Their new outreach was to the east in Siberia, and by the 1700s to Alaska.

Protestants did not get involved in overseas missions until more than a century after the Reformation. Finally, with the emergence of Pietism, the continental Moravians and Lutherans began sending missionaries in the 1700s. In Great Britain, it was William Carey who began the effort. As a young Baptist shoemaker, he came to the conviction that God wanted him to travel to India with the message of Christ. His elders assured him that it could not be done and that, if God wanted it done, he surely would not choose *you*, young man! But Carey pressed on, actually traveling to India himself.

Why did the missionaries go, often at great discomfort and danger to themselves? Of course, there were unworthy reasons, as all human decisions are ambiguous. But on the positive side, missionary spirituality included love for the people served, courage in facing the unknown, confidence in God's provision when human help often failed, and, ultimately, a sense of humor over the tangled human condition, with all its different customs and languages.

Mission spirituality includes both the spirituality of the missionaries themselves and that of their supporters at home. A certain global perspective is one aspect of such a spirituality. Many people first became aware of the world outside their own country by hearing missionaries describe their "mission field." Another aspect is fervent prayer, especially intercessory prayer. So many people at home have trusted that their requests would make a difference halfway around the world, and there is abundant anecdotal evidence of their effect.

The analog to missionary spirituality is that of the peoples who were first won to Christianity through the missionaries' efforts. Unfortunately, very little of their spirituality has come down to us. It has only been in the twentieth and twenty-first centuries that most of the indigenous Christian movements in different continents have finally developed a distinctive voice. We turn next to that time period.

Spiritual Practice

1. Seventeenth- and eighteenth-century Christians were faithful in **journaling**. They recorded not only the outer events of their lives but also their inner thoughts and feelings. Ron Klug writes that there is no wrong way to keep a journal; the best method for you is best found by you. He lists many sorts of functions that a journal can fulfill. It can help you make decisions, sort out your relationships, preserve your stories, and develop your ability to see and hear.

Putting feelings on paper is one way to get them out where you can deal with them. When I have written out a problem, it does not have the same power over me. It can be especially helpful to write out prayers. Experiment by writing the longings of your heart in a prayer to God. It takes longer than speaking, of course, but this gives you time to ponder. You can say what you want to say in your deepest heart.

2. A **spiritual mentor or director** can be an important help in the spiritual journey. Hearing your story from the outside gives balance and judgment for a wise listener that is often impossible to achieve for oneself. This relationship helps a person have a feeling of accountability for his or her

spiritual practices. The guilt and shame that we seek to hide can be accepted, discussed, and sometimes healed in a situation of trust and openness. The gifts and possibilities we are not aware of can be pointed out. Encouragement when life is tough can be very important. Most of all, the grace of God, which we seem to forget again and again, flows through.

Notice that spiritual direction is not therapy; it differs from psychological counseling or pastoral counseling. Spiritual direction is aimed not at solving a particular problem but at helping you see God's ways with you and hear God's voice for you. Your spiritual director is a companion who walks with you on your spiritual journey of life. The main activity of such a spiritual mentor is to listen, and often you reach greater clarity just by talking through the situation. But the mentor also asks questions, leading you to see elements in the situation that you did not see before. Occasionally, the mentor may also teach, by making you aware of some of the spiritual practices described in this book.

The "soul friend," or spiritual director, can be a specially trained counselor or, more informally, a respected friend. Some spiritual directors see their clients about every three weeks. Some receive a fee for their work, while others do not. Serving as a companion to another wayfarer is holy work and, especially gratifying when the discernment of God's gracious leading bears fruit.

3. One of the special practices of Pietism and Methodism was gathering in small groups for **Bible study and prayer**. There is a special dynamic in small groups that is not present in large groups or when you are alone. Agree with some of your friends to gather in someone's living room to study the Bible, pray, and share your experiences. This is a way of developing friendships while learning more and deepening your prayer concerns. Many printed guides are available for such groups.

4. **Keep the Sabbath**. The reformed tradition, especially the Puritans, are known as Sabbatarians. You probably will not want to observe the Lord's Day the way they did, but there is great value in considering the wisdom of the Jewish tradition of resting one day in seven. This is not an arbitrary law but a healthy practice. One might look at the Sabbath commandment among the Ten Commandments as the first labor legislation. Masters were prohibited from working their servants and their animals day after day, week after week with no day off.

So why not give yourself a day off? Why not set aside a day for doing the important things and not the urgent things? Wouldn't you really like to rest, attend to relationships, pray, worship, help those in need, and generally stand back from the pressure cooker for a while? If you are a student or a teacher, wouldn't it feel good to have a period of time when you deliberately set aside all the reading and writing that hangs over your head, in order to tackle it freshly after that time of rest is over? Making it a consistent practice to have a time of rest and renewal can help to reduce the pressure in your life. You will live longer.

The time you choose is up to you. Maybe you want to start with half a day. Maybe you want to choose the traditional Jewish Sabbath, from sundown Friday to sundown Saturday.

5. **Sing!** The Walkman tends to make us passive with music. Singing itself is great physiologically as well as emotionally and spiritually. When we sing praise to God, it lifts us right out of our self-centered world with its problems. It widens our view of reality and helps us stop telling lies about ourselves—that we are no good. Praise glorifies the God who made all creation good—and you are not an exception! (Oh, yes, you may truly be a "miserable sinner," a "wretch like me," but God is greater than all that and has delivered us.) Sing in the shower, on a walk, and especially in the church assembly.

6. **Listen to** or **play** or **sing** some of Bach's music. Find out about his texts. I will never forget singing this Easter text in a church choir:

> Christ Jesus lay in death's strong bands
> For our offenses given;
> But now at God's right hand he stands
> And brings us life from heaven.
> Therefore let us joyful be
> And sing to God right thankfully
> Loud songs of hallelujah!
> Hallelujah![21]

Aids for the Exercises

Bakke, Jeannette. *Holy Invitations: Exploring Spiritual Direction.* Grand Rapids: Baker, 2000.

Baldwin, Christina. *Life's Companion: Journal Writing as a Spiritual Quest.* New York: Bantam, 1990.

Barry, William A. and William J. Connolly. *The Practice of Spiritual Direction.* New York: Seabury, 1982.

Edwards, Tilden. *Spiritual Director, Spiritual Companion: Guide to Tending the Soul.* New York: Paulist, 2001.

———. *Spiritual Friend.* New York: Paulist, 1980.

Guenther, Margaret. *Holy Listening: The Art of Spiritual Direction*. Cambridge, Mass.: Cowley, 1992.

Klug, Ronald. *How to Keep a Spiritual Journal*. Minneapolis: Augsburg, 2002.

Leech, Kenneth. *Soul Friend: The Practice of Christian Spirituality*. San Francisco: Harper, 1980.

Moon, Gary W. and David G. Benner, eds. *Spiritual Direction and the Care of Souls: A Guide to Christian Approaches and Practices*. Downers Grove, Ill.: InterVarsity, 2004.

Reiser, William E. *Seeking God in All Things: Theology and Spiritual Direction*. Collegeville, Minn.: Liturgical Press, 2004.

Sellner, Edward C. *Mentoring: The Ministry of Spiritual Kinship*. Cambridge, Mass.: Cowley, 2002.

Suggested Reading

Anonymous. *The Way of a Pilgrim and the Pilgrim Continues His Way*. Trans. R. M. French. New York: Seabury, 1952.

Bosch, David J. *Transforming Mission: Paradigm Shifts in Theology of Mission*. Maryknoll, N.Y.: Orbis, 1991.

Erb, Peter C., ed. *Pietists: Selected Writings*. Classics of Western Spirituality Series. New York: Paulist, 1983.

Francis de Sales. *Introduction to the Devout Life*. Garden City, N.Y.: Image Books, 1972.

Fremantle, Anne, ed. *The Protestant Mystics*. New York: New American Library, 1964.

Guyon, Jeanne-Marie Bouvier de la Mothe. *Madame Guyon: An Autobiography*. Chicago: Moody, n.d.

Kierkegaard, Søren. *Provocations: Spiritual Writings of Kierkegaard*. Compiled and edited by Charles E. Moore. Farmington, Pa.: Plough, 1999.

Spener, Philip Jacob. *Pia Desideria*. Minneapolis: Fortress, 1989 (1964).

Steere, Douglas V., ed. *Quaker Spirituality: Selected Writings*. Classics of Western Spirituality Series. New York: Paulist, 1984.

Tomkins, Stephen, *John Wesley: A Biography*. Grand Rapids: Eerdmans, 2003.

Chapter 8

The West since 1900

As we move into the twenty-first century, the start of the past one hundred years seems far in the past. So much has changed in the last decades. In Europe and America, we have gone from optimism to despair and back several times. We have been disillusioned by two world wars and a Great Depression. We have seen the horrors of Auschwitz and Hiroshima, and we have heard of Stalin's genocide in the Ukraine. Wars in Vietnam and Iraq have disillusioned many. We have lived under the mushroom cloud and seen the Soviet Empire rise and fall. Amazingly, South Africa has emerged from Apartheid in a peaceful transition. We have traveled to the moon and seen the beauty of the earth from space, a beauty that we perceive to be threatened by ecological disaster. The population of the earth has increased sixfold, along with hunger, malnutrition, and poverty. Christianity has spread to about a third of the human population, making its biggest gains in Africa while receding in its former home of Europe.

A new consciousness has been emerging in this past century. We are now looking at reason and science with more nuanced valuation. We are struggling to find new gender balance in our society and a new psychological appreciation for the depths of the human, an appreciation introduced to us by Sigmund Freud, Carl Jung, and others.

The churches of the world have developed new ecumenical relationships since a famous meeting of missionaries in 1910 in Edinburgh. Now, the World Council of Churches, founded in 1948, is well over half a century old. The Catholic Church has changed since the Second Vatican Council in the 1960s, from monolithic isolation to dialogue with other Christians, with modern society, and with other religions. These moves have been tempered by the longest-reigning pope in the century, John Paul II.

We live in a world much more closely connected by communications media and by economic interdependence than the world at the start of the twentieth century. But we have not made very much progress toward eliminating war or poverty. The Arab-Israeli dispute continues. African populations throughout the continent are stirring for more democracy after half a century of independent but authoritarian governments.

Europe, the continent considered to be most Christian in previous centuries, had a difficult time in the twentieth century. World War I shattered the optimism of the first decade; the Great Depression and World War II devastated the middle of the century. The horrors of the Holocaust, the growth of Marxist atheism, secularism, and many intellectual challenges to the truth of Christianity have left a continent nominally Christian, with only a remnant serious about Christian spirituality. Yet that remnant has been both innovative and devoted to the study of the tradition.

I have attempted to analyze some of the important new developments leading up to the present, using the template introduced at the beginning of this book. I have organized the writers and movements into four sections according to their major emphasis: our relations to God, to self, to others, and to creation. There is considerable overlap, as most of the writers appreciate more than one relationship. This chapter will include both European and North American developments among the Orthodox, Roman Catholic, and Protestant traditions since 1900.

Relating to God

God the Holy Spirit:
Holiness, Pentecostal, and Charismatic Movements

A family of new movements stemming originally from the eighteenth century focused new attention in the twentieth century on God the Holy Spirit. Pentecostalism was arguably the most important new development of the 1900s, as, starting from zero, it became the most rapidly growing type of Christianity in the world. It was inspired by primitive Christianity as seen in the Acts of the Apostles; the experience of the earliest church seemed such a contrast to twentieth-century churches.

This was not the first or the last attempt to recapture the harmony and power of primitive Christianity. For example, the Restorationist movement of the nineteenth century in the United States had led the Disciples of Christ and the Churches of Christ to attempt to free the church of denominationalism and to worship as the earliest Christians worshiped. A more radical example is the Bruderhof, a community founded in 1920 who see the key to early Christian authenticity in the sharing of goods, in pacifism, and in group discipline.

Pentecostalism itself developed out of various Holiness movements. To tell their story, we need to move back before 1900. One stream of Holiness movement was non-Wesleyan, represented by the Keswick Convention in Britain, a mostly Anglican movement. This stream eventually affected the great evangelist Dwight L. Moody, in 1871, and through him the Moody Bible Institute in Chicago. The characteristic phrase of this stream is "the Higher Life"; it does not teach sinless perfection.

A second stream followed Wesley's teaching of entire sanctification, when the Methodist churches had lost interest in it. Many evangelicals felt a longing for "something more" than the justification by grace they had experienced at conversion. They found the power to live the new life expected by these groups, a life of holiness, avoiding the pleasures of the world and devoting themselves to evangelism and social reform. They found power in an experience of total surrender to God and, according to the Methodist branch of the movement, a life of sinless perfection thereafter.

The mother of this branch of Holiness tradition was **Phoebe Palmer** (1807–74). She grew up in a Wesleyan household and longed for entire sanctification, which came to her only after her three infant children had all died. She devoted herself to a ministry of preaching, organizing, and writing. Her first book, *The Way of Holiness*, was followed by a defense of women in ministry, *The Promise of the Father*. She is known today especially for one of the five hundred hymns she composed: "Blessed Assurance, Jesus is mine!" She collaborated with the text writer, her blind friend Fanny Crosby.

Three authors who are still popular among evangelicals came from this Holiness stream of spirituality. In *The Christian's Secret of a Happy Life*, written by **Hannah Whitall Smith** (1832–1911), personal surrender to Christ is the secret, whether life goes well for you or not. There is some similarity here to Mme. Guyon from France in the 1600s (see chapter 7). One of the most enduring devotional books to come out of the Holiness movement was *My Utmost for His Highest* by **Oswald Chambers** (1874–1917). Chambers's wife, Gertrude, assembled his lectures at the Bible Training College in London into the book, which contains a year of daily readings. Here is a sample of his core assertion:

> The imperative need spiritually is to sign the death warrant of the disposition of sin, to turn all emotional impressions and intellectual beliefs into a moral verdict against the disposition of sin, [namely], my claim to my right to myself. Paul says, "I have been crucified with Christ"; he does not say, "I have determined to imitate Jesus Christ" or, "I will endeavor to follow Him" but, "I have been identified with Him in His death." . . . Haul yourself up, take a time alone with God, make the moral decision and say, "Lord, identify me with your death until I know that sin is dead in me." Make the moral decision that sin in you must be put to death. . . . It is not just a question of giving up sin, but of giving up my natural independence and self-assertiveness, and this is where the battle has to be fought. It is the things that are

right and noble and good from the natural standpoint that keep us back from God's best. . . . Beware of refusing to go to the funeral of your own independence.[1]

Finally, from the Holiness movement came two other popular devotionals. Lettie Cowman (1870–1960) assembled *Streams in the Desert* and *Springs in the Valley* from Scripture and other sources. She and her husband helped to found the Oriental Mission Society in 1907.

The pivotal moment in the development of a new style of Christian spirituality occurred in a storefront church on Azusa Street in Los Angeles (see map 7) in 1906. At that time, a black Holiness evangelist, **William Seymour** (1870–1922), introduced both black and white seekers to "baptism with the Holy Spirit" and speaking in tongues. The movement spread with lightning speed, growing quickly in North and South America and even in Europe. Two later Pentecostal leaders were Smith Wigglesworth (1859–1947), an English evangelist who traveled the world, and Donald Gee (1891–1966) and David Du Plessis (1905–87), who represented Pentecostalism in ecumenical circles at midcentury.

There were some hints of the transition from Holiness to Pentecostalism in advance, but what was new in Pentecostalism was the replacement of Wesley's "second blessing" with the biblical "baptism in/with the Holy Spirit" (see Luke 3:16; Acts 1:5). Furthermore, the outward sign of the baptism was speaking in tongues followed by the spiritual gifts listed by Paul in 1 Corinthians 12, among them prophecy and healing. Today it is claimed that Pentecostal denominations are the fastest-growing part of Christianity.

Earliest Pentecostalism was multiracial, but as the movement spread and solidified into American denominations, black and white followers generally organized separately. Both segments were despised and rejected by the established churches because they were mostly poor, uneducated people. Pentecostalists charged that the churches had lost the power of the Holy Spirit. Over the decades, Pentecostalism became more moderate as its members gained in affluence, just as Wesley's followers had. They began to found colleges and build handsome churches. The more extreme emotional outbursts in services, which had led to their nickname "Holy Rollers," became less frequent.

In the 1960s and 1970s, large numbers of Protestants and Catholics, and even a few Orthodox Christians, were led by the neo-Pentecostal, or charismatic, movement to the same experiences as "classical" Pentecostalism. Unlike the people affected in the first few decades of the century, these charismatics remained in their historic denominations instead of starting new ones. They did not necessarily accept the fundamentalism and the list of forbidden activities of the original Pentecostals, but they did begin to take evangelism, healing, and praise very seriously.

The movement had its greatest success, surprisingly, among Roman Catholics. This branch had its origins in the Cursillo movement, which developed in the late 1940s in Spain during a time of considerable political pressure on the church and the need for renewal. The *cursillo* (which means "little course" in Spanish) is a carefully planned weekend followed by small group meetings. It seeks to convert the retreatant to a conscious and deliberate discipleship to Jesus Christ. The Cursillo movement spread not only to many other countries but also to other denominations over time, including American Catholics, who in the late 1960s began to seek baptism in the Spirit and to speak in tongues. The hierarchy saw to it that priestly guidance was given to what was essentially a lay movement that began in universities. Cardinal Suenens and Pope Paul VI blessed the movement. The Protestant churches reacted much more cautiously and sometimes with hostility. The more conservative churches were, surprisingly, the most critical. Many fundamentalists were utterly opposed.

What is Pentecostal or charismatic spirituality? It focuses on the love of God seen to be present and active. The practice of speaking in tongues is experienced as an assurance of God's love. "Letting go" to allow the Spirit to guide the sounds from the mouth is a form of surrender to God. Answers to prayers for healing of physical or emotional problems also underline the presence and power of God. The Holy Spirit, brought into prominence in this movement, nevertheless takes second place to Christ as the savior and friend of the worshiper. The group is the locus for hearing the Word of God through both Scripture and prophecy. Prophecies are sometimes cast in the form of the biblical prophets, "My people, hear my voice. . . ." It is understood that God is actively communicating with the group in these spontaneous messages, which are subject to the norms of Scripture and the judgment of the leadership. In this way, the movement is similar to the Quaker form of worship. The traditional suspicion of education and intellectual endeavor in the earliest Pentecostalists has diminished, but there is still a sense that the anointing of the Spirit is more important than academic degrees for leadership.

Much of the Catholic and Protestant charismatic renewal has been eclipsed by a new nondenominational charismatic spirituality. The Vineyard movement and many independent congregations add a charismatic flavor to traditional evangelicalism. But the drama and the controversy of early Pentecostalism has been renewed by the "Toronto Blessing," a movement that has included extended "holy laughter" as well as dancing, barking, and "being slain in the Spirit." This movement began in the Toronto Airport Vineyard Church in 1994 and has quickly spread to selected congregations throughout the world.

God of the Bible

Many spiritual writers have emphasized the importance of Scripture as the revelation of God in their spirituality. Such writers include theologian Karl Barth (1886–1968) and evangelist Billy Graham (1918–). Perhaps most widely published in the twenty-first century, however, is **Eugene H. Peterson** (1932–), a spiritual writer of the Presbyterian persuasion who was also, until recently, James M. Houston Professor of Spiritual Theology at Regent College, Vancouver. He was pastor for twenty-nine years of Christ our King Presbyterian Church in Bel Air, Maryland. Peterson's spiritual writings include *Earth and Altar: The Community of Prayer in a Self-Bound Society*; *A Long Obedience in the Same Direction*; *Traveling Light*; *Take and Read: Spiritual Reading, An Annotated List*; and *The Contemplative Pastor*.

His *Subversive Spirituality* is a collection of shorter pieces that illustrate his main themes. Peterson's writing is often directly connected to the Bible. For example, he writes on "Saint Mark: The Basic Text for Christian Spirituality" and on "Jeremiah as an Ascetical Theologian." Here is a sample:

> Spirituality is always in danger of self-absorption, of becoming so intrigued with matters of soul that God is treated as a mere accessory to my experience. This requires much vigilance. Spiritual theology is, among other things, the exercise of this vigilance. Spiritual theology is the discipline and art of training us into a full and mature participation in Jesus' story while at the same time preventing us from taking over the story.[2]

Peterson is not afraid to speak boldly and controversially from his biblical posture. For example, he writes:

> First overwhelmed and then considerably angered by the shopkeeper mentality of so many pastor colleagues, I felt the need to establish God-attentiveness and God-responsiveness in my own life and repudiate religious marketing entirely. . . . My conviction is that the pastor must refuse to be shaped by the culture, whether secular or ecclesiastical, and insist on becoming a person of prayer in the community of worship. This is our assigned task; anything less or other is malpractice.[3]

Peterson has published a version of the Bible called *The Message*, in which he translates Romans 12:1-2, a key text about Christian spirituality, as follows:

> So here's what I want you to do, God helping you: Take your everyday, ordinary life—your sleeping, eating, going-to-work,

and walking-around life—and place it before God as an offering. Embracing what God does for you is the best thing you can do for him. Don't become so well-adjusted to your culture that you fit into it without even thinking. Instead, fix your attention on God. You'll be changed from the inside out. Readily recognize what he wants from you, and quickly respond to it. Unlike the culture around you, always dragging you down to its level of immaturity, God brings the best out of you, develops well-formed maturity in you.[4]

God of Theology

A more intellectual approach to our relation to God is found among the theologians who also care deeply about spirituality. Among these are the European Catholics Karl Rahner and Hans Urs von Balthasar.

Karl Rahner (1904–84) is among the greatest of the twentieth-century theologians as well as among the most prolific; it is said that he has more than four thousand written works to his name! But he is also an important spiritual writer.[5]

Rahner was a Jesuit, but he found the older, strict theology of his Jesuit teachers oppressive. Rahner managed to master the medieval tradition so thoroughly that when he showed his "progressive" side, none of his detractors could better him in the use of the traditional sources. He was very influential at the Second Vatican Council, but he came close to being silenced by the church. Fortunately, a special petition to Pope John XXIII resulted in the church not enforcing the order.

Rahner had a distinguished academic career. After earning his doctorate in 1936, he taught at Innsbruck, Vienna, Munich, and Münster. He was invited to lecture at many of the major universities of the world. His essay "On Prayer" was delivered in bombed-out Munich in 1946. Later it sold more than one hundred thousand copies in Germany. Here are some samples from Rahner's writings:

> Laugh. For this laughter is an acknowledgment that you are a human being, an acknowledgment that is itself the beginning of an acknowledgment of God. For how else is a person to acknowledge God except through admitting in his life and by means of his life that he himself is not God but a creature that has his times—a time to weep and a time to laugh, and the one is not the other. A praising of God is what laughter is, because it lets a human being be human.[6]

> Make everyday life your prayer. Pray for this great art of Christian living, as difficult to master as it is essentially simple in itself. Pray

in everyday life, and so make everyday life your prayer. The sorrowful and fleeting days of our life, passed in monotony and banality, in commonplace pursuits and in toil, will merge with the day of God, the great day that has no evening.[7]

A theologian of similar stature to Rahner, **Hans Urs von Balthasar** (1905–88) was more conservative than progressive. Like Rahner, he wrote an extensive theological opus but also addressed the practicalities of prayer and daily spiritual life. One of his main emphases was the importance of beauty and a vision of the beauty of God. In the three main values—truth, goodness, and beauty—he asserted that it is only in beauty that truth is good and that goodness is true. If love is the center of Christian spirituality, it consists in truth, beauty, and goodness. Balthasar became friends with Karl Barth and was the spiritual director of Adrienne von Speyr (1902–67), a Swiss physician and author. He wrote more than a thousand books and articles but is not well known among English readers.

God of Literature and Imagination

At mid-century a group of literary persons gathered in an Oxford pub to read one another's fiction. They called themselves the "Inklings."[8]Among them were C. S. Lewis (1898-1963), J. R. R. Tolkien (1892-1973), Dorothy L. Sayers (1893-1957), and Charles Williams (1886-1945). G. K. Chesterton (1874-1936) had been a strong influence on Lewis. This group produced works that took the spiritual realm seriously, but each in a different way. Lewis has perhaps become the best known of them because of his seven children's stories about Narnia, his space trilogy, and his many essays about Christian themes. He described his conversion to Christian faith in *Surprised by Joy*, and he described the demonic realm perhaps better than any theological treatise in *The Screwtape Letters*, a fictional correspondence between a chief demon and his underling. Lewis's imagination has made the Christian message credible for many in the twentieth century.

God of Spiritual Practices

Among the many twentieth-century writers on mysticism, perhaps the most influential in the English-speaking world was **Evelyn Underhill** (1875–1941). She became a mystic in the philosophical, Platonic sense before being baptized as a Christian in adulthood. The person who influenced her most became her spiritual director, Baron **Friedrich von Hügel** (1852–1925). He was a modernist Roman Catholic lay theologian and philosopher of religion living in England.[9] Von Hügel's *Letters to a Niece* demonstrates his heart in the course of spiritual direction. He urged Underhill to ground her mysticism in a concrete church community and go to serve the poor in East London. She did so, and it humanized her.

Underhill is best known for her major study *Mysticism*, first published in 1911, and her later work *Worship*, published in 1936. She drew many people's attention to the classical mystical texts. She devoted herself to a ministry of personal spiritual direction from her home and through retreats at the village of Pleshey, northeast of London. A new harvest of her spirituality has more recently been reaped from her retreat lectures.[10] Underhill's interest in spirituality and mysticism was not merely academic; she was also actively involved with the practical problems of real people.

In the Orthodox world, twentieth-century Christians experienced great suffering under the Bolshevik regimes, especially that of Stalin. A new but limited freedom for spiritual pursuits arrived as the Soviet Empire disintegrated at the end of the century. Of the Russian diaspora, perhaps the best-known writer in English is **Anthony Bloom** (1914–2003), known as Metropolitan Anthony of Sourozh. He grew up in Russia and Persia as an atheist until age fifteen. Then he had a direct experience of Christ while reading the Gospel of Mark, which changed his life forever. After training and serving as a physician, he became a priest of the Russian Orthodox Church in England, then archbishop, and finally metropolitan. His best-known book is *School for Prayer* (1970), which is often recommended as a beginner's guide to prayer.

Thomas Merton (1915–68), arguably the greatest Catholic spiritual writer of the century, could be placed in any of the four parts of this chapter. He was a man of three continents. He spent his boyhood and early manhood in Europe, most of his adulthood in North America, and his last weeks in Asia, where he died.

The child of a father from New Zealand and a mother from the United States, "Tom" was born in Prades, a small city near the Pyrenees Mountains in southern France. He grew up first in French schools, then in English ones, culminating in a short time at Cambridge University.

After he studied English literature at Columbia University, Thomas Merton made the decisive step of seeking baptism in a small Roman Catholic church near the campus. Despairing of a world rapidly moving toward the Second World War, he gave himself to one of the strictest, most separate of religious orders, the Trappists, whose Gethsemani Monastery in Kentucky he had visited on a retreat (see map 7). Entering the monastery on December 10, 1941, he felt happy and at peace.

The abbot asked him to write about a number of saints, and seeing his extraordinary gifts, he also asked him, against Merton's own will, to write an autobiography. The resulting book, *The Seven Storey Mountain*, became a best seller in 1948 and thus made Merton known not only in the United States but around the world. The book seemed to be a twentieth-century *Confessions*, like that of St. Augustine (see chapter 4). Here was the story of a worldly young man who radically changed direction, leaving the world behind to devote himself to God.

The Seven Storey Mountain had given Merton a national audience during the 1950s, but his perspective on the world changed during that decade:

> In Louisville, at the corner of Fourth and Walnut, in the center of the shopping district, I was suddenly overwhelmed with the realization that I loved all those people, that they were mine and I theirs, that we could not be alien to one another even though we were total strangers. It was like waking from a dream of separateness, of spurious self-isolation in a special world, the world of renunciation and supposed holiness. The whole illusion of a separate holy existence is a dream. . . .
>
> This sense of liberation from an illusory difference was such a relief and such a joy to me that I almost laughed out loud. And I suppose my happiness could have taken form in these words: "Thank God, thank God that I *am* like other men, that I am only a man among others." To think that for sixteen or seventeen years I have been taking seriously this pure illusion that is implicit in so much of our monastic thinking![11]

Merton's view of the world and its relation to the monastery changed so radically that he was no longer pleased to be known as the author of *The Seven Storey Mountain*. That book expressed a spirituality that he no longer believed. He saw now that as a monk, he was still in the world: he had not escaped it. And he saw his responsibility in that world to be wider than prayer for it:

> The spiritual life is not a life of quiet withdrawal, a hothouse growth of artificial ascetic practices beyond the reach of people living ordinary lives. It is in the ordinary duties and labors of life that the Christian can and should develop his spiritual union with God. . . . Christian holiness in our age means more than ever the awareness of our common responsibility to cooperate with the mysterious designs of God for the human race. This awareness will be illusory unless it is enlightened by divine grace, strengthened by generous effort, and sought in collaboration not only with the authorities of the Church but with all men of good will who are working for the temporal and spiritual good of the human race.[12]

As a participant in the world, Merton felt called to express his views, which went against the grain of American society. For the rest of his life, Merton wrote prolifically, publishing about forty books, poetry as well as essays, inspirational books, and especially journals and articles, hundreds of them. The journals reveal a searching and wide-ranging intellect, with profound and sometimes humorous and wry insights into life. They do not tell us much about the intimate life Merton shared with God, but they reveal an eye for the ironies of life.

The articles address the major social issues of the day; this was a new chapter in Merton's development. He came out for the civil rights movement, against the cold war, against nuclear weapons, and eventually against the Vietnam War. All of these were at one time lonely and unpopular stands, and the Catholic Church felt betrayed by its "poster boy." The censors attempted to shut him up, but he circulated mimeographed articles to a wide circle of friends.

Merton was an early advocate of Christian dialogue with people of other faiths. He remained thoroughly Christian but explored what Christians could learn about the spiritual life from Buddhists, Hindus, Jews, and Muslims.

As a monk, Merton was first professed as a member of the order, was then ordained a priest, and then served as novice master, teaching new monks, some of whom had been attracted to the order by his own writings. Later, he became the spiritual director of many in the monastery. He gradually desired to become a hermit within the order and eventually obtained permission from his abbot to live alone in a small house on monastery grounds while still participating in the seven-times-daily regimen of prayers.

The third continent, Asia, engaged Merton's attention from the 1950s forward. He began to study Zen Buddhism, Taoism, and Hinduism. He found a deep fellowship with the monks of these traditions, in their rejection of the values of much of Western society, the goals of wealth, power, and pleasure. Merton's one and only long trip from the monastery was his last. He was able to visit California, Alaska, India, Ceylon (now Sri Lanka), and Thailand on this journey. Near Bangkok (see map 10), he was accidentally killed by touching a faultily wired electric fan. He died twenty-seven years to the day after his entry into the monastery. After his death on December 10, 1968, many more of his writings were published, and his journals continue to inspire new books in the twenty-first century.

Centering prayer has become a familiar spiritual practice in many cities. Basil Pennington (1931–) and Thomas Keating (1917–) are two American monks who have written extensively on centering prayer. The term is meant to describe an apophatic type of meditation, without images. Thus its main antecedents in the tradition are *The Cloud of Unknowing* and the writings of John of the Cross.

Through books and conferences, Pennington and Keating are teaching people how to center themselves by quietly being in the presence of God, without petition. It is a difficult mental discipline that they teach, to be free of thoughts, simply present to God. They teach the use of a special word of one's own choice, not as a mantra but as a homing device: when one's thoughts go astray, one comes back to God's presence by reminding oneself with this special word.

John Main (1926–1982) entered the Benedictine Order after other careers in the British Foreign Service and at Trinity College, Dublin. He later founded the Benedictine Priory of Montreal. From there his followers, notably Lawrence Freeman, started the World Community for Christian Meditation.

Main's approach to spirituality centers on meditation using a mantra. His suggested word for repetition in meditation is the Aramaic *Maranatha*, meaning "Come Lord; Come Lord Jesus." His teaching is very simple, and he urges on his disciples the need for childlike simplicity. As one meditates for half an hour each morning and evening, one will enter a silence. Then, after a long period, the silences will grow longer. These are the times when one may be experiencing the very heart of God.

John Main led group meditation many times in Montreal, using music, humor, and teaching to aid the process. He would sit by a stereo playing relaxing music and then would turn it off and give a brief instruction. The instructions he gave during his last year of life are collected in *Moment of Christ: The Path of Meditation*.[13] He also published *The Heart of Creation*, *Word into Silence*, and *Word Made Flesh*.

Late in the twentieth century, the **Labyrinth** movement affected many denominations. Built into the floor of the Chartres Cathedral in France is a stone design that was originally used for medi- tative walking but is now often covered with chairs. This forgotten feature has been revived in Grace Episcopal Cathedral in San Francisco. With the leadership of Lauren Artress, not only has the cathedral built two labyrinths, itself but it has become a center for promoting the use of labyrinths interna- tionally and gives advice on how to build and teach about labyrinths.[14]

The spiritual practice involved is meditative walking. The labyrinth is not a maze, which confuses the searcher, but rather a very clear path from the periphery to the center and back out again. With the accompaniment of music, a group of people can walk the labyrinth, meeting one another on the way, or a person can walk alone. It is a practical way of using the body in meditation. The walk assumes added significance when considered as a metaphor for the journey of life. The walk inward becomes a journey of purification; meditation in the center is compared to illumination; and the journey outward becomes union, a return to service in the world for the walking meditator, who is refreshed and healed.

The values of many spiritual disciplines appear in the writings of **Richard J. Foster** (1928–), who first became well known through his *Celebration of Discipline*, published in 1978.[15] In this book, Foster describes twelve spiritual disciplines, which are divided into three types: the inward, the outward, and the corporate disciplines. The opening chapter on spiritual disciplines as a door to liberation sets forth the need for disciplines as well as a theology concerning their role. While Foster believes that only by God's grace do we live the Christian life, he also asserts that the disciplines are needed to receive that grace in the continual fashion necessary for the Christian journey.

> Picture a long, narrow ridge with a sheer drop-off on either side. The chasm to the right is the way of moral bankruptcy through human strivings for righteousness. Historically this has been called the heresy of moralism. The chasm to the left is moral bankruptcy through the absence of human strivings. This has been called the heresy of antinomianism. On the ridge there is a path, the Disciplines of the spiritual life. This path leads to the inner transformation and healing for which we seek. . . . We must always remember that the path does not produce the change; it only places us where the change can occur. This is the path of disciplined grace.[16]

One value of this best seller is its clear demonstration that the disciplines include the community and the world. Spirituality is intended to work itself out in daily life among others.

Foster founded an organization called Renovare, which promotes teaching about the spiritual life in local congregations. He will be remembered not only as a best-selling author but also as the founder of an institution that focuses on ordinary people in Christian parish churches.

Relating to the Self

Jesus said, "Love your neighbor as yourself." Implied in such love is self-care, nurture of the self, and healing. In this section, we will consider special twentieth-century movements and writers who deal with the self in the context of spirituality.

Employing Psychology

The twentieth century was distinctive for the development of the new fields of psychology and psychoanalysis. By the middle of the century, the general public was thinking in psychological terms and listening respectfully to the results of psychological research. Since spirituality has to do with the human person, even the soul, its interests overlap with psychology, which is literally the "study of the soul." Early in the 1900s, a great rift occurred between the two, which still has not been fully overcome. Psychologists and psychoanalysts were frequently opposed to religion as unscientific, neurotic, and harmful to human well-being in general. Christians did not trust therapists. Today the situation has improved. Psychologists are perhaps less defensive about their discipline as a science, and Christians have seen the value of psychological concepts and therapies.

Among those who worked in the field of psychology, the most influential for Christian spirituality is **Karl G. Jung** (1875–1961). The son of a minister, Jung was born and spent most of his life in Switzerland. In 1909, he titled his doctoral dissertation "On the Psychology and Pathology of So-Called Occult Phenomena," which reflected a long interest in spiritual realities outside of as well as within Christianity.

Jung's writings were the basis for the development of the Myers-Briggs Type Indicator, a widely used resource in spiritual direction. An understanding of the types of personality dynamics has been found helpful in choosing and practicing spiritual disciplines, such as prayer. An older typology based in Sufi tradition is the Enneagram, a circle of nine types, which is also used in spiritual direction.

Morton Kelsey (1917–2001), an Episcopalian priest and former professor at Notre Dame University, was a major American spiritual writer who explicitly stated his debt to psychology, and especially to Karl Jung. When writing on meditation, Kelsey voiced his frustration that other writers had not seen the value of the psychologists:

> I found next to nothing written about prayer and meditation that took into account the discoveries about the human soul made by depth psychology in the ninety-five years of activity. Freud, Adler, Jung, Maslow, Carl Rogers and Rollo May might as well not have existed for all the importance they seem to have for most writers on prayer. Yet the masters of the devotional life and the depth psychologists need each other. They have each discovered something of the reality of the human soul, and each discipline has something important to say to the other. There is a burning need to see meditation in this new light.[17]

Kelsey's manner of meditating uses images, which he notes is different from centering prayer. Kelsey is quite clear that not everyone will find his own method the most helpful; he notes that his wife uses centering prayer, which appeals more to her.

Kelsey wrote more than forty books, many of them on subjects that others do not dare to touch. His writings on dreams are one of the few treatments of the subject from a Christian and Jungian point of view. He also wrote about speaking in tongues, a subject ripe for dialogue between psychologists and charismatics. A personal favorite, however, is his account *Healing and Christianity*, which gives a brief history of Christian involvement in both physical and emotional healing.

Addressing Addictions

In the United States in the 1930s, "Bill W." and "Dr. Bob"—William Wilson (1895–1971) and Robert Smith (1879–1950)—founded Alcoholics Anonymous (AA). Both were deeply influenced by the Oxford Group, later known as Moral Rearmament, which took Christian principles with absolute seriousness.[18] A thorough discussion of the influences that shaped AA indicates both Christian and secular movements.[19] The two men deeply believed in the message of the gospel, but they and other alcoholics did not find help in the churches and conventional Christianity. They developed groups for alcoholics that accepted all people, as the churches never did. Here are the twelve steps that they developed, based in part on the eight principles of the Oxford Group:

1. We admitted we were powerless over alcohol, that our lives had become unmanageable.
2. Came to believe that a Power greater than ourselves could restore us to sanity.
3. Made a decision to turn our will and our lives over to the care of God *as we understood Him.*
4. Made a searching and fearless moral inventory of ourselves.
5. Admitted to God, to ourselves, and to another human being the exact nature of our wrongs.
6. Were entirely ready to have God remove all these defects of character.
7. Humbly asked Him to remove our shortcomings.
8. Made a list of all persons we had harmed, and became willing to make amends to them all.
9. Made direct amends to such people wherever possible, except when to do so would injure them or others.
10. Continued to take personal inventory and when we were wrong promptly admitted it.

11. Sought through prayer and meditation to improve our conscious contact with God *as we understand Him*, praying only for
knowledge of His will for us and the power to carry that out.

12. Having had a spiritual awakening as the result of these steps, we
tried to carry this message to alcoholics and to practice these
principles in all our affairs.[20]

These steps obviously include wisdom from the tradition of Christian
spirituality. Some have found these steps in the Bible as a whole;[21] others, in
the Beatitudes from the Sermon on the Mount (Matthew 5). Nevertheless,
the authors felt it necessary to expand the concept of God into what is commonly called one's "Higher Power," since many alcoholics could not relate to
the usual picture of God.

Over the years, the original twelve steps have been supplemented by a
literature incorporating basic attitudes, prayer, and meditation. One of the
most widely used texts in the spirituality of AA is the "Serenity Prayer,"
which is the first part of a longer prayer composed by theologian Reinhold
Niebuhr (1892–1971): "God grant me the grace to accept with serenity the
things I cannot change, courage to change the things I can, and wisdom to
know the difference."[22] In recent decades, this literature has increasingly
caught the attention of Christian spiritual directors and pastors. Perhaps
there is some possibility of more cooperation between the churches and AA.

One of the elements in this interest is the insight about the ubiquitous
nature of addiction—that is, what AA pioneered for one kind of addiction is
relevant for others, and not only for the obvious ones, such as drugs, gambling, and overeating.[23] It turns out we do not consciously choose the com-
pulsive behaviors we find in ourselves; they relate to Paul's lament in
Romans, "For I do not do the good I want, but the evil I do not want is what
I do" (Romans 7:19).

The twelve steps are a program that includes several features of earlier
spirituality, such as a soul friend, daily examen, restitution, surrender to God,
and sharing your belief with others. It focuses on the discovery and overcoming of irrational, harmful habits that have at their root the insistence that
"I am God." The root of addiction is seen to be spiritual, and healing begins
by surrender to grace, the gift of God.

Ministering Healing

Virtually all Christians pray for healing in some way or at some time. The
impetus for such prayer in the twentieth and twenty-first centuries has come
from a number of sources, but perhaps none as widespread as the charismatic
renewal. The antecedent influence for many in the United States was **Agnes
Sanford** (1897–1976), born in China of missionary parents, the wife of an
Episcopal clergyman, and with him the founder of "Schools of Pastoral

Care." Her first writings, including her *Healing Light*, preceded the charismatic renewal, but she influenced many within it and joined it in her later years. Among her titles are *The Healing Power of the Bible*, *The Healing Gifts of the Spirit*, and many others, including a novel, *The Lost Shepherd*. Sanford emphasized the willingness of God to heal and the need for emotional as well as physical healing. She invited the person to visualize the healing taking place, and to visualize the person wrapped in the love of God. She coined the phrase "healing of memories" for an emotional release from past wounds through the re-imaging of the event in the presence of Jesus. Her loving approach was quite different from the bombastic mid-century scenes of Oral Roberts healing people on television.

Positive Thinking and Self-Esteem

One of the more controversial movements in American spirituality has been the "positive thinking" school of thought first developed by **Dr. Norman Vincent Peale** (1898–1993). As pastor of an influential New York congregation, he wrote *The Power of Positive Thinking* in 1952. It sold more than 20 million copies, promoting the idea that our thoughts need to be positive if we are to accomplish our goals. Later he founded *Guideposts* magazine.

This school of thought is similar to the approach taken in much "success"-oriented literature available in bookstores. It does not seem to be distinctly Christian, and its main focus may directly contradict the cross of Jesus and the concept of grace; rather, it focuses on the commercial and material rewards that so many seek. But the Christian promoters of this idea have had success themselves in reaching and influencing the American population.

Robert H. Schuller (1926–) is known for his television program *The Hour of Power* and for his congregation, the Crystal Cathedral, in Garden Grove, California. A minister of the Reformed Church in America, he has demonstrated his ability to communicate with the California culture. He is the author of many books and is acquainted with celebrities.

Schuller prefers the term *possibility thinking* to *positive thinking* and focuses on what the psychologists have called self-esteem. Schuller believes that a new reformation is needed in the way the church thinks or that it will fall by the wayside:

> Self-esteem then, or "pride in being a human being," is the single greatest need facing the human race today.[24]

> I call upon the church to make a commitment to remodel itself until it becomes the best thing that has ever happened to the human race. The church becomes the best friend for all people when we

proclaim the Gospel of Faith—Hope—and Love which truly stimulates and sustains human self-esteem.[25]

In the last decade of the twentieth century, the Chicken Soup series, a
popular series of anthologies, ran to more than 15 million copies. The series
consists of popular spirituality aimed at Americans who want something
short and uplifting. The sales of this series, and its expansion to television,
indicates Americans' desire for success and self-esteem as much as it does
their hunger for the spirit.

Relating to Others

Relating to other people is an essential part of the spiritual life. We relate to
individuals, to communities, and to society as a whole for inspiration and
correction. We are called to love, in a variety of ways, all people in the world.
Some are friends; some, family. Some are like us; some are not. Some share
our faith in Christ; others have faith in other traditions or ideologies. It is
impossible here to discuss all the permutations, but the most important relationships are organized, in wide variety, from the most personal spiritual
direction, through the church communities, to the peoples of the world.

Spiritual Direction

One of the most widely known spiritual writers of the century, **Henri
Nouwen** (1932–96), was trained in pastoral care in the United States. By his
writing, he helped to transform the field from dependence on psychology to
an appreciation of spiritual care.

Nouwen was born to a pious family in Nijkerk in the Netherlands. He
was an energetic child who played at being a priest from age six. Nouwen had
a stable Roman Catholic home and felt an early calling to the priesthood. His
education continued in both theology and psychology, partly in the
Netherlands and partly in the United States. Perhaps it was his fourth book,
The Wounded Healer, a book about pastoral care published in 1972, that first
made him well known. His second book, *Thomas Merton: Contemplative
Critic*, was published in the same year in the United States.

Three of Nouwen's spiritual journals describe major periods of ministry: *Genesee Diary* concerns his search for spiritual direction from Father
John Eudes Bamburger during his monastic sabbatical at Genesee Abbey,
New York; *Gracias!* describes his Latin American encounter with the poor
and with Gustavo Gutiérrez; and *The Way to Daybreak* reveals his identification of mentally handicapped people as the poor whom he finally felt called
to serve. He died in the fall of 1996, after writing about forty books on the
spiritual life.

Two major changes in Nouwen's spiritual journey should be noted here. First, he initially became socially engaged in 1965 when he marched with Martin Luther King Jr. in Selma, Alabama. Second, in the mid-1970s, he came to a change in the way he wrote. No longer did he try to describe spiritual principles or practices in the abstract; rather, he began to write about them in the concrete context of his own experience. Much of Nouwen's success as a writer comes from his ability to name common feelings and experiences in a very open and honest fashion. The intellectual brilliance of Merton the poet can be off-putting, despite his gregariousness and good humor; in contrast, the frankness of Nouwen the counselor invites identification with another wounded, stumbling human being.

> We cannot force God into a relationship. God comes to us on his own initiative, and no discipline, effort, or ascetic practice can make him come. All mystics stress with an impressive unanimity that prayer is "grace," that is, a free gift from God, to which we can only respond with gratitude. But they hasten to add that this precious gift indeed is within our reach. In Jesus Christ, God has entered into our lives in the most intimate way, so that we could enter into his life through the Spirit. . . .
>
> So, the paradox of prayer is that it asks for a serious effort while it can only be received as a gift. We cannot plan, organize or manipulate God; but without a careful discipline, we cannot receive him either. This paradox of prayer forces us to look beyond the limits of our mortal existence.
> —Henri J. M. Nouwen, *Reaching Out*

Spiritual direction has become an established practice not only in Roman Catholic circles but in Anglican and Protestant ones as well. Among the writers who have added greatly to this field are Gerald May, Tilden Edwards, and Kenneth Leech.

Tilden Edwards (1935–) and Gerald May (1898–) teach at one of the newer schools for training spiritual directors, the Shalem Institute. Kenneth Leech (1939–) is an Anglican priest who serves not in a comfortable suburb or university but in East London, an area much in need of Christian ministry. The first volume of Leech's trilogy, *Soul Friend*, is one of the basic books about spiritual direction. His second, *True Prayer*, focuses on that most basic of the Christian disciplines. Third, *Experiencing God: Theology as Spirituality* addresses the issues about God, the subject and object of the spiritual life. He writes,

There is indeed considerable evidence not of God's death, but rather of his absence and of the continued, and at times frenzied, quest for his presence by many people.[26]

Of the upsurge in interest in spirituality there can be little doubt. The urgent need is for spiritual discrimination and discernment between the phony and the authentic, between the false gods and the true God. What is certainly clear is that the uncritical espousal of the total secularization of the West, widely held in the 1960s, is wrong.[27]

The Christian Community: Ecumenical Spirituality

The movement for Christian unity known as ecumenism did not begin in the twentieth century. Ever since there have been divisions in the churches, there have been those who have prayed for their reunion. For example, Philip Melanchthon, the young associate of Luther, tried hard to reconcile Lutherans with others. But in the twentieth century, ecumenism developed not only major institutions but widespread practice of prayer among denominations. We have mentioned that the Pentecostal/charismatic movement, the centering prayer movement, and the practice of walking the labyrinth, among others, have become part of many denominations.

What is of special interest to us here is the growth of a movement of prayer for Christian unity. A week specially devoted to this cause was started in 1908, then approved by Pope Pius X in 1909. At that time, many Protestants understood Roman Catholic ecumenism to mean that Protestants should "come home" to Rome. But **Abbe Paul Couterier** (1881–1953), who was experienced in building understanding between French Catholics and Reformed churches, was able to convince Protestants to adopt the same week, January 18–25, for the purpose of prayer for unity. Since 1966, the Vatican and the World Council of Churches have planned and promoted the week together.

Orthodox, Catholics, and Protestants in the current century have learned to pray together on many levels at meetings, conferences, and retreats. Many believe that it is only prayer that has kept the movement going despite many obstacles. As yet there has been little approved sharing of Holy Communion, but much intercommunion has taken place informally.

One very special expression of ecumenical spirituality is the community of Taizé in France. Founded by Roger Schutz and Max Thurien, Taizé is a semimonastic order with members from both Catholic and Protestant traditions. The Orthodox have also made their contribution. At a service led by Brother Roger in a packed Episcopal cathedral in Edinburgh, I watched as many non-Orthodox believers joined in kissing a large cross-shaped icon lying in the middle of the church floor, as a prayer of solidarity with Russian Christians.

To the amazement of many Christians, one of the most important contributers to ecumenical spirituality was a pope. **Pope John XXIII (Angelo Roncalli)** (1881–1963) was one of the most popular popes of the twentieth century. A fat man who was not ashamed of his body, he exuded goodwill to all.

It is a remarkable fact that Angelo Roncalli, Vatican diplomat in Turkey and France, and later patriarch of Venice, always preferred common people. He once said: "This morning I must receive cardinals, princes and important representatives of the Government. But in the afternoon I want to spend a few minutes with some ordinary people who have no other title save their dignity as human beings and children of God."[28] The son of a peasant family, he never forgot his origins and never apologized for them.

John XXIII is remembered for calling the Second Vatican Council, which began in the fall of 1962. Through this council, John permitted refreshing voices and movements that had previously not been allowed to surface to become officially recognized in the Roman Catholic Church. These movements included the scriptural movement, the liturgical movement, and the ecumenical movement. One book recalls the following episode: "'The Council?' he said as he moved toward the window and made a gesture as if to open it. 'I expect a little fresh air from it. . . . We must shake off the imperial dust that has accumulated on the throne of St. Peter since Constantine.'"[29] John also said: "We are here on earth not to guard a museum, but to cultivate a garden flourishing with life and promised to a glorious future."[30]

In 1993, a fresh voice spoke from Lemmon, South Dakota (see map 7), a place that few Americans had heard of before reading *Dakota: A Spiritual Geography*, written by **Kathleen Norris** (1947–).[31] Here was a New York writer who had moved to the Great Plains and rediscovered Christian faith. The book suggested that place was important to spirituality and spent a good deal of time describing the climate, landscape, and people of the plains. But it also described how this lapsed Presbyterian found renewal, especially by Benedictine monks! Kathleen Norris saw the unity of Christian faith and made an adult choice to adopt it as her own. Here is an example, from another book by Norris, of her own observation of the present situation in the United States:

> The human need for religion did not disappear between the seventeenth century and the present day. If anything, its suppression as a respected form of emotional and intellectual engagement has resulted in a dramatic eruption of religion's shadow side, an America that is not a secular society, as some claim, but a land of

myriad vague spiritualities, mostly individual and even secular in that they disdain the conventionally religious, anything related to church-going and other traditional practices of the Christian faith.[32]

Norris's *Amazing Grace: A Vocabulary of Faith* deals with important religious terms in her usual frank manner, weaving parts of her own story into a fresh understanding of the terms:

Perfection, in a Christian sense, means becoming mature enough to give ourselves to others. . . . This sort of perfection demands that we become fully ourselves as God would have us: mature, ripe, full, ready for what befalls us, for whatever is to come. When I think of perfection in this sense, I am far from Martha Stewart land. I am thinking of an acquaintance, Catherine LaCugna. . . . Now, whenever I recite the prayer that ends the church's liturgical day, "May the Lord grant us a peaceful night, and a perfect death," it is her death that I think of. A perfect death, fully acknowledged and fully realized, offered for others.[33]

Norris represents the rediscovery of Catholic spirituality by a contemporary Protestant. She has opened up a two-way street between these two traditions in a personal way by describing her own experiences and thus allowing the two to appreciate each other within the Christian spiritual family.

The Christian Community: The Saints and the Blessed Virgin Mary

The Apostles' Creed affirms belief in "the communion of saints." Protestant interpreters understand the word *saints* to include all Christians, as Paul seems to do in the addresses of his letters. Paul addresses all the Christians in Corinth, for example, as saints, even though their community life was far from holy! Yet they are holy because their sins have been forgiven. Protestants, starting with Luther, do honor the saints but are not very clear about how the living now relate to the dead.

Orthodox and Catholic Christians understand "communion of saints" to mean that we who are living now are somehow united with those who have gone before us, especially those selected as heroic in their holiness. For Roman Catholics, these saints are defined by the Vatican and are available to answer prayer by interceding with God. Among all the saints, the most popular is the blessed Virgin Mary, the mother of Jesus. The devotion to Mary as part of Christian tradition goes very deep and has developed differently in different cultures through the ages. She presents a feminine face of the Divine.

In *Mary through the Centuries,* Jaroslav Pelikan demonstrates the continuity and the varieties of devotion to the mother of Jesus.[34] She has been pictured more than any other woman. Among her titles are the Second Eve, the Theotokos, the mater Dolorosa, the Mediatrix, and the Queen of Heaven. Pelikan points out that Marian doctrine in the Roman Catholic Church is a prime example of spirituality leading theology, not vice versa, for it has been popular devotion that has run ahead of official dogma and led the popes eventually to make pronouncements about the Blessed Mother, notably about her immaculate conception, in 1854, and her assumption to heaven, in 1950.

Previous devotions to Mary may be found in other chapters of this book, but here we wish to focus on twentieth-century developments. One such development has been pilgrimages to sites of apparitions of the Virgin. Mary appeared to Juan Diego in Guadeloupe, Mexico, in 1531 and to Bernadette Soubiroux at Lourdes, France, in 1858. The striking fact is that these sites of previous apparitions became thriving pilgrimage sites in the twentieth century.[35] In these places, the devotion to Mary herself, and not just to the occasional healing, is at center stage.

New apparitions appeared in the twentieth century, among them to Lucia, Francisco, and Jacinta at Fatima, Portugal, in 1917 and to six young people in Medugorje, Croatia, in 1981. These are now international pilgrimage sites for people from all continents.

John Paul II (Karol Jozef Wojtyla) (1920–) has had one of the longest papacies, which marked its twenty-fifth anniversary in 2003. Although John Paul II was a participant in Vatican II, his policies have been in a very different direction from those of John XXIII. He is perhaps best known for his world travels, the attempted assassination in 1981, his opposition to the Iraq war of 2003, and his conservative views on sexual matters.

Pope John Paul II revived Marian devotion, which went into a period of decline after Vatican II:

> Thanks to Saint Louis of Montfort, I came to understand that true *devotion to the Mother of God is actually Christocentric, indeed it is very profoundly rooted in the Mystery of the blessed Trinity,* and the mysteries of the incarnation and Redemption. And so, I rediscovered Marian piety, this time with a deeper understanding.[36]

The World: Justice, Peace, and Love

The ethical requirement is a constitutive element of Christian spirituality. Its roots lie in the Old Testament, epitomized by the well-known quotation from Micah (6:6-8):

> He has told you, O mortal, what is good;
> and what does the LORD require of you

> But to do justice, and to love kindness,
> and to walk humbly with your God? (verse 8)

Seeking justice and peace and showing kindness to those in need follow naturally from walking with God. Here we shall note a few of the many recent Christians who have stood against economic and social injustice, racial injustice, and gender injustice.

Peace and Justice
In Europe, one of the outstanding Christian theologians and martyrs was **Dietrich Bonhoeffer** (1906–45). His context was the tumultuous history of Germany in the first half of the twentieth century.

Bonhoeffer grew up in an intellectual family who did not understand his desire to study theology. He studied in New York City at Union Theological Seminary from 1930 to 1931 and appreciated African American worship in Harlem. He served a congregation in London, planning to study with Gandhi in India, but it was not to be. The Nazis had taken over the German government and church, but Bonhoeffer, resisting them, returned to teach in a small secret seminary in Finkenwalde (see map 6). Bonhoeffer was not only a lecturer; he also gave spiritual direction to his students.

While in Germany, Bonhoeffer wrote his provocative commentary on the Sermon on the Mount, *The Cost of Discipleship* (more recently published as *Discipleship*). Like Kierkegaard almost a century earlier, he castigated his own Lutheran tradition for preaching "cheap grace," an easy, uninvolved Christianity. The whole nation, he said, has been baptized with little sense of the meaning of being Jesus' disciple. Rather, he said, "whenever Christ calls us, his call leads us to death."

When the Gestapo closed the Finkenwalde seminary, Bonhoeffer described his teaching there in *Life Together,* a book that radically analyzes the basis of Christian community. The book describes the spiritual practice he taught his students: pondering short passages of Scripture, meditating, and memorizing.

Bonhoeffer was invited back to teach at Union Seminary in 1939, a safe haven from the horror of Nazi rule. But he left New York after a month, believing that he could have no authentic role in rebuilding Germany after the war if he did not live through the terror himself. Along with other family members, he became involved in a plot to overthrow the Nazis by assassinating Hitler. Later Bonhoeffer was arrested, served other prisoners' spiritual needs, and finally was executed by the Nazis a few days before the Americans liberated his prison.

Some have come to know Bonhoeffer exclusively through *Letters and Papers from Prison*, published after his death by his friend Eberhard Bethge.

The letters introduced new phrases, such as "religionless Christianity," "secular holiness," and "man come of age." Bonhoeffer was critical of "religion" as a replacement for the living God and decried the "God of the gaps," a God who was used only to explain what science could not yet explain. This pushed God to the periphery of life, when God belonged to the center. For Bonhoeffer, God in Christ suffered with the world, and Christians were called to suffer with those who had no voice. While continuing the daily readings and hymns in Tegel prison, he wrote on July 21, 1944:

> During the last year or so I've come to know and understand more and more the profound this-worldliness of Christianity. The Christian is not a *homo religious* but simply a man, as Jesus was a man—in contrast, shall we say, to John the Baptist. . . . [I mean] the profound this-worldliness, characterized by discipline and the constant knowledge of death and resurrection. I think Luther lived a this-worldly life in this sense. . . .
>
> I discovered later, and I'm still discovering right up to this moment, that it is only by living completely in this world that one learns to have faith. One must completely abandon any attempt to make something of oneself, whether it be a saint, or a converted sinner, or a churchman (a so-called priestly type!), a righteous man or an unrighteous one, a sick man or a healthy one. By this-worldliness I mean living unreservedly in life's duties, problems, successes and failures, experiences and perplexities. In so doing we throw ourselves completely into the arms of God, taking seriously, not our own sufferings, but those of God in the world—watching with Christ in Gethsemane. That, I think, is faith; that is *metanoia* [repentance]; and that is how one becomes a man and a Christian (cf. Jer. 45!). . . .
>
> May God in his mercy lead us through these times; but above all, may he lead us to himself.[37]

We hear in Bonhoeffer echoes of Luther's theology of the cross. Both emphasize the suffering and powerlessness of God. Bonhoeffer is critical of any spirituality that leads a person to be caught up in oneself, without involvement and action in this world; no sentimentality and no "pie in the sky" spirituality will do.

Catherine de Hueck Doherty (1896–1985), an aristocratic Russian who became a penniless refugee, brought to Canada and the United States a passionate heart of care for the poor and the Russian tradition of hermitage. One of her twenty-two books, *Poustinia: Encountering God in Silence, Solitude and Prayer*, describes personal retreats (*poustinia* in Russian means "desert").

It is an excellent guide to spending time as a hermit with the one goal of spending time alone with God. Doherty became a Roman Catholic in 1920 in England. After working in Harlem, in New York City, Doherty founded the Madonna House in Ontario, a lay order of more than two hundred people spread among twenty-three field houses throughout the world.

Doherty has many similarities to her contemporary **Dorothy Day** (1897–1980), whom she knew. Both are now being proposed for canonization as saints. Day is better known in the United States as the founder of the Catholic Worker movement. She identified with the poor from an early age but only gradually became the Catholic prophet of her time. Trained in journalism, she founded the *Catholic Worker* newspaper with Peter Maurin in 1932, at the depths of the Great Depression. The paper, which competed with the Communist *Daily Worker*, had a religious radical viewpoint favoring labor and eventually opposing war. The newspaper spawned a number of hospitality houses across the country. Day was arrested many times for protests against her country's wars. Her autobiography is titled *The Long Loneliness*.

Day's spirituality involved a commitment to peace and justice that was not comfortable for middle-class Catholics nor for their priests and bishops. As a later social protester, Daniel Berrigan, wrote: "Dorothy had written about, defended, explained, the following: cotton pickers, braceros, prisoners and exprisoners, families of every condition, the unemployed, priests and nuns, scholars, native Americans, monks, alcoholics, addicts, slum folks, auto workers, coal miners. Among others. She stood with them."[38] Day wrote in her autobiography: "We have all known the long loneliness and we have learned that the only solution is love and that love comes with community."[39]

A Southern Baptist who is widely influential but may not come to mind immediately as a spiritual writer is former U.S. president **Jimmy Carter** (1924–). Carter received the Nobel Peace Prize in 2003 for his work for peace. In addition to building houses for Habitat for Humanity, leading diplomatic efforts to reconcile enemies, and helping Africans to overcome widespread illnesses, Carter has been writing books, among them *Living Faith*; *Sources of Strength: Meditations on Scripture for a Living Faith*; and *The Virtues of Aging*.

More radical is **Jim Wallis** (1955–), founder of *Sojourners* magazine, who calls evangelicals to political commitments far from the conservative "Christian Coalition." Wallis expects discipleship to include action with and for the poor. He is a columnist, the founder of a network of churches from all backgrounds named Call to Renewal, and the author of several books, including *Faith Works*.

Whereas the preceding writers and leaders have addressed the issues of peace and justice by seeking to change patterns of behavior in large groups, the more typical manner of showing Christian love has been by helping individuals who are sick, poor, or physically or mentally handicapped. Two outstanding leaders will complete this section.

Mother Teresa of Calcutta (1910–97) introduced herself this way: "By blood and origin I am all Albanian. My citizenship is Indian. I am a Catholic nun. As to my calling, I belong to the whole world. As to my heart, I belong entirely to the heart of Jesus."[40]

One of the most widely known Christians of the twentieth century, Teresa was born in a small country among a people only 10 percent Christian. Agnes Gonxha Bojaxhiu was born Albanian but later became a citizen of India. While being sent for rest to Darjeeling, she experienced the "call within a call" on May 10, 1946, to found the Missionaries of Charity:

> It was on the train, on September 10, 1946, that she received her second call—"the call within the call," as she refers to it: "And when that happens the only thing to do is to say 'Yes.' The message was quite clear—I was to give up all and follow Jesus into the slums—to serve Him in the poorest of the poor. I knew it was His will and that I had to follow Him. There was no doubt that it was to be His work. I was to leave the convent and work with the poor, living among them. It was an order. I knew where I belonged but I did not know how to get there."[41]

Teresa planned an order with a fourth vow: "wholehearted free service to the poorest of the poor." She led a retreat on "I thirst," the words of Jesus on the cross. Now, in every Missionaries of Charity chapel, one will find beside the crucifix the words "I thirst": it means first of all the thirst of Jesus for us, and then ours for him.

Teresa was not a writer of books, but many of her speeches and shorter writings have been compiled into devotional books. Here is a sample:

> The greatest disease in the West today is not TB or leprosy; it is being unwanted, unloved, and uncared for. We can cure physical diseases with medicine, but the only cure for loneliness, despair, and hopelessness is love. There are many in the world who are dying for a piece of bread but there are many more dying for a little love. The poverty in the West is a different kind of poverty—it is not only a poverty of loneliness but also of spirituality. There's a hunger for love, as there is a hunger for God.[42]

Teresa was awarded the Nobel Peace Prize in 1979 and died on September 5, 1997. Her body was carried through the streets of Calcutta on the same gun carriage that had carried the bodies of Mahatma Gandhi and Jawaharlal Nehru.

Jean Vanier (1928–) is known primarily as the founder of l'Arche. Started in 1964, l'Arche is now an international network of communities for the mentally handicapped. It was in such a community that Henri Nouwen spent his last years serving as a priest. Vanier brings a refreshing emphasis on community in a society and spiritualities devoted to the individual. His own repute is such that he was invited to give a major address to the gathering of the Anglican bishops of the world at Lambeth in 1998:

> Almost everything I say here is the result of my own experience of life in l'Arche, the community in which I have been living for nearly twenty-five years. . . . L'Arche is special, in the sense that we are trying to live in community with people who are mentally handicapped. Certainly we want to help them grow and reach the greatest independence possible. But before "doing for them," we want to "be with them." The particular suffering of the person who is mentally handicapped, as of all marginal people, is a feeling of being excluded, worthless and unloved. It is through everyday life in community and the love that must be incarnate in this, that handicapped people can begin to discover that they have a value, that they are loved and so are lovable.[43]

Race

Many North Americans question the relation of Christianity to other religions, including Native North American cultures and religions. Many American Indians and a number of non-Indians are thinking deeply about the relationship between Christianity and the religions of Native peoples. Many are asking if the commonalities of these two have been overlooked. Others are calling for a Native spirituality within Christianity. Especially attractive are the traditional Indian reverence for "all my relatives" (all living creatures and even all things in nature) and the honored roles for women in these religions. Many Native Americans who are Christian are seeking a spirituality that will combine their traditions with the gospel of Jesus.

One twentieth-century influence from Native Americans has been a reputed speech by **Chief Noah Seattle** (or Sealth) (d. 1866), who was baptized in the Catholic faith in the 1830s. Chief Seattle led his people in prayer often after that time. But he did not write the speech often attributed to him in which he called on the Europeans to care for the land. It was composed for a video in the 1980s.

The African American population is now overwhelmingly Christian and has been nourished down through the centuries by a spirituality of endurance, liberation, and celebration. African Americans have suffered unspeakably from slavery and then discrimination. Those sufferings have produced a community drawn together in worship that reaches the heart. James Cone, who earlier wrote hard-hitting books of black liberation theology, turned to an analysis of the spirituality of the black church. He saw in the music and preaching of the Christian community the core of values that has sustained African Americans.

At the end of the century, **Howard Thurman** (1899–1981) became better known than he ever was during his lifetime. He had a prestigious career teaching at Howard University and Boston University, where he served as Professor of Spiritual Disciplines and Resources and Dean of the Chapel. He was also founding minister in San Francisco of the Church for the Fellowship of All Peoples. Today Thurman's writings have been rediscovered by those who did not know him in person. It is said that Martin Luther King carried Thurman's *Jesus and the Disinherited* in his briefcase. Thurman combined spiritual practice and racial integration.

Martin Luther King Jr. (1929–68) is the best-known African American worldwide. It is no accident that the civil rights leader was also a Baptist preacher. His vision of the mountain the night before his death testifies to spiritual roots that sustained his quest for justice through militant nonviolence. His *Letter from a Birmingham Jail*, explaining why he chose to break the law for the sake of justice, and *Strength to Love*, indicating the spiritual basis for a long-term struggle, both testify to a spirituality that was expressed in his public actions. King wrote:

> The first twenty-four years of my life were years packed with fulfillment. I had no basic problems or burdens. . . . It was not until I became part of the leadership of the Montgomery bus protest that I was actually confronted with the trials of life. . . . We began to receive threatening telephone calls and letters in our home. . . .
>
> In this state of exhaustion, when my courage had almost gone, I determined to take my problem to God. My head in my hands, I bowed over the kitchen table and prayed aloud. The words I spoke to God that midnight are still vivid in my memory. "I am here taking a stand for what I believe is right. But now I am afraid. . . . I am at the end of my powers. I have nothing left. I've come to the point where I can't face it alone."
>
> At that moment I experienced the presence of the Divine as I had never before experienced him. It seemed as though I could hear

the quiet assurance of an inner voice, saying, "Stand up for right-eousness, stand up for truth. God will be at your side forever." Almost at once my fears began to pass from me. My uncertainty disappeared. I was ready to face anything. The outer situation remained the same, but God had given me inner calm.

Three nights later, our home was bombed. Strangely enough, I accepted the word of the bombing calmly. My experience with God had given me a new strength and trust. I knew now that God is able to give us the interior resources to face the storms and problems of life.[44]

King has now been made a national hero, but in his own day he was very controversial. We must not forget his spiritual roots and his boldness in challenging society's norms when he is reshaped now as a secular main-stream leader.

Cesar Chavez (1927–93) was a pious Catholic social activist who organ-ized the United Farm Workers in California. He was a nonviolent leader, a deeply spiritual person, who frequently used fasting to bring attention to his cause. Chavez is considered the greatest Latino-American leader in history.

Gender
The churches of the West are currently in the midst of a serious reevaluation of their spiritual roots in response to the new consciousness among women. In the United States, the radical feminism of the few in the 1970s has devel-oped into a more widespread women's movement in the churches, which is influencing not just personnel policies and the language of hymns but also the way we think about God. Women's Christian spirituality has become a major development.

Feminism in spirituality values women as full partners with men in the quest for wisdom of God; the equality in leadership of the human commu-nity; the self-nurture that is necessary to reach out to those who are disad-vantaged and stand with them; and a responsible, caring dominion within the creation. Feminists, both women and men, have devoted themselves to dis-covering the contributions of women in the past, including women of the Bible—notably, the women disciples of Jesus—and the women down through the centuries who have made significant contributions to spiritual-ity. Feminists have also attempted to change society's concept of women so that they will be taken seriously as teachers, leaders, and sustainers of the human community and of the Christian communities.

One of the most notable current writers of feminist Christian spiritual-ity is **Joan Chittister**, a Benedictine nun, columnist, founder of Benetvision, peace activist, and author of more than twenty books. She has written on the Rule of St. Benedict, daily spiritual reflections on Scripture, the desert fathers and mothers, the Apostles' Creed, personal struggles, the role of women in the Roman Catholic Church, and a feminist approach to spirituality. Since the term *feminist* is used by different writers in a wide variety of ways, I quote here some of her pointed comments on the subject:

> It isn't femaleness that counts, it's feminism—those qualities in both women and men that make feeling, compassion, heart, and service as important as reason, strength, law, and power.[45]

> [Feminism] is geared to the creation of a society that rejects decisions, roles, and categories based on sex alone. Feminism regards the human race as one humanity in two genders and sets out to make the fullness of humanity available to both of them.[46]

> Feminism . . . is a way of seeing. It is a new worldview. It is an attitude toward life. It values things differently than did its forbears. It gives honor where honor has far too long been lacking. It looks with new respect at values traditionally held by women or called feminine, whether, as a matter of fact, anything can rightfully be labeled specifically feminine or not. . . . Qualities derided or disregarded in culture because they are feminine are . . . the very qualities lacking in society today, the very reason that culture is teetering on the brink of its own destruction.[47]

Chittister reminds us that spirituality is about real life, not about an escape: "The truly spiritual person, tradition teaches us, knows that spirituality is concerned with how to live a full life, not an empty one. Real spirituality is life illumined by a compelling search for wholeness. It is contemplation at the eye of chaos. It is life lived to the full."[48]

Much of the history of Christian spirituality, with some notable exceptions, has been developed and reported by men. A thorough change in tone is needed so that the concerns of women are also addressed. A fresh view of the relation of the sexes in spirituality is emerging, in which the female as well as the male character of God is recognized and in which the gifts of women are recognized along with those of men. Writers such as Chittister aid that emerging view.

Many other women scholars have remained within the Christian church and sought reform within it along feminist lines. Perhaps none of these is better known or more prolific than **Rosemary Radford Ruether** (1936–).

She is a Roman Catholic lay theologian and mother of three. Ruether teaches in a Methodist seminary, Garrett-Evangelical, and is thus largely out of the reach of the Roman Catholic hierarchy. Although she does not commonly write under the heading of "spirituality," she assured this writer that, for her, theology includes spirituality and ought not be separated from it.

Ruether brings to her feminist position an ethical perspective that is common among Christian feminists, a concern for all people, especially people of color, gays and lesbians, and economically disadvantaged groups. She applies the liberation theology of Latin America to all peoples in North America. She has also been an outspoken critic of Israeli oppression of Palestinians and has taught for ten years at the Howard School of Religion, one of the leading African American seminaries in the United States. The breadth of Ruether's vision is seen in the following statement from her widely known book *Sexism and God-Talk:*

> In reflecting androcentrism (males as norms for humanity), women must also criticize all other forms of chauvinism: making white Westerners the norm of humanity, making Christians the norm of humanity, making privileged classes the norm of humanity. Women must also criticize humanocentrism, that is, making humans the norm and crown of creation in a way that diminishes other beings in the community of creation.[49]

Ruether represents the social-prophetic side of Christian feminism. She is unafraid to criticize the oppressive powers of our time and in this way conforms her practice to the prophets, except that she focuses on gender oppression, which they did not. Other feminist writers take different perspectives. Among the other influential writers at the close of the twentieth century were Anne Carr and Elizabeth Johnson.

Two kinds of writers of women's spirituality have emerged. One type wishes to remain within the Christian tradition, reforming it to avoid dualisms and hierarchies and to value experience highly, especially the experiences of women, including women from other cultures. This means reading the Bible with different eyes, looking for the women, asking how events looked from their point of view. It also means being skeptical of the Christian tradition as a whole, looking for obvious and not so obvious ways in which males have undermined Paul's assertion that in Christ Jesus "there is neither male nor female" (Galatians 3:28).

A second kind of women's spirituality has left Christianity behind. Finding the Bible and the theological tradition of the churches too patriarchal, a number of women have started their own spiritual groups. Some of them worship the Mother Goddess of older religions, some practice a modern revision of witchcraft, and others simply look for healing ideas, including New Age materials.

Feminism within and outside the church is a global phenomenon. Women of color have sometimes dissociated themselves from the term *feminism*, using *womanist* (black) or *mujerista* (Latino) theologies instead to express the distinctive character of their struggle for liberation as nonwhite women. African and Asian women have joined women of the Americas and Europe in calling for a new status for women in spirituality, theology, and church life.

A number of men have responded to the women's movement with neither full rejection nor full acceptance of their stance. Some have modeled a men's movement on the women's movement. The "liberation" of men, as with women, has included consciousness raising, group meetings, criticism of societal stereotypes, and an attempt to rediscover the essential masculine. The movement is not satisfied with the common images of masculinity in our culture. The damaging things that men do are sometimes related to the psychological training of boys and to the "father wound," the absence of the father from the life of the boy. A new word in the lexicon to parallel *misogyny* is *misandry*, the hatred of the masculine.

Sam Keen is one writer able to articulate a man's need for liberation from domination by female power, symbolized by his word WOMAN. He also introduces a criterion that acts as a critique of various feminist positions. One section of his book *Fire in the Belly: On Being a Man,* is called "Ideological Feminism—No! Prophetic Feminism—Yes!" He explains: "Prophetic feminism is a model for the changes men are beginning to experience. Ideological feminism is a continuation of a pattern of general enmity and scapegoating that men have traditionally practiced against women."[50]

What do these perspectives mean for Christian spirituality? A number of writers have taken up the task of exploring the questions involved, and a major movement among evangelicals has emerged. One of the issues, as for feminist spirituality, is the image of God. Should we abandon the traditional liturgical and spiritual language for addressing God (or even the very word *God*) in light of the critique of patriarchy? One of the most thoughtful responses to this question is given in Brian Wren's *What Language Shall I Borrow? God-Talk in Worship: A Male Response to Feminist Theology.*[51]

David James, building on Wren and others, asks and answers: "*Is a masculine God necessary for masculine spirituality?* The answer is 'yes.' . . . The conclusion of the authors represented in these pages is that masculine images of God are a rich source of reflection for men. To eradicate them from the religious consciousness would be as great an act of gender-violence as any ever perpetrated by patriarchy."[52]

An alternative view is offered by conservative writers and by the movement called Promise Keepers. Founded by football coach Bill McCartney of the University of Colorado, the Promise Keepers idea first emerged on March 20, 1990. Its form has been large sports stadium rallies to call men to faith in Jesus Christ and to responsibility within their families.

The Promise Keepers rallies have been criticized by feminists, who see them as an assertion of male power; by liberal Protestants, who do not approve of their ideals; and by men from liturgical backgrounds who find the free-wheeling and highly expressive style of worship off-putting. The relation of the Promise Keepers to feminism is not officially hostile, but some spokespersons have gone beyond the group's official policy in statements that seem to put women in second place.

Meeting Other Religious and Spiritual Traditions

As the world has grown smaller, Christians have become more and more aware of other religious and spiritual traditions. A spectrum of opinion can be discerned in how much Christians themselves make use of spiritual practices and read spiritual writers from other traditions. Some Web sites warn against the pollution of the clear Christian stream by many of the writers already discussed in this book, on the ground that they are heretical. The other end of the spectrum would include people who seek, like the Bahai faith, to bring all religions into one. Many Christians will want to take a middling stance, welcoming what can be learned from other traditions but retaining loyalty to the Bible, to Jesus, and to the Christian church. It is necessary for this group to evaluate carefully whether to adopt practices based in other belief systems.

Pope John Paul II's conservatism can be seen in his warnings about not just theology and ethics but also spirituality:

> For this reason it is not inappropriate *to caution* those Christians who enthusiastically *welcome certain ideas originating in the religious traditions of the Far East*—for example, techniques and methods of meditation and ascetical practice. In some quarters these have become fashionable, and are accepted rather uncritically. First one should know one's own spiritual heritage well and consider whether it is right to set it aside lightly. . . . A separate issue is the *return of ancient gnostic ideas under the guise of the so-called New Age.* . . . [Gnosticism is] in distinct, but not declared, conflict with all that is essentially Christian.[53]

His cautionary comment may be directed toward the following writers, who have explored the boundaries of different religious traditions and found that borrowing from them has enriched their spirituality.

India provoked in Christian missionaries a profound engagement between Christian and Hindu spiritualities. **Bede Griffiths** (1906–93) began his journey in Britain and finished after many travels in India. At Oxford, he was not popular for supporting the miners' strike in 1926: "By that time I was disillusioned with all of civilization, not just what I was and lived through. I think T. S. Eliot's *Wasteland* and *The Hollow Men* brought out the sense that civilization was collapsing. That made us turn to poetry, to art, to music, to another world altogether."[54]

In Griffiths's third year at Oxford, C. S. Lewis became his tutor. Griffiths writes: "Of course, he was a big influence on my becoming a Christian. We were almost contemporary with that. We began to discover the Christian background of English literature. . . . That's how we grew. I owe a tremendous amount to his influence in my becoming a Christian—actually, I believe it was mutual. We shared with each other."[55]

As he grew in Christian life, after a period in the Anglican Church, Griffiths became a Roman Catholic, professed as a Benedictine monk in 1936, took the name Bede, and was ordained a priest in 1940. For the next fifteen years, he was a Benedictine in the United Kingdom. At this time, he wrote an autobiography.[56]

But his whole life took a change in direction when he decided to go to India in 1955. After visiting and working in a number of communities and founding an ashram, in 1958 Griffiths left the Benedictines and the Roman Catholic Church for the Thomas Christians who follow Syrian Orthodoxy. Finally, not satisfied, he came to Shantivanam (in Tamil Nadu) in 1968 with two other monks and founded his own ashram.

Looking back on his experience of so many years, Griffiths reflects on some of the early themes of his life and exhorts those of us in the West:

> I feel that India gave me the other half of my soul. My life in England, first of all, was dominated by the intellect, by the rational mind. I went from school to college and I passed exams in Latin and Greek, and so on. I was always searching to get beyond the mind. . . . But whereas that was something rare in England, in India it was the norm—the natural order of society. . . . I think I can say that I was discovering the feminine because the masculine mind dominates in Europe and was dominating my mind. The feminine is the intuitive, the sensitive, and also the sensual mind—in a sense, the whole bodily life. Christianity tends to put this down; India has accepted it totally. In India it is all integrated: the sensual and the spiritual. I still go on discovering that other half all the time.[57]

Griffiths founded the Society for the Renewal of Contemplative Life in California in September 1992. He said, "Contemplation is the awakening to the presence of God in the human heart and in the universe which is around us. Contemplation is knowledge by love."[58] He died in his ashram in May 1993, surrounded by faithful devotees.

We turn now to a Jesuit in India, **Anthony De Mello** (1931–87), whose teachings and stories have become favorites with many around the world.

"What attracted so many to [De Mello's] person and his ideas was precisely that he challenged everyone to question, to explore, to get out of prefabricated patterns of thought and behavior, away from stereotypes, and to dare to be one's true self—in fine, to seek an ever greater authenticity."[59]

De Mello went through various phases of teaching. He first was a gifted promoter of the Ignatian spiritual exercises. Then he developed two different approaches to spirituality, each called a *sadhana*. The first was influenced by a popular book of the time, *I'm OK, You're OK*, but the second reversed his judgment: "I am whatever I am, and I feel whatever I feel, and it's fine. I need not be OK in order to be OK if you follow me; I may not be OK, and that is perfectly OK with me."[60]

One of De Mello's accomplishments was introducing the Jesus Prayer (see chapter 5) to the Indian Catholic Church. He himself learned the prayer from *The Way of a Pilgrim*. De Mello both contributed out of the store of Christianity—in this case, Orthodox Christianity—and borrowed from Indian wisdom, especially in his stories. He believed in spiritual growth by story. Here is one of his favorite stories, an excellent one for affluent Christians:

> A monk in his travels found once a precious stone and kept it. One day he met a traveler, and when he opened his bag to share his provisions with him, the traveler saw the jewel and asked the monk to give it to him. The monk did so readily. The traveler departed overjoyed with the unexpected gift of the precious stone that was enough to give him wealth and security for the rest of his life. However, a few days later he came back in search of the monk, found him, gave him back the stone and entreated him: "Now give me something much more precious than this stone, valuable as it is. Give me that which enabled you to give it to me."[61]

From Japan, **William Johnston** (1925–) has written extensively about Christianity and Zen Buddhism. He sees strong connections between the spirituality of *The Cloud of Unknowing* and other apophatic Christian texts and Zen. He has been writing and living in Japan over a long career, demonstrating the compatibility of these two major streams of spirituality.

In America and Europe, a spiritual movement commonly called New Age arose in the second half of the twentieth century. An eclectic movement, it includes elements from old and new, including astrology, European paganism, Native American practices, theosophy, and so forth. Not unified in any way, the movement raised the awareness of ordinary people about spirituality while clearly (or unclearly) distinguishing itself from Christianity.

Relating to Creation

One distinctive development in twentieth-century spirituality was a new appreciation for the natural world and the role of human beings in enhancing or destroying it. The threat of a nuclear winter, then the threat of global warming, and the awareness of the extinction of species and of pollution of land, sea, and water have focused urgent attention on ecology in ways not seen in previous history. Some have blamed Christianity for this situation, seeing the religion as exploitative. The text from Genesis 1:28—"Be fruitful and multiply, and fill the earth and subdue it; and have dominion over the fish of the sea and over the birds of the air and over every living thing that moves upon the earth"—has come in for a great deal of criticism and reexamination. Does it give moral justification for the exploitation of the earth, for the consumerist lifestyle so typical of developed economies? Or, have science, technology, and commerce worked together to bring us to the present impasse? Ecological spiritualities make clear that ecology is a spiritual matter, not just a technological one: people need conversion to a different way of perceiving the world if they are going to act for the health of the earth.

More than any other spiritual writer of the twentieth century, **Pierre Teilhard de Chardin** (1881–1955) focused our attention on the creation, and thereby on the relation of science and religion. Teilhard came from a large family but lived to experience the deaths of almost all his siblings. He also observed gory wounds and psychological trauma as a stretcher bearer in World War I. Yet his teachings were consistently optimistic, not seeming to take human pain and sin seriously. Although most of his writing was done in the first half of the century, he did not become known until the second half, after his death. This delay was caused by censorship by the Roman Catholic Church and his superiors in the Jesuit order. For most of his life, he was forbidden to publish and was virtually exiled from his native France. He chose to live in northern China, where he engaged in geological and paleontological work.

It was at the point of original sin that Teilhard got in trouble with his superiors in 1924 and agreed not to publish his ideas. His books that were published later include *Mass on the World, The Phenomenon of Man, The Divine*

Milieu, *The Heart of Matter*, and *Hymn of the Universe*. The themes of these books are seen in one of his early poems, "Hymn to Matter" (1919):

I bless you, matter, and you I acclaim: . . .
I acclaim you as the divine milieu, charged with creative power, as the ocean stirred by the Spirit, as the clay molded and infused with the life by the incarnate Word. . . .
Raise me up then, matter, to those heights, through struggle and separation and death; raise me up until, at long last, it becomes possible for me in perfect chastity to embrace the universe.[62]

The Divine Milieu: An Essay for the Interior Life was written in 1927 but not published until 1957. He addresses the book to waverers who stand on the threshold of the church: "These pages put forward no more than a practical attitude—or, more exactly perhaps, a way of teaching how to see. . . . If you are able to focus your soul's eyes so as to perceive this magnificence, . . . your one thought will be to exclaim: 'Greater still, Lord, let your universe be greater still, so that I may hold You and be held by You by a ceaselessly widened and intensified contact!'"[63]

He died on Easter day, April 10, 1955. Teilhard was very much discussed at the time of Vatican II. He brought a fresh vision of the nature of the world, focused on the central image of fire and the dynamic of evolutionary change. It was highly speculative, but he was attuned to the issues of the interior life, which are connected to his theories.

In the 1990s, Teilhard's vision of a geosphere growing to a biosphere and in turn developing a noosphere (a sphere of mind) led to renewed interest in his theory as applied to the Internet. As some saw the interconnection between people revolutionized by the new technology, the noosphere provided a concept to explain the wonder of a new step in human evolution.

A second figure from the twentieth century is **Matthew Fox** (1940–), who champions "creation-centered spirituality" or, simply, "creation spirituality." The concerns of this school are wider than ecology alone, but there is a strong emphasis on the ecological theme in Fox's writing. Fox is a controversial figure, having been expelled from the Dominican Order and the Catholic priesthood in 1993. He became an Episcopal priest in San Francisco in 1994. Fox wrote an account of these events in his *Confessions: The Making of a Post-Denominational Priest*.[64]

Why were Fox's critics so adamant that he was no longer teaching the Orthodox Christian faith? To them, he seemed to set aside the major theme of Christian salvation, what he calls redemption/fall-centered spirituality—that is, in spite of his calls to reject dualisms and to work as a both/and theologian,

Fox cut the Christian faith into two opposing sides and called for the victory of one over the other. He seemed to set the first article of the creeds (on creation) over against the second article (on redemption).

Let us get a taste of the passion of this spiritual reformer from his early book *On Becoming A Musical Mystical Bear: Spirituality American Style*:

> For we have numerous instances in Western spiritualities of a life-denying rather than a life-affirming spirituality. And the fact is that these, more than the Jewish spirituality of life-affirmation (which we should recall Jesus came out of), have held dominance in Western civilization. Repression, not expression; guilt, not pleasure; heaven, not this life; sentimentality, not justice; mortification, not developing of talents: these are the earmarks of what Western spirituality has for the most part done. . . . The spiritualities of Plato, Augustine, and Denis [Pseudo-Dionysius] can lead to life-denial and deep human pessimism. Yet they have invariably been the more popular and influential spirituality in Christianity.[65]

Rosemary Ruether, whom we met earlier in this chapter, is an ecofeminist and has written about the connections between patriarchy and the destruction of the natural environment. For example, she writes: "Domination of women has provided a key link, both socially and symbolically, to the domination of earth, hence the tendency in patriarchal cultures to link women with earth, matter, and nature, while identifying males with sky, intellect, and transcendent spirit."[66]

Ruether then goes on to indicate the spiritual roots of our problem and what can be done about it:

> A healed relation to each other and to the earth then calls for a new consciousness, a new symbolic culture and spirituality. We need to transform our inner psyches and the way we symbolize the interrelations of men and women, humans and earth, humans and the divine, the divine and the earth. . . . Rather we must see the work of eco-justice and the work of spirituality as interrelated, the inner and outer aspects of one process of conversion and transformation.[67]

Finally, we note an ecological writer who is not as well known as Ruether or Fox but who wants to stay much closer to the traditional posture of Christian spirituality. Charles Cummings, in *Eco-Spirituality: Toward a Reverent Life*, proposes a new paradigm that is neither the fall/redemption tradition of Catholic tradition nor Fox's creation spirituality but a synthesis of both.[68] Christians who share some of Fox's criticisms of the tradition but who demur from his rejection of the centrality of the cross will find Cummings's approach more acceptable.

Cummings offers a helpful survey of the developments, both scientific and spiritual, that led us to our present crises and offers suggestions for spiritual practice. Among many other suggestions, he calls for Christians to simplify their lives. This includes consuming less of the world's resources through eating lower on the food chain, using public transport instead of private cars, and resisting the tendency to throw away what can be reused into our vast and growing landfills. Thoughtful Christians in the developed world share Cummings's concerns, but only a few practice care for the earth as a spiritual discipline.

Spiritual Practice

1. The **prayer of yielding or surrender** is found in many spiritual traditions. For Kierkegaard, one first has to have a self to surrender before this is possible. To be a self means not to be a passive part of the crowd, not to be shaped by the world, but to be one's true self. Discovering that true self is a lifelong quest, as is surrendering it to God. But the lifelong must find actuality in the present and be repeated again and again. One of our highest forms of worship is to offer ourselves to God:

> I appeal to you therefore, brothers and sisters, by the mercies of God, to present your bodies as a living sacrifice, holy and acceptable to God, which is your spiritual worship. Do not be conformed to this world, but be transformed by the renewing of your minds, so that you may discern what is the will of God—what is good and acceptable and perfect. (Romans 12:1-2)

> Merciful Father, we offer with joy and thanksgiving what you have first given us—our selves, our time, and our possessions, signs of your gracious love.

> Blessed are you, O Lord our God, maker of all things. Through your goodness you have blessed us with these gifts. With them we offer ourselves to your service and dedicate our lives to the care and redemption of all that you have made, for the sake of him who gave himself for us, Jesus Christ our Lord. Amen.[69]

Hannah Whitall Smith, Phoebe Palmer, and other Holiness leaders found their deepest happiness in being "on the altar" as an offering to God. This sort of surrender of one's will to God cannot be manufactured. As you look back on your life, can you recall times when you have become *willing* rather than *willful* toward God, when you have "let go and let God," when you have said "here am I" in the sense of total willingness? If so, **write** about how that felt. If not, write what it might mean for you right now—what you think God wants from you right now, what objections and fears you might have, what it is that tugs you to give in to God.

What would it mean to do this every morning?

Note that I find a certain danger in this spiritual practice: I might begin to think that I am justified, made right with God, by my own offering of myself, instead of receiving Christ's offering for me. I might base my spiritual life on what I do instead of what God does for me. I could become legalistic with myself instead of feeling the freedom to give myself away out of love from God and for God. This danger is present for all spiritual practices, but it seems to me to be a special and subtle danger here.

2. If tongues is one of your gifts, use it in **prayer**. Use this gift when you do not know how to pray a prayer of intercession, or when your heart is too full of praise for ordinary words. Two people, one in South Africa and one in India, have told me how they use tongues to pray silently all day long. This is another way to fulfill Paul's word about praying constantly.

3. Try out a **centering prayer** or the mantra prayer of John Main. Many Christians have found this a helpful practice when they have only known verbal prayer previously. Start by quieting yourself, as in the first exercise in chapter 1. Then choose a word that is spiritually powerful to you, perhaps *Jesus* or *Spirit* or *love* or *peace*. Give your loving attention to God without attempting to speak to God. Just be in the presence. When your thoughts wander, use your special word to bring you back. If you find this difficult, John Main's method may be easier. Repeat constantly the mantra "Maranatha" in four slow syllables. The chant can help to keep your mind at home. Again, what you are aiming for is simple presence with God, so that God's healing may go deeper and deeper in your soul.

4. **Study** the twelve steps used with Alcoholics Anonymous. Consider how they apply to you, whether or not you are addicted to alcohol. No one is superior to someone who is addicted; addiction is not a moral fault but a disease. Those who follow the steps do not consider themselves "cured." They are "recovering" alcoholics, not "recovered" alcoholics. Likewise, Christians are in the process of recovering from sinning and from being sinned against. Perhaps you have some addictions of your own. Think of your behavior and consider whether you may be addicted to pornography,

shopping, gambling, eating, or some other activity. **Pray** the steps meditatively, and let them lead you to action.

5. **Take action for social justice**, as so many in this chapter have done. Do not allow your spirituality to be an inward, private matter only. Stand up for what is right! The other practices in this book can make you strong to oppose injustice at home, at school, in the workplace, and yes, in politics. Take care what you purchase, to support a fair wage for the people who make your clothes, shoes, and household items. Buy from local farmers. It takes more effort, but it feels so much better than the plastic convenience of a huge store. Everything you purchase is a vote for the way in which the item was produced.

In our day, when citizens of democratic states have influence on national policies, **writing letters** can be an important spiritual exercise. Advocating the rights of those who have been denied is being a kind of preventive "good Samaritan." For example, Bread for the World advocates for the hungry both in the United States and globally. Amnesty International advocates for prisoners of conscience who are often tortured or who have "disappeared." The Children's Defense Fund stands for the rights of the young. Writing letters is an effective way to stand up for justice and love in our world of poverty, refugees, and prisoners.

6. **Study, pray,** and **write** to understand who you are as a gendered person. What does it mean in your spiritual life to be a woman or a man? How do you relate to God as masculine and feminine? Pray and meditate on what it would mean for you to address God with feminine terms. Does it make you uncomfortable? Why? Does it set you free? Why? If both men and women are made in the image of God, then we must both reflect something in God's nature. Our cultural stereotypes say that women are weak, tender, nurturing, and emotional while men are strong, tough, goal oriented, and rational. God is not subject to our cultural stereotypes, and neither are we.

7. **Consider the animals.** If you have pets, observe what you can learn from them spiritually. They are a different species from you, but you offer them hospitality. You and they are both creatures of the one God. They are often very dear to us, almost like a human person. Raise your pets in prayer, pondering what you can learn from them.

Do the same for the wild animals. We are to be stewards of God's creation. What does the existence of wild animals mean for your home on earth? Did God make them only for human use, or do they have meaning in and of themselves?

Aids for the Exercises

Bondi, Roberta C. *Nick the Cat: Christian Reflections on the Stranger.* Nashville: Abingdon Press, 2001.

Main, John. *John Main: Essential Writings.* Ed. Laurence Freeman. Maryknoll, N.Y.: Orbis Books, 2002.

Keating, Thomas. *Foundations for Centering Prayer and the Christian Contemplative Life: Open Mind, Open Heart; Invitation to Love; The Mystery of Christ.* New York: Continuum, 2002.

Suggested Reading

Allchin, A. M. *The Kingdom of Love and Knowledge: The Encounter between Orthodoxy and the West.* New York: Seabury, 1982.

Brown, Robert McAfee. *Spirituality and Liberation: Overcoming the Great Fallacy.* Louisville: Westminster, 1988.

Cummings, Charles. *Eco-Spirituality: Toward a Reverent Life.* New York: Paulist, 1991.

Dyrness, William. *Learning about Theology from the Third World.* Grand Rapids: Zondervan, 1990.

Elie, Paul. *The Life You Save May Be Your Own: An American Pilgrimage.* New York: Farrar, Straus and Giroux, 2003.

Ferguson, Duncan, ed. *New Age Spirituality: An Assessment.* Louisville: Westminster John Knox, 1993.

Merriman, Brigid O'Shea. *Searching for Christ: The Spirituality of Dorothy Day.* Notre Dame, Ind.: Univ. of Notre Dame, 1994.

Timmerman, Joan H. *Sexuality and Spiritual Growth.* New York: Crossroad, 1992.

Underhill, Evelyn. *Mysticism: A Study in the Nature and Development of Man's Spiritual Consciousness.* New York: Dutton, 1961 (1911).

Chapter 9

The Non-Western World since 1900

A s we turn to the non-Western continents of the world, I want to emphasize my belief that the Western world, the so-called first world, needs the two-thirds world, or so-called third world, in order to develop an authentic and vital spirituality. A very good general guide to this process is William Dyrness's book *Learning about Theology from the Third World*.[1] Dyrness describes African theology as focused on Christianity and culture, Latin American theology as centered on the political setting, and Asian theology as focusing on the transcendent as its main theme. These are overgeneralizations, as Dyrness realizes. His point, however, is that Christians in the West can no longer afford to leave out of consideration the contributions and challenges of Christians from these continents—that is, these Christians have both gifts to offer from their own cultural backgrounds and hard questions to ask of the affluent Christians of the West.

A helpful way to distinguish interactions between culture and Christianity includes four types of interactions: transcultural, contextual, countercultural, and cross-cultural. *Transcultural* aspects of Christian tradition are found in every culture—for example, an ethic of love, a belief in Jesus as Lord and Savior, the presence of God in worship. *Contextual* elements are those that have been absorbed from the indigenous culture in the practice of Christian faith—for example, African dances in worship, Asian architecture in buildings, American music in hymnody. *Countercultural* elements in Christianity offend the local culture, as indeed the message of the cross will offend every culture. The churches have not always done well in refusing to adapt to such indigenous practices as consumerism, racism, and sexism. And finally, *cross-cultural* elements are those borrowed from another culture for the sake of appreciation—for example, Americans singing South African hymns, Nigerians using European prayers, Thai Christians adopting American musical instruments.

Each of us tends to view reality according to our own limited experience. That experience may be limited to our own country, our own denomination, even our own congregation, family, or neighborhood. It is very important that we all take a wider view. With regard to Christian spirituality, we may be missing some of the most important developments far from our experience. If you are reading this book in the West—that is, in North America or Europe—it is possible that you are not aware of what is happening in the rest of the world, or as it is known by other names, in the third world, the two-thirds world, the developing world, the global south. And if you are reading this book in the global south, you may be surprised to read about the "Global North," which we have here been calling the West.

It is because of developments in the global south that Christianity continues to grow in numbers. From about half a billion Christians in 1900, the faith grew to 2 billion in 2000 and now increases by about 25 million each year.[2] This numerical increase has not meant a percentage increase, however; Christianity has remained at about 33 percent of humankind, which now numbers over 6 billion. It is becoming more and more recognized that the centers of Christianity are moving to the global south. The population of Christians in the developing world increased from 83 million in 1900 to 1.1 billion in 2000. The increase has been most dramatic in Africa, where there were 10 million Christians in 1900 and 330 million in 2000.[3]

Meanwhile, Muslims increased not only in number but in percentage, going from about 200 million (12.3 percent) in 1900 to about 1.2 billion (19.6 percent) in 2000. It is projected that these percentages will increase in the twenty-first century, to 22.8 percent in 2025 and 25 percent by 2050.[4]

The actual practice of Christianity has slipped drastically in Europe in the face of secular thinking. Christianity remains very strong in the United States, despite some decline in the major denominations.[5] The departure of European Americans from the churches will be countered by the new influx of immigrants. A great deal has been made of the influx of persons of non-Christian religions, making America more diverse religiously.[6] It is important for American Christians to demonstrate hospitality and welcome the newcomers from other faiths. Though there is truth in this analysis, it tends to forget that many, perhaps most, of the immigrants are Christians. The largest part of immigrants to the United States is from Latin America, where more than 90 percent of people profess Christian faith. Many African immigrants also bring their Christianity with them. A little known fact is that most Arab Americans are Christians from Lebanon.

Where Christianity is really growing is in Africa, Latin America, and Asia. The churches planted in these continents over the past centuries have accelerated their growth since the late twentieth century as their leadership was gradually put in the hands of indigenous persons. Perhaps missionaries from these countries will re-evangelize Europe in the future. The number of Christians in the global south has been increasing rapidly, both by conversion and by birth to Christian families. Philip Jenkins's *The Next Christendom* has illuminated this fact. His book gives both support and critique to the hour-glass image we looked at in chapter 1. The development of Eastern Orthodox, Roman Catholic, and Protestant Christianity has the hourglass shape; what it does not take into account is the Eastern Christianity of the Oriental Orthodox Churches. We will discuss these churches briefly here in this chapter.

When we look for written descriptions of non-Western Christian spiri-tuality, we find far fewer books and far fewer indigenous writers. There are several reasons for this. First and foremost is the lack of wealth in the global south. Many people do not have money to buy books; therefore there are few publishers and few writers. The differences in currency valuations and the corruption in post offices may also mean that books published in the West are too expensive or are easily stolen from the mail.

Latin America

Roman Catholic Christianity came to Latin America with the conquistadors and since then has spread at least nominally to most of the population. It was a very special Spanish spirituality that accompanied the conquerors. They saw Jesus as the wretched sufferer who modeled a life of suffering for his fol-lowers. The manner in which the faith was imposed on the native population stands as one of the worst examples of religious imperialism.

In many countries, the ordinary people did not understand the faith, and it became an overlay on their previous beliefs. A kind of duality developed in which traditional divinities and practices were mingled with Roman Catholic spirituality, often resulting in a haphazard contextualization of the faith.

In Mexico, the **Virgin of Guadalupe**, who appeared to Juan Diego in 1531, is an example of a combination of indigenous and imperial spiritual-ity. The Virgin appeared to him on the very hill, Cerro de Tepeyac, where a traditional female divinity, Tonantzin, the Mother of the Gods, associated with the moon, had welcomed pilgrims until the Spanish forbade it. When the Virgin instructed Juan Diego to ask the local bishop to build a church on this sacred hill, the bishop was skeptical. Eventually, he was convinced by a miracle: Juan found roses growing in the midst of winter, carried them to the bishop in his cloak, and his cloak became the canvas for the image of the Virgin. This cloak can still be viewed today in the Basilica of Guadelupe, in the northern part of Mexico City (see map 8), unfaded after all these years. Some 10 million people visit the shrine each year, about half of them near the time of the Guadelupe festival, December 12. On a recent visit, I observed a man walking on bloody knees to the shrine, fulfilling a vow to the Virgin.

Guadelupe/Tonantzin is an indigenous goddess and the mother of Jesus. Her image, found all over Mexico and widely in Latin America, bears no infant Jesus but stands on the moon. She is the patron saint of Mexico and enjoys widespread loyalty and devotion.

Liberation Spirituality

The church in Latin America came to be a bastion of support for the European populations that held and still hold the land and economic power. In some countries, 2 percent of the people owned 90 percent of the land. The question of social justice was muffled by the cultural captivity of the church hierarchy.

But in the mid-twentieth century, a few priests started "base Christian communities," which involved the poor people in Bible-based group meetings that enlivened faith and called into question the economic order. The *camposinos*, or peasants, learned to read and to think critically about their lives. This grassroots movement gave birth to a new kind of theology, liberation theology.

Among the first leaders to become well known was **Dom Helder Camara** (1909–99), bishop of Recife, Brazil, and author of *A Thousand Reasons for Living*, among many other books. Camara's passion for the poor met with criticism from the Vatican but inspired many others across the continent. He was quoted as saying, "When I give bread to the poor, they call me a saint; but when I ask why people are poor, they call me a communist."[7]

Liberation theology eventually was adopted by professional theologians and is now well known throughout the world. It advocates a new way of doing theology—that is, from the perspective of the poor, from the "bottom up." It employs Marxist analysis to reveal the injustice and conflict in the human situation, followed by the Christian Gospel to promise hope for liberation from oppression in the historical future. This theology has been criticized from both Catholic and Protestant conservative perspectives on several accounts. It has seemed to some to tend toward a secular theology of social and economic revolution without any transcendent or specifically spiritual content.

Gustavo Gutiérrez (1928–), in *We Drink from Our Own Wells*, describes a liberation spirituality that must give the critics pause. The problematic elements of liberation theology hardly appear in Gutiérrez's book. There is nothing of Marxist analysis here. It is clear that spirituality is for personal and communal relationship to God, and not simply for political revolution. Gutiérrez is known as a theologian who lives simply among the people of Peru, practicing what he advocates in his writing.

His book is valuable in many ways. Speaking from the perspective of the Latin American poor, Gutiérrez finds traditional Catholic spirituality to fall short on two counts: it is geared to a minority, namely the religious orders, and it is too individualist and interior. Gutiérrez calls for a spirituality for all the people that includes practical action for liberation on a communal level. Drawing on the Bible and on selected figures from the history of European spirituality, he calls for a wholistic view of the Christian life, consisting of a trinitarian "Encounter with the Lord," "Walking in the Spirit," and a "Journey to the Father."[8]

The special marks of liberation spirituality as set forth in *We Drink from Our Own Wells* are conversion (the necessary break with the past, which occurs again and again), gratuitousness (the free, unearned grace of God), joy in suffering and martyrdom (which come in the struggle for liberation), spiritual childhood (which Gutiérrez sees as necessary for a commitment to the poor), and community (as the proper context for solitude).

One of the attractive features of the book is the seriousness with which Gutiérrez takes the Bible. In the course of his discussion, he also deals at length with Paul's understanding of flesh, spirit, and body. He shows that Paul is not following Neo-Platonist denigration of the body but is using the term *flesh* in a different sense. This section would be helpful in many books on spirituality, and it is unfortunate that these findings of critical word study were not available centuries earlier.

Similar in tone is Jon Sobrino's *Spirituality of Liberation*.[9] This book is a fresh and serious challenge to others to rethink spirituality on biblical, liberationist lines in their own settings.

As mentioned earlier, one of the main vehicles for liberation theology is the "base community," in which poor *camposinos* gather to discuss the Bible. We have a remarkable document of such discussion in Ernesto Cardenal's *The Gospel in Solentiname*. Cardenal was a former student of Thomas Merton. The four volumes are a reconstruction of Cardenal's experience as a priest in a village in El Salvador, in which he recounts biblical texts and the comments on them made by the people.[10] Here is a sample of comments about the Christmas story in Luke 2:

> Pedro Rafael Gutierrez spoke again: "I think that in this earthquake the ones who are suffering most are the rich, and I'm going to tell you why: Acahualinca has never had any water, any electricity, any milk, any rice, any beans. Now this Christmas the rest of them don't have any either. But the poor have been without food and electricity for a long time. All their Christmases have been like this. The radio talks about people going out into the street without shoes or clothes, and how the hell long have the poor people gone without shoes and clothes?"
>
> "They've been like that since the birth of Jesus. . . ."

Felix spoke again: "I'm going to tell you one thing. Listen to me, Pedro. The rich never suffer. The government puts a five per cent tax on business. And are they the ones who pay it? It's the poor. . . . "

"He came to share the lot of the poor. And Joseph and Mary were turned away from the inn because they were poor. If they'd been rich they'd have been welcomed in."

"God wanted his son to be born in a pigsty, in a stable. . . . He wanted his son to belong to the poor class, right? If God had wanted him to be born to a rich lady, that lady would have had a room reserved at that hotel. Especially arriving in her condition."

"I see in this the humility of God. Because it was his son, and his mother had him just like any dog. And Jesus came to free the world from these injustices (which still exist). And he came so that we could be united and struggle against these injustices. . . . With today's Gospel, it seems to me that no poor person should feel looked down upon. It seems to me that it's clear that a poor person is more important than a rich one. Christ is with us poor people. I think we're worth more. To God. To the rich we aren't worth a thing, good only to work for them. . . . Jesus was rejected in Bethlehem because he was poor, and he goes on being rejected in the world for the same reason. Because when you come down to it the poor person is always rejected. In our system, that is."[11]

The world's attention to liberation thought was heightened by the El Salvadoran assassinations of Bishop Oscar Romero in 1980, of four women in religious orders in 1980, and of six Jesuits, their housekeeper, and her fifteen-year-old daughter in 1989. Many, like me, have visited the bedroom of Father Stan Rother, fondly referred to as Padre Aplàs, who was murdered in his bed in Santiago Atitlan, Guatemala, in 1981 for his advocacy for the common people.

The opposition of Pope John Paul II has reduced the impact of liberation theology in Latin America since his papacy began in 1978. Coming from an anti-Communist posture in Poland, the pope did not want to see anyone in the church favoring Marxism. However, the pope did call for criticism of economic injustices related to capitalism and the globalization of the world economy. The questions raised by liberation theology will continue.

The challenge of liberation spirituality for North Americans is twofold: Is our spirituality so individualized and psychologized that it excludes issues of justice? Are we prepared to share power with groups that have been disempowered, either within our own societies or in the two-thirds world?

Pentecostalism

The vast majority of Latin Protestants are Pentecostalists, whose rise in the Western hemisphere has been dramatic. The Pentecostal version of Christian spirituality does not depend on learning or wealth; rather, it is simple and experiential. Globally, Pentecostalism has grown from virtually nothing in 1900 to more than half a billion believers in 2000, and it is projected to increase both its numbers and percentages in the twenty-first century.[12]

Here begins a first person description of Pentecostal worship in Brazil by the U.S. theologian Harvey Cox:

> The Pentecostal congregation called Amor de Deus meets in the huge courtyard between two adjoining apartment houses in a part of Rio de Janeiro where peeling lower middle-class tenements meld almost imperceptibly into a dilapidated slum. On this clear, cool Sunday night in June, some 600 people are crowded into the area, most seated on folding chairs and long wooden benches, but many standing. Guitarists strum vigorously. . . .
>
> Benedita's testimony was not unusual. At least not at first. . . .
>
> When she was twenty-six . . . God spoke to her, the Holy Spirit entered her life, and she felt the joy of salvation.
>
> "Alleluia!"
>
> But then, Benedita began to weave into her narrative some observations about the cruel way Brazilian society treats poor people. She mentioned corrupt politicians and big businesses.[13]

In this account, Cox has mentioned some distinctive characteristics of Latin American Pentecostalism—the humble economic station of those involved, the urban setting, and the typical activities in a Pentecostal service, which include singing, speaking in tongues with interpretation, and testifying. What amazed Cox was the social awareness of Benedita's testimony, a combination of economic criticism with Spirit-filled worship. Many Latin American Pentecostal churches are not simply about pie-in-the-sky-by-and-by, keeping poor workers in their place. Rather, they are about a present experience of God that energizes them to oppose the oppression of the rich. Walter Hollenweger gave evidence of Pentecostal overcoming of racism twenty years earlier, supporting Cox's evidence.[14]

On the other hand, Pentecostalism in Guatemala seems to be very inward looking and has been given a bad name by the atrocities committed in the 1980s by General Rios Montt. Clearly, differences exist across the continent in the temper of Pentecostalist spirituality.

Africa

This section discusses four main developments in African spirituality: (1) the spirituality of ancient African churches, (2) liberation concepts in the African setting, (3) the movement to contextualize African Christianity, and (4) the spirituality of African indigenous churches.

Ancient African Churches

Two ancient African churches continue to the present day: the Coptic Church of Egypt and the Ethiopian Orthodox Church. Both are closely related, and both have come through long periods of persecution and isolation. It was my privilege to attend two weekday "Bible studies" by Pope Shenoudah III in the Cathedral of St. Mark in Cairo (see map 9). He has been a leader of the renewal of the church in the last several decades. In a gathering of thousands of people who welcomed him with applause and cheers, he patiently answered questions sent in to him on a wide variety of subjects and then led the whole crowd in a careful consideration of the meaning of the Bible for today.

Perhaps the most striking spiritual practice of the Copts is fasting. They fast more than two hundred days a year, including all Wednesdays and Fridays, as did early Christians. Much of the present vitality of the Coptic Church depends on monasteries in the desert, where laypeople go for worship and blessings. Very dear to Egyptian Christians is the account of the escape into Egypt by Joseph, Mary, and the infant Jesus (Matthew 2:13-23). Many places have been designated as a resting place of these refugees, including sacred sites up the Nile River. These are places of pilgrimage and prayer as well as stops for tourists from abroad.

The Ethiopian Church is much like the Egyptian, with frequent fasts, important monasteries, and impressive liturgies. It has also developed special dances for its musical leaders and claims the presence of the original ark of the covenant.

Liberation Spiritualities

The second development, liberation, finds a very similar expression to that of Gutiérrez in a volume by Archbishop **Bukole Wa Ilunga,** *Paths of Liberation: A Third World Spirituality.* Both are Catholic authors who in the post–Vatican II setting give considerable attention to the Bible. Both are proposing serious changes for their countries on the basis of experience of oppression and of a longing for freedom. Ilunga expresses the essence of freedom as that which enhances life, a central theme in many accounts of African traditions.

The first third of Ilunga's book boldly portrays the problems of Zaire (now D. R. Congo). He not only decries the damage to his people brought by years of colonial alienation and recent foreign manipulation, but lays out the responsibility of present-day Zairians for the crushing poverty of the country. Written during the reign of President Mobutu, Ilunga's book criticizes Mobutu's policy of "Authenticity" for not leading back to true African roots. Rather, it became a political shibboleth behind which all sorts of schemes to defraud people were hatched. Ilunga describes the growth of government corruption leading to paralysis of the economy, both on high and low levels. The root problem, Ilunga concludes, is human sin: "the underlying cause of all the things that do not work."[15]

His prescription, based on a lengthy discussion of the Bible, is that personal liberation must go hand in hand with social and political liberation. Personal corruption can undo the best efforts of plans for development. If individuals are not freed from sin, even the most just system will not liberate the poor. On the other hand, an unjust system is sinful as well, enslaving all those who suffer under it.

Under the banner of Black Theology, significant development of the liberation theme took place in southern Africa. The Black Theology and Black Consciousness movements, in tandem with similar movements in the United States, articulated a theological opposition to the apartheid system. *Apartheid* (pronounced "ah-PAR-tate") is an Afrikaans word that means "separateness." Apartheid had roots far back in the immigration of Europeans to South Africa beginning in 1652. The system was codified into law following the victory of the Nationalist Party in 1948. Although supported by the Dutch Reformed Church in South Africa, it was clear to all others, especially the nonwhite population that suffered under this system, that the system was unjust, immoral, and sinful. The churches of English background spoke up against apartheid from the beginning but were unable to take decisive action against it. These churches, whose members were mostly black, nevertheless included many white people of British descent whose economic interests led them to support apartheid at the polls while condemning it in church resolutions.[16]

Many courageous individuals opposed the system, including **Alan Paton** (1903–88), whose novels, beginning with *Cry, the Beloved Country*, described the pain and suffering caused by the system. Deeply Christian, Paton held a vision of deep compassion for all sides. Paton comes from the British side of the white population. From the Afrikaner side, Beyers Naude (1915–2004) suffered rejection by the Dutch Reformed Church and eventually banning (house arrest) by the South African government.

Another of the courageous Afrikaners who broke with apartheid was **John de Gruchy**. This theologian and scholar of Dietrich Bonhoeffer's legacy (see chapter 8) gathered an engaging, challenging collection of spiritual writings under the title *Cry Justice!*[17] A special characteristic of this daily devotional guide is the inclusion of songs and artwork, as well as prayers and meditations, from South African Christians. The book contains the music and words for the powerful hymn "Nkosi Sikele' iAfrika," which is sung all over southern Africa. Composed by Enoch Sontonga in the Xhosa language at a Methodist mission school in 1897, it was adopted as the official anthem of the African National Congress in 1912 and later as the national anthem of South Africa. I have always been deeply moved when hearing this anthem. Here is an English translation:

> Lord, in your mercy bless Africa
> Lift up the horn of her power and strength.
> In your love and kindness hear our prayer,
> Father look on us, and bless your family.
> Come, Spirit come—come and bless us
> Come, Spirit come—come and bless us
> Father, look down, and bless Africa,
> Father look on us, and bless your family.[18]

The most well known of the Christian opponents of apartheid is **Desmond Tutu** (1931–), former archbishop of Johannesburg and winner of the Nobel Peace Prize. Tutu has written a number of short books that contain sermons and meditations appealing for both justice and reconciliation. He is known not only for leading marches and conducting mass funerals for the victims of apartheid but also for his spiritual leadership. He is known to be a person of prayer, rising very early each morning to spend an hour or more with God.

Apartheid was officially ended in 1994 following the release of Nelson Mandela from twenty-nine years of imprisonment. The laws that codified apartheid in the 1950s were rescinded, and in multiracial elections, the people of South Africa chose Mandela as prime minister. He proved to be one of the greatest African rulers in living memory.

After independence, Desmond Tutu chaired the Truth and Reconciliation Commission, a dramatic attempt to heal the wounds of the apartheid era. Although far from perfect, it was a courageous attempt to bring confession and forgiveness to a divided land. Spiritual principles were the basis for a social justice event, as Tutu describes it in *No Future without Forgiveness*.[19]

Contextualization

The third main theme in African Christian spirituality is contextualization. What will a Christianity that is fully African look like? The quest for an indigenous cultural expression of Christianity has led theologians to reevaluate the primal religions, to show new interest in the ancient African churches of Egypt and Ethiopia, and to carefully study the African indigenous churches.

Missionaries from the North Atlantic countries generally taught Christianity on the basis of their own post-Enlightenment, "modern" assumptions and addressed the kinds of questions they were accustomed to at home. Christianity became a "classroom religion" for many people. It taught reading and writing and the correct answers to the questions in the catechism, whether Catholic, Reformed, or Lutheran, but it often did not address the questions that Africans raised then and continue to raise now, explicitly or implicitly.

Christianity was attractive to Africans because of the impressive age of its scriptures, the possibility of confidence in the love of the Creator, and the promise of secure and eternal life after death. But post-Enlightenment missionary Christianity did not have much to say about issues of daily concern; the status of the ancestors; the role of spirits and divinities; contact with the unseen world through visions, dreams, and animals; and, especially, matters of health and fertility. These issues had already been secularized in Europe and North America, and whether knowingly or unknowingly, missionaries became the agents of secularization in Africa.

The contrast between an indigenous spiritual worldview and a Western secular worldview became vividly apparent in the ministry of **William Wade Harris** (1866–1929).[20] A forty-seven-year-old Liberian, Harris was called while in prison to be a prophet. He discarded all Western clothing and set off walking near the Atlantic across Ivory Coast, preaching to indigenous peoples that they should abandon their old gods and be baptized in the name of the Father, Son, and Holy Spirit. Harris walked all the way to Gold Coast (now Ghana) and back across Ivory Coast to Liberia in the years 1913 to 1915. It is said that more than one hundred thousand people responded to this African prophet, with his bamboo cross, turban and robe, calabash rattle, and bowl of baptismal water!

There had been a few missionaries in Ivory Coast for about twenty years, but they had found little success in convincing people to accept a "modern" worldview. Harris, however, spoke to the people within their own worldview. He believed in the power of the gods and spirits and in the possibility of miracles. His demonstration of "signs and wonders" like those in the Acts of the Apostles convinced many people to burn their old images and amulets and to be baptized by Harris. Unlike the missionaries, he did not demand any book learning before baptism. Through baptism, people felt immediately defended from the revenge of their abandoned gods by the spiritual power of the new God who loved them.

Harris was not concerned about denominations. Some of those he baptized became Catholic, others became Methodist, and still others started indigenous churches. He kept the local communities together instead of separating out individual converts, as the missionaries did. He also permitted and practiced polygamy, a traditional form of African marriage.

Harris was unknown to Western missionaries for many years. Later missionaries and Africans themselves referred to him as an example of the movement to indigenize Christian theology in Africa. The Catholics and Protestants in the second half of the twentieth century devoted themselves to replacing the European "clothes" in which they had received the gospel with African ones, in worship, architecture, art, philosophy, and yes, spirituality. This effort, largely carried out by professors and pastors, has resulted in a large number of books and some influence on local congregations. For example, during my own decade of service in Nigeria, I saw a gradual acceptance of drums and dancing in worship services, but conservatives were not happy about it. The missionaries of my era were all in favor of African cultural expressions, but conservative church leaders were not always willing to change. I recall one pastor's wedding where the bride, groom, and African guests were dressed up in their best Western clothes, but all the missionary guests wore African garb!

African Indigenous Churches

The fourth feature of African spirituality is the emergence of African indigenous churches, or AICs. Starting in the late 1800s, some Christians broke away from the missionary-led denominations to form their own churches of various sorts. Some were almost completely modeled on the originating church, but with black leadership. Others developed new spiritualities that were more in tune with African traditional religions. They did not consciously set out to do this, as they were very much against the continued practice of these religions by their followers. Rather, they sought a third way, for example, by forbidding the use of both Western and traditional medicine in favor of prayer alone. There were a great variety of such churches; David Barrett counted some six thousand of them already in 1968.[21] Today the number has increased exponentially. For example, in Ibadan, Nigeria, one can observe—just by walking around a single block—more than twenty different independent churches, most of them only a single congregation with an evangelist/healer leading his or her flock. But many of the independent churches are very large organizations started by major prophets.

The example of the prophet Harris is not unique. Other prophets also emerged in Africa during the twentieth century, and they founded major church bodies. Almost all of the Nigerian founders came from the Anglican Church, and their churches are commonly called Aladura churches—that is, churches of pray-ers. Garrick Braide (ca. 1882–1918) founded Christ Army Church in the Niger Delta. Joseph Babalola (1904–1959), a driver of heavy machinery, became a minister of healing in the 1930s, leading a revival of the Yoruba people that opened the way for many new churches. Moses Orimolade, who was later called Baba Aladura (Praying Father), and Christiana Abiodun Akinsowan began one of the most colorful of the Nigerian churches in 1925, the Cherubim and Seraphim. Josiah Ositelu (1902–66), seer of thousands of visions, founded the Church of the Lord (Aladura) in Nigeria.

Simon Kimbangu (1889–1951), who after miracles of healing was imprisoned for decades by the Belgians in Zaire, founded the Church of Christ on Earth by Simon Kimbangu, which has grown to more than 5 million members and secured a place in the World Council of Churches. **Isaiah Shembe** (1867–1935), a Zulu in South Africa, founded the Nazarite Church. There are many other churches and founders. None of them set out deliberately to "accommodate" Christianity to African culture, but all of them did an "end run" around Western ideas of Christianity. In seeking to be faithful to the Bible and to the Spirit, they did produce a form of Christianity that was indigenous to Africa, a "contextualized" faith. The churches founded by these prophets and others are now looked upon as providing clues for the contextualization of spirituality in the mission-founded churches.

The African indigenous churches portend a special type of spirituality that is strange to the European individualist, rationalist spirituality of recent centuries. Major themes for the African churches include an affirmation of life in this world as well as beyond the grave; the role of the living dead in the communion of saints; the importance of healing; and the presence of the Spirit to work in power. Some of these themes are found in Pentecostal Christianity on all continents, but others are distinctive to Africa.

African Christianity has both gifts and challenges for first world Christians. I see the gifts as (1) a sense of the presence of God in all things, (2) an experience of the Spirit of God for power to meet the challenges of life, (3) a strong emphasis on the community, and (4) an eagerness to celebrate in music and dance the glory of God. The challenges for Westerners, on the other hand, are to stand up for Africa, the overlooked continent, and to make policies that will enable this troubled continent to overcome poverty, AIDS, illiteracy, corruption, and civil wars. The suffering of African peoples has been immense since the late twentieth century. Only with determined, long-range effort will Africans be able to solve their problems and will Westerners be able to learn from African spirituality.

Asia

The world's largest continent also has the most people, but it has the smallest percentage of Christians. Christianity began in Asia, but its thought forms seem quite different from those of the ancient civilizations of India and China. On this continent lie some of the most difficult cultural challenges to an indigenous Christian spirituality. As with the other continents, I will not attempt any sort of completeness in this discussion, but select a few highlights.

Ancient Churches

The ancient churches still exist in minority situations in India, Syria, Iraq, Iran, Lebanon, and Palestine. Among the Jews present at the Pentecost event were Arabs (Acts 2:11). Today many of these Christians are members of the Middle East Council of Churches. Their spirituality goes very deep, honed by centuries of persecution. Theirs is a liturgical spirituality shaped by the prayers and eucharist of their gathered worship.

Perhaps least known to Christians in the United States are the Palestinian Christians, who still maintain the churches of Bethlehem and Nazareth. These Christians have suffered greatly from the Israeli occupation and from suspicions among their Muslim neighbors. Some of them have taken courageous stands for peace between Israel and Palestine.[22]

The Thomas Christians mentioned in chapter 4 are still alive and thriving in Kerala State, India. Their prayers include bowing to the ground and using candles and icons. They have developed a strong reputation in the World Council of Churches for learning and for ecumenical leadership.

Japan

Anyone who has read the whirlwind theological tour of Asia described in *Waterbuffalo Theology*, by **Kosuke Koyama** (1929–), must recognize the great diversity among peoples who have different climates and cultures (see map 10). Koyama sketches the very different situations in Singapore, Thailand, China, Hong Kong, the Philippines, Indonesia, Burma, Vietnam, Japan, and Taiwan. In the situation of northern Thailand, where he is writing, he speaks of a "monsoon orientation" as "cyclical cosmic regularity and its saving dependability without hurry and without argument."[23] How different from the spirit of the industrialized countries, including his own homeland, Japan! This difference is indicated in the meditations he titles *Three Mile an Hour God*.[24] Koyama is intensely aware of the cultural differences within Asia as well as those between Asia and the West. His conversational style, freehand drawings, and witty remarks show a down-to-earth spirituality.

Koyama calls for quite a different direction in spirituality from the Latin American and African sources we have discussed. His is not a spirituality of social justice or of contextualization but a spirituality of the cross, as the place where a God of history expresses wrath about human sin. Koyama is not trying to blend together Asian religions and Christianity but is focusing on the very stumbling block that Paul wrote about: the cross. In his *No Handle on the Cross*, Koyama rejects human attempts to control God or to reduce the offensiveness of the Christian message by taking the spotlight off the cross of Jesus.

Sometimes Koyama sounds very much like Luther's "theology of the cross" as opposed to a "theology of glory." He may have been influenced by his compatriot **Kazoh Kitamori** (1916–), author of *Theology of the Pain of God*, written in 1946. After the suffering of the Second World War, Kitamori proposed the pain of God as a third member of a necessary triad that includes the love of God and the wrath of God. In writing this way, he opposes the theology of the Greek fathers, who insisted that God could not suffer. Kitamori writes of a mysticism of suffering: "We become united with the pain of God through our pain, and we are united with God through the joined pains."[25]

Kitamori may have influenced the writer of the most influential book in modern Japanese Christian writing, *Silence*. **Shusaku Endo** (1923–96), a Catholic, set his novel in seventeenth-century Japan, when Christians, who had multiplied to some three hundred thousand after the visit of Francis Xavier in 1549, were suddenly persecuted after 1614. Endo's main character, a Portuguese Jesuit named Sebastian Rodrigues, faces the government's demand to renounce his faith by trampling on an image of the crucified Christ, a "fumie." If he does apostasize (renounce his faith), Christian peasants suffering under torture will be released. At this point, the silence of God, which has troubled Rodrigues through all his time under persecution, is broken. The face of Christ appears to him and permits him to trample on Christ's face in order to save the peasants. The implication of this is explained by one interpreter as follows:

> The triumphant Christ of the West, dominant in the mind's eye of Rodrigues until now, has shifted to a kenotic Christ, emptied and broken. The silence of God, then, is broken in no triumphant blaring of horns or in a show of divine might, but in a paradox and mystery of divine suffering. God is not silent to suffering, but is suffering alongside creation. The beatific vision, the face-to-face encounter with God, is turned upside down. The suffering Christ who encourages so-called apostasy embodies a radical image of God. This is a necessary picture.[26]

Another Japanese leader from the twentieth century is **Toyohiko Kagawa** (1888–1960). Though he came from an affluent family, he chose to live in the slums of Kobe to minister to the poor. On his first day there, he found himself sharing his very small space with a man with skin disease, who was followed by other homeless persons who moved in with him. Kagawa was not only a social activist but a poet:

> "He cannot save Himself" —
> Long ago
> The crowds
> Reviled a Man
> Who came
> To save them.
> And I,
> Who fain would follow Him,
> Am spent.
> For I can see
> No hope
> For the slums
> Because that,
> First of all,
>   This thing
>   Is wrong —
>   That men
> Should crowd
> Thus in the dearth,
>   And dark
>   And dirt —
> Should crowd and throng...
>
> But oh,
> The pity, the pity!
> My people
> Must stay
> In the city;
> So this six-foot shack
> That shelters me
> Is the only place
> Where I want to be.[27]

Kagawa organized labor and peasant unions to improve their very difficult lot. He was arrested by the Japanese government several times in the 1940s under suspicion of spreading peace propaganda. World War II seemed to destroy all his work, yet he reorganized and aided in the rebuilding of Japan, remaining a preacher even though he was offered a high political office. He was devoted not only to evangelizing the Japanese population but to building a just society, which he considered the kingdom of God on earth. He asked: "Who will accomplish the successful reconstruction of the economic system, if the Christians do not try to serve in this way? The spirit of brotherhood and love which is at the heart of Christianity is the promise of hope for the new order."[28]

If a single word were chosen to summarize Kagawa's spirituality, it would be *love:*

> Love alone introduces God to me. Love is my sanctuary—in factory, field, city street; in bedroom, office, kitchen, sickroom. I have my sanctuary everywhere I go in the universe. Where Love is, there God is. . . . Love is the ultimate religion. Classify me not by creed: I belong to nothing but Love. Jesus it was who taught that it should be so. Jesus never said that men were to be shunned for their creeds. Love is the ultimate revelation, the final sanctuary.[29]

China

China, the world's largest nation, has a long and varied history of Christian spirituality. The Nestorian Christians established churches from 653 to 845 but then were totally suppressed under the Tang dynasty. Later, Franciscans and Jesuits visited the royal courts. Among these was Matteo Ricci (see chapter 6). It was in the 1800s that Protestants first came to China. Robert Morrison came in 1807 and, after years of patient scholarly work, translated the Bible into Chinese. After 1860, after two opium wars, which were a kind of economic rape, Western powers forced the Chinese to accept missionaries. Missionary work in China was tainted by these events. A huge number of foreign missionaries arrived, with good intentions, and built schools, clinics, and churches. All of this work was uprooted by the Communist movement, starting in the early 1920s by the New Culture movement, which was virulently anti-Christian, and finally in the Communist takeover in 1949 and the Cultural Revolution of 1966. Christianity was seen as the tool of the capitalist imperialists. Religion in general was seen as superstition that must be eradicated for the progress of the nation, which must rely on scientific principles.

So, Chinese Christians had to face a hostile government during almost all of the twentieth century, and very many were imprisoned, tortured, disgraced, and killed for their faith. That faith has persisted through the fires of persecution, however; and since the Cultural Revolution ended in 1976 with the death of Mao, Christians have been able to reorganize and grow at a rapid pace. The Communist government has insisted on regulating the churches and allows only Protestants who are part of the Three-Self Patriotic movement to conduct open services and train pastors. Attendance at these open churches in the cities is overwhelming. Meanwhile, Roman Catholics must affiliate with the Catholic Patriotic Association, which seeks to cut all ties to Rome. Others who worship in houses are still persecuted and must meet in secret.

Because of this situation, no one knows the extent of Christianity in China today. Estimates range from 5 to 100 million Christians; perhaps 50 to 60 million is close to the mark. These Christians must be very careful about contact with foreign Christians. They are, in fact, proving that Chinese Christianity is indigenous to China and not dependent on the West. They have survived the harshest persecution and thereby have left behind all that is not essential to Christian spirituality: church buildings, church institutions, public acceptance. These were all destroyed during the Cultural Revolution.

What is essential did remain and grow, apart from any support of foreigners: the Bible, the community, the family. What is it that has continued to attract Chinese people to faith in Jesus Christ? Many of them say that it is joy. Though public preaching is not permitted, new Christians say that they have observed a joy in the life of Christians that contrasts with the bleak joylessness of the Communist ideology.

The Chinese example is a challenge to affluent Christians elsewhere in the world. They have followed a spirituality of the cross: suffering, endurance, patience, poverty. In the course of their trauma, they have left Western denominations behind. A North American interprets this challenge as follows:

> There may be elements in our culture—its commercialism, consumerism, greed, and hedonistic values—that are also alien to Christianity, but the threat is more subtle and difficult to handle. In our interpretation of Christianity it is so terribly important to make the distinction between what is "Christian" and what is "culture." This may not always be possible, but the attempt must be made. Christianity must not be made a captive to any culture—East or West, capitalist or communist.[30]

On the other hand, the Chinese example raises for Christians the question of the importance of contact with others of the faith throughout the world. A temporary isolation may be necessary because of critics in the Chinese government, but Christian spirituality does need encouragement and interchange with an ecumenical, worldwide community.

India

In India we see a development outwardly similar to African contextualization but quite different in content. The development of a friendly Christian relationship to Hinduism goes in the direction of a mysticism not character-istic of Africa. Drawing on the resources of Ramanuja (1017–1137), Sadhu Sundar Singh (1889–1929), and Krishna Pillai (1911–48), **A. J. Appasamy** (1891–1975) developed a Christian spirituality in the *bhakti* tradition of Hinduism. *Bhakti* refers to the way of salvation by devotion rather than by the other two major paths in Hinduism: knowledge and moral achievement. It is the path that seems closest to the Christian concept of salvation by grace. Starting from his doctoral dissertation at Oxford, Appasamy related the mes-sage of the Gospel of John to Indian mysticism. He was friendly to the use of Hindu terminology and practice (see also pages 172–73 on Griffiths and de Mello).

A more recent collection of Indian Christians' writings includes this paragraph, indicating a direction for Indian Christian spirituality:

> The insistence of self-consciousness and individuality as meaning personality is a modern Protestant variation, not belonging to the ancient Catholic theology which is more in accordance with Indian metaphysics. We are too much burdened by our consciousness and self-consciousness. I desire to be rid of this growth—a sickly growth of the ego. I desire to be made one with the Christ, losing my abnormal self-consciousness, exclusive and well, and so-called rationality, in the ocean of his life. . . . We should receive the immor-tal Christ as the Universal Spirit of beauty love and truth (*sat, chit* and *anandom*) and not as a separate individual spirit.[31]

Stanley Samartha reflects on the funeral rites he witnessed for a man who was given both Christian and Hindu ceremonies:

> The Christian service was *formal,* orderly, well-structured, and with the minister in his robe, there was no doubt that it was official. In contrast the Hindu rite was *informal,* less rigid, with hardly any words uttered and no priest being present. The whole group partic-ipated in the rite.
>
> One could not but become aware of the *silence* that dominated the Hindu rite. No speeches were made, no *mantras* recited and, . . . there was no singing. The Christians, on the other hand, seemed to be very uneasy about any periods of silence. . . .
>
> Except, of course, for the sign of the cross and flowers there were no other visible *symbols* which could add to the meaning of the Christian service. Hindus had a number of them, all taken from nature itself—flowers, coconut, *tulsi* leaves, water from the river Ganga, the bamboo framework, banana leaves and, of course, fire.[32]

Samartha would also favor a more indigenous Christian Spirituality.

So you, the reader, have now followed me uphill and down through a brief history of Christian spirituality. Given this history, where are we in the present, and what does the future portend? This will be the subject of our final chapter.

Spiritual Practice

1. **Meet a person** born in another country who is now your neighbor as a resident of the United States. Notice people in your daily life who are recent immigrants. Show hospitality to such people in appropriate ways as the opportunity arises. Sometimes a smile can mean a lot. See if you can become known to such a person in a way that allows you to ask about religion in the person's home country. Most people from Africa and Asia are quite open about their faith, rather than being offended or ashamed as many Americans are. If you identify as a Christian and the person does too, see if you can learn more about what the Christian life is like in that person's culture. If you find that the person is from a different religion, see it as an opportunity to learn more about that religion. Do not try to force the conversation, but allow your own faith to emerge naturally at the right time.

2. **Study** in books and on the Internet one country that interests you. Learn to know the culture, history, and religious situation of that country. If you belong to a church, find out if the church has missionaries there. Consider traveling to that country to experience the life of the people and the life of the church firsthand.

3. **Study** and **pray** to consider how to relate to persons who come from a non-Christian tradition. Your conclusions may lead you to be more liberal or more conservative, but consider the options carefully, knowledgeably. In my opinion, it is too easy to say that all religions are alike and are equal. It is also too easy to say that only your religion is right and that all others are in darkness. For spirituality, one of the main issues is whether you incorporate practices from other faiths into your own practice. I am convinced that this can be helpful if done with care. I admire the practices of other faiths. Here are some examples: Jews have a lot to teach Christians about the spirituality of the home. Muslims are faithful to pray five times a day in prayers of praise. Hindus have given the world the physical and spiritual disciplines of yoga. Buddhists focus on meditation and therefore have much to teach about the methods and techniques of this practice, which is part of all world religions. Native Americans show reverence for the natural world, not rape or indifference. In all these cases, I believe Christians

can learn a great deal from other traditions for spiritual practice while remaining faithful to their own tradition by their faith in Jesus as the world's Lord and Savior.

4. **Study**, **pray**, and **write** to consider how liberation theology and spirituality might apply to you. Where do you see oppression in your own life and in the life of the world? Is there a message of Jesus that will set free the oppressed? If you come from the middle class, consider what Jesus might look like to a person without your economic privileges. Why is it that so many of the world's Christians, from the first century to the twenty-first, have been poor people? How can you become a minister to the people Jesus loved, to the poor, sick, and rejected?

5. **Study**, **pray**, and **write** so that you become aware of the ways Christianity has been contextualized or has falsely accommodated itself in your own culture. It has been contextualized out of its ancient Jewish context in order to make it understandable to you, so that you do not need to leave your culture behind in order to be a Christian. But it may have been falsely accommodated to your setting if its basic values or beliefs have been forgotten or compromised in order to make it more acceptable to people in your culture. If you are in the United States, consider the contextualizing of Christianity into your language and your post-Enlightenment culture. Consider your individualism, your consumerism, your attitude toward what is foreign. Consider Jesus' values about peace, love, and what is important in life. Make some judgments about these matters, and live according to your convictions, not just according to the Christian subculture of your country.

Suggested Reading

Brown, G. Thompson. *Christianity in the People's Republic of China.* Atlanta: John Knox, 1983.

Chao, Jonathan, ed. *The China Mission Handbook: A Portrait of China and Its Church.* Hong Kong: Chinese Church Research Center, 1989.

Costa, Ruy O., ed. *One Faith, Many Cultures : Inculturation, Indigenization, and Contextualization.* Maryknoll, N.Y.: Orbis, 1988.

Cox, Harvey. *Fire From Heaven: The Rise of Pentecostal Spirituality and the Reshaping of Religion in the Twenty-first Century.* Reading, Mass.: Addison-Wesley, 1995.

Donovan, Vincent J. *Christianity Rediscovered: An Epistle from the Masai.* Notre Dame, Ind.: Fides/Claretian, 1978.

Dyrness, William. *Learning about Theology from the Third World.* Grand Rapids: Zondervan, 1990.

Fung, Raymond, comp. and trans. *Households of God on China's Soil.* Geneva: World Council of Churches, 1982.

Gutiérrez, Gustavo. *We Drink from Our Own Wells: The Spiritual Journey of a People.* Maryknoll, N.Y.: Orbis, 1984.

Hollenweger, Walter J. *Pentecost Between Black and White: Five Case Studies on Pentecost and Politics.* Belfast: Christian Journals Ltd., 1974.

———. *Pentecostalism: Origins and Developments Worldwide.* Peabody, Mass.: Hendrickson, 1997.

Ilunga, Bakole Wa. *Paths of Liberation: A Third World Spirituality.* Maryknoll, N.Y.: Orbis, 1984.

Kitamori, Kazoh. *Theology of the Pain of God.* Richmond, Va.: John Knox, 1958.

Koyama, Kosuke. *Waterbuffalo Theology.* London: SCM, 1974.

———. *Three Mile an Hour God.* London: SCM, 1979.

Neal, Marie Augusta, S.N.D. *A Socio-Theology of Letting Go: The Role of a First World Church Facing Third World Peoples.* New York: Paulist, 1977.

Rakoczy, Susan, ed. *Common Journey, Different Paths: Spiritual Direction in Cross-Cultural Perspective.* Maryknoll, N.Y.: Orbis, 1992.

Romero (film). Directed by John Duigan. Los Angeles: August Entertainment, 1989.

Shorter, Aylward. *African Christian Spirituality.* New York: Macmillan, 1978.

Stauffer, S. Anita, ed. *Christian Worship: Unity in Cultural Diversity.* Geneva : Department for Theology and Studies, The Lutheran World Federation, 1996.

Stoner, John K., and Lois Barrett. *Letters to American Christians.* Scottdale, Pa.: Herald, 1989.

Tromph, G. W., ed. *The Gospel Is Not Western: Black Theologies from the Southwest Pacific.* Maryknoll, N.Y.: Orbis, 1987.

Trout, Jesse M. *Kagawa, Japanese Prophet.* New York: Association, 1959.

Chapter 10

Where Do We Go from Here?

here are many ways of analyzing the story I have just told. It is an incomplete story, unwieldy, with rough edges. Each of us will draw our own conclusions as to what is to be treasured and what is to be tossed. The basic premise of this overview is that we who live today are in continuity with the past and with others throughout the world. There are no "good old days" in the sense of sentimental longing for a perfect time. Rather, the story goes on with ever new challenges and hopes. We have the privilege of knowing the story better than any previous generation. How we understand it, however, is not automatic and easy.

The Story

Christian spirituality is a style of walking in the Holy Spirit. It therefore involves the whole of life, not some private segment. It is the way we relate to God, to ourselves, to others, and to the creation as well as their relation to us. The Bible gives a series of normative principles, positive and negative examples of life experience, and the gospel of Jesus Christ, on which all else depends.

The early centuries of Christianity were characterized by an expansion to many cultures: Asian, African, and European. Within the Roman Empire and in other places, severe persecutions marked Christianity from the beginning. The Jewish affirmation of creation was frequently dimmed and sometimes lost, leaving a legacy of denigration of the body, of sexuality, and of women in the tradition. The spiritual and moral disciplines of the faith—as well as the growth of mystical communion, or union, with God—were emphasized by many writers.

The eastern part of the Roman Empire, later called Byzantine, developed in different ways from the West, with an emphasis on the resurrection as victory over death and on the *theosis* (or divinization) of humans, rather than the focus on sin and forgiveness as in the West. The icon and the Jesus

Prayer, in the context of the divine liturgy with its Eucharist, came to characterize Eastern spirituality, which has constantly renewed itself by going back to the tradition.

Monasticism in the West was a lay protest movement that engendered much Roman Catholic spiritual writing. The ideals of the orders expanded into service for the world with the mendicant orders of the thirteenth century and the Jesuits in the sixteenth. The "love of learning and the desire for God" were developed in the monasteries.

Protestants emerged to challenge the whole Catholic structure, including its assumptions about spirituality. Their main point was "grace alone, faith alone, Scripture alone." Protestants started afresh, with various degrees of borrowing from Catholic spirituality but always rooted in their understanding of biblical teaching.

The modern age was a time for throwing off the "superstitions" of both Catholics and Protestants, or at least fitting them into a new understanding of the role of reason. The traditions developed Puritanism, Pietism, evangelicalism on the Protestant side, as well as the maverick Kierkegaard. The Catholics centered into personal spirituality, especially the French school, preceded by a maverick of their own, Pascal. During this time, Christianity began to spread to continents other than Europe, but the non-European contributions to the universal church were not usually appreciated.

The twentieth and early twenty-first centuries have seen the development of Christian faith on a global scale, in some sense fulfilling the promise of the first centuries. It is time now for Christians in Europe and North America to listen not only to the writers of the past but also to peoples of the present from different cultural traditions. Euro-Americans need to hear the voices of Native Americans and African Americans. The role of women in the historical development of Christianity and in the present has been seriously neglected; the male-dominated tradition has a great deal to learn from women. We can hope for a future of mutual understanding and cooperation, though that will not happen without painful struggles toward reconciliation.

Global Christian Community

One basic premise of this discussion is that Christianity is by nature a global rather than a European faith. We have looked at a few developments in selected continents to show that Christians can learn from one another across cultural, linguistic, and racial lines.

But we must also say that even this glimpse of the variety of spiritualities leaves us with certain pressing questions. Among the first is the question of *unity in diversity*. Given that there are different styles of Christian living, can one speak of Christianity as a single religion? Is not there a serious tension between the social activism of liberation theology and the quiet mysticism of Asian Christian mystics, who have used the methods of Hinduism or Buddhism?

A related question is how to evaluate different schools of spirituality from different cultures. Our basic stance in this book has been appreciation, welcoming the riches of different cultures to the Christian global family. But each of us in our own churches must make choices about the lifestyles we adopt. This also applies cross-culturally. What are *the criteria* for deciding if a given spirituality is authentically Christian, and if it is worthy to be emulated outside its own home? If North Americans have much to learn from Latin Americans, do Asians and Africans also have much to learn from each other as well?

Are the criteria for evaluating a spirituality the same or different from those for evaluating a theology? I would expect an authentic theology to reflect the Scriptures; to give a central role for Jesus as the Christ; to value faith, hope, and love; to be understandable within its culture; and to challenge the idols of that culture. Are there additional criteria for spiritualities?

A third question is the way of *transmitting spiritualities* cross-culturally. Writing books can be helpful, but books seldom communicate beyond the specialist reader. Music, art, and stories are effective ways of conveying the spirit of another people. The exchange of living persons is perhaps the best means of sharing spiritualities. How can we more effectively share with one another what the Spirit has given us?

Finally, one of the fundamental issues for our future discussions will be if and how the Christian church can learn from *non-Christian movements and religions* to enhance its own spirituality. Has God given wisdom to other religious traditions? If so, how can Christians value and learn from them without diluting the integrity of their own tradition? I believe that there is much that has already been learned from other traditions in the past that we take for granted as Christians today. But there have also been cases in which adopting a spirituality from the outside has led to a distortion of the gospel, for example, Neo-Platonism in European Christianity.

What Is Needed in Our Day?

Just as each period and culture in the history of Christian spirituality is unique, so we as individuals are different from one another. In our thirst for God, we need not all drink from the same kind of cup, glass, or goblet. A survey like this is intended not only to display the varieties of containers but also to raise questions about their appropriateness for a given setting. Not all of them will be appropriate for North America at the start of the twenty-first century.

First of all, we need much more courageous leadership in the churches to teach and practice the spiritual life. Many people have the impression that attendance at Sunday morning worship is all that the church asks, that this is the limit of its vision of the Christian life. Rather, the churches must find a way to make clear that the Sunday morning liturgy is important for the spiritual life, *in the context of* other spiritual practices. The church must strengthen its adult education so that people feel free to explore and study, not that there is one correct answer for every question. People need to know that not all spiritual practices are fitting for every person; how we pray will be different for each person. But there must be a clear understanding that communal, family, and personal practice are important.

A Christian spirituality for our time must keep the four relationships *in balance*. Neglecting creation can result in a disparagement of the self as well. Separating the creation relationship from the others, however, can lead to fanatical views about animal rights. Each of the four needs the others.

We also need a *listening spirituality*. We must be willing to hear the voices from continents and ages other than our own. It will be important that we also listen judiciously to peoples of other faiths. In North America, this especially means listening to the Native peoples of the continent and to people recovering from addictions. Without abandoning Christian commitments, it is possible to learn about spirituality that is ecologically healthy and wholistically physical.

The focus of Christian spirituality must be *trinitarian*. A strong emphasis on the Creator needs to supplement our clear, central devotion to Jesus Christ as incarnate redeemer, servant, healer, and friend. The role of the Holy Spirit needs strong emphasis not only for the use of the spiritual gifts of many kinds but also for the sense of the presence of a powerful and loving God.

The basis of our spirituality in *God's passionate love* must be preserved against the constant tendency to make spirituality into a meritorious work. There is no doubt that we are called upon to respond to God's love. From the perspective of the onlooker, the behavior of the Christian is what counts; spirituality is a behavior, insofar as it involves praying, sharing one's goods, meditating, advocating the rights of the oppressed, going on retreats, receiving the sacraments, living simply, witnessing for the faith, reading the Bible, and so forth. Yet all of this is grounded not in our worthy intentions but in God's forgiveness, God's empowerment, God's creation.

The Christian tradition has had serious blind spots. It is not that we in our day have none, but distance gives us a better perspective on those of other ages and cultures. One of those has been the acceptance of social norms about women that Jesus would not have approved. Another is the use of creation not as good stewards but as exploiters. A third is the affirmation of a proper self-love, which nourishes and has patience and forgiveness for oneself. Each of these blind spots was overcome in some part of the tradition, yet on the whole, I believe the tradition still needs correcting.

A Personal Word

As I sit before my computer, surrounded by books, on a snowy Minnesota day, I am very much aware that this account of the tradition is only an introduction. It has been very good for me to do the reading that undergirds this telling of the story, but there is so much that I either want to read or ought to read. This distinction is because different parts of the tradition will be more helpful, more valid, more vivid, than others.

I have tried to give a balanced account of the Orthodox, Catholic, and Protestant traditions. Including elements from all of them is important, just as it is important to be aware of the whole Bible. Some parts that may not seem very useful at one time may be just what is needed at another. I remember, for example, the Lamentations and lament psalms, and how they fit with what contemporary psychologists have learned about our need to grieve. I recognize the increasing role of Orthodox icons and the Jesus Prayer for Western Christians. I think of the spiritual power of African and Latin American Christianity for renewing North American Christians. Each of us needs the others, across time and space.

We have looked now at the story of Christian spirituality in many ages and lands. It has been an introduction to a world of study and prayer that invites us to drink deeper. Our thirst for God reflects a chronic dehydration, but God is longing to give us drink.

What then shall we do? Having a wider horizon for our practice of the Christian life, it is up to each of us to select, to experiment, to evaluate, and to adapt. A kind of knowledge is available to us from books, but personal knowledge, the kind that really counts, can come only from experience.

We are all thirsty for God, for Spirit, for love. That thirst does not end while we are in this life; we long for more of God, more of Spirit, more of love. The old hymn says it well:

> I love to tell the story,
> For those who know it best
> Seem hungering and thirsting to hear it like the rest.[1]

Yet I believe that there will be a consummation when, as Julian wrote, "all shall be well, and all shall be well, and every manner of thing shall be well," and we shall know God as fulfilled Love forevermore.

Spiritual Practice

1. Go on a **pilgrimage**! Choose a place that will be meaningful to you, near or far. Perhaps it is as close as the place that God spoke to you at an earlier age. Perhaps it is the grave of someone you love. Perhaps it is the locale of a great spiritual writer who is introduced in this book. I have found it very moving myself to visit the sites of the spiritual mentors who have gone ahead. I have sat in C. S. Lewis's pew in his Anglican church. In his own bedroom, I have touched the Bible John Wesley used. I have prayed at the site of a Latin American martyr. My hair has stood on end at Buchenwald concentration camp. I have visited the house where St. Ignatius lay in bed recovering from his battle wound. I have looked out the window of the room where Luther translated the New Testament. All of these and more have made the story of Christian spirituality come alive for me. If approached in the attitude of a pilgrim instead of a tourist, these places make concrete what one has learned from books like this one and can produce awe, praise, or sorrow, depending on the place.

Another kind of pilgrimage is to offer support by your presence to people in suffering. For example, you might visit Palestine and Israel as a pilgrim both to pray at the sites of biblical events and to show awareness of the Christians in this troubled region. The indigenous Christians are often overlooked by American Christians. Paying attention to them is a way of affirming that they matter, that we are all together in the body of Christ.

2. Choose one of the persons or movements in this book, and **engage** them at a deeper level. It is possible to have a rich dialogue with a person from the past. Read the books, pray the prayers, and engage the Spirit. Imagine the person alive before you, and create a conversation with him or her. What would he or she ask if acting as your spiritual director? What do you want to ask to attain his or her wisdom?

3. Consider all the ways your spiritual practices can interact with **modern media**. How do spiritual practices enrich your use of the Internet, the movies, television, or recorded music? The methods of *lectio divina* can be used to consider a movie. Your prayer life can be enhanced by the Internet.

Aids for the Exercises

Blythe, Teresa, and Daniel Wolpert. *Meeting God in Virtual Reality: Using Spiritual Practices with Media.* Nashville: Abingdon, 2004.

Cousineau, Phil. *The Art of Pilgrimage: The Seeker's Guide to Making Travel Sacred.* Berkeley, Calif.: Conari, 1998.

Forbes, Cheryl. *Notes of a Reluctant Pilgrim: The Idea of Pilgrimage in Everyday Life.* Grand Rapids: Zondervan, 1992.

Appendix: Time Line

	(about 50–130)	New Testament
A.D. 100	(about 100)	Odes of Solomon
	(about 157)	Montanus
	(160?–220?)	Ignatius of Antioch
	(160?–225)	Tertullian
	(185–254)	Origen
A.D. 200	(250–353)	Antony
	(296?–373)	Athanasius
A.D. 300	(306?–373)	Ephrem
	(330–379)	Basil of Caesarea
	(345?–399)	Evagrius of Pontus
	(360?–432)	John Cassian
A.D. 400	(480?–547)	Benedict
A.D. 500–1000	(1090–1153)	Bernard of Clairvaux
	(1033–1109)	Anselm of Canterbury
A.D. 1100	(1109–1179)	Hildegard of Bingen
	(1170?–1221)	Dominic Guzman
	(1181/2–1226)	Francis of Assisi
	(1193–1253)	Claire of Assisi
A.D. 1200	(1225–1274)	Thomas Aquinas
	(1260–1328?)	Meister Eckhart
	(1293–1381)	Jan van Ruysbroeck
	(1296–1359)	Gregory Palamas
A.D. 1300	(1353–1416?)	Julian of Norwich
	(1380–1471)	Thomas à Kempis
A.D. 1400	(1483–1546)	Martin Luther
	(1484–1531)	Ulrich Zwingli
	(1491–1531)	Ignatius of Loyola
	(1496–1561)	Menno Simons
A.D. 1500	(1509–1564)	John Calvin
	(1515–1582)	Teresa of Avila
	(1542–1591)	John of the Cross
	(1555–1621)	Johann Arndt
	(1567–1622)	Francis de Sales
	(1575–1629)	Pierre de Berulle
	(1593–1633)	George Herbert

A.D. 1600	(1611–1691)	Lawrence of the Resurrection
	(1623–1662)	Blaise Pascal
	(1624–1691)	George Fox
	(1628–1688)	John Bunyan
	(1635–1705)	Philip Jacob Spener
	(1648–1717)	Mme. Guyon
	(1651–1715)	François Fenelon
	(1663–1727)	August Herman Francke
A.D. 1700	(1703–1791)	John Wesley
	(1707–1788)	Charles Wesley
	(1720–1772)	John Woolman
	(1725–1807)	John Newton
	(1731–1805)	Macarius of Corinth
	(1749–1809)	Nicodemus of the Holy Mountain
	(1759–1833)	William Wilberforce
	(1799–1873)	Henry Venn
A.D. 1800	(1813–1855)	Søren Kierkegaard
	(1866–1929)	William Wade Harris
	(1870–1922)	William Seymour
	(1875–1941)	Evelyn Underhill
	(1881–1955)	Pierre Teilhard de Chardin
	(1881–1963)	Pope John XXIII
	(1886–1968)	Karl Barth
	(1888–1960)	Toyohiko Kagawa
	(1897–1980)	Dorothy Day
	(1898–1963)	C. S. Lewis
A.D. 1900	(1904–1984)	Karl Rahner
	(1906–1945)	Dietrich Bonhoeffer
	(1910–1997)	Mother Teresa
	(1915–1968)	Thomas Merton
	(1920–)	Pope John Paul II
	(1926–1982)	John Main
	(1928–)	Gustavo Gutiérrez
	(1928–)	Richard J. Foster
	(1929–1968)	Martin Luther King Jr.
	(1929–)	Kosuke Koyama
	(1931–)	Desmond Tutu
	(1932–1996)	Henri Nouwen

Glossary

anamchara. A Celtic word for "soul friend," a spiritual companion and guide.

anchorite, anchoress. A man or woman who chooses to live alone to pray and meditate.

Anglican. Relating to the Church of England.

apatheia. Literally "passionlessness." In practice, freedom from those passions that drive one away from God.

apophatic. An approach to spirituality that emphasizes the mystery of God and therefore strips away all words and metaphors for God in order to meet God in silence and darkness. *See* kataphatic.

cenobitic. Communal monasticism as opposed to individual; opposite of eremitic.

Chalcedon. A church council in 451 that defined Jesus Christ as one Person with two natures, human and divine.

charism, charismatic. A charism is a gracious gift from God, such as those discussed by Paul in 1 Corinthians 12. Charismatic Christians value and employ these gifts. Charismatic may more specifically refer to those people in historic denominations who employ these gifts, in distinction from Pentecostalists, who have founded denominations that employ them. In a wider sense, every Christian is charismatic, having received such gifts.

contextualize. To develop a form of Christianity that is culturally fitting.

docetic. Refers to the idea that Jesus only appeared to be human; affirms that spirit must not come into contact with body; one aspect of Gnosticism.

Eastern Orthodox. Those churches such as Greek Orthodox or Russian Orthodox that accept the first seven ecumenical councils as valid, including the definition of Chalcedon. (Roman Catholics accept more councils than seven.)

ecumenical. *1.* Referring to the whole inhabited world; universal. *2.* The movement to unite different Christian denominations.

eremitic. The form of monasticism in which persons live alone. The word *hermit* comes from this word.

Gnosticism. A variety of religious movements judged to be heretical by the early church. They denied the goodness of the world and taught a secret knowledge for escaping from creation at death.

Hellenism. A general word for the Greek culture spread widely by Alexander the Great in the fourth century B.C.

icon. A painting of a religious figure that serves as a point of contact with the worshiper; an object of devotion, but not worship, that affirms the incarnation of Christ.

incarnation. The teaching that the Word became flesh in Jesus of Nazareth; a strong affirmation of the goodness of human, physical life. Not to be confused with *re*incarnation in Hinduism.

Jansenism. A religious movement in seventeenth-century France that taught the predestination of the saved and the unsaved.

justification. Being made right with God; or the declaration that one is righteous on the basis of Christ's death and resurrection; a gift to be received by faith.

kataphatic. An approach to spirituality that makes full use of words and images to describe God. *See* apophatic.

liberation theology. A movement that sees the goal of the gospel as human freedom from spiritual, political, and economic oppression. May be applied by any oppressed group, e.g., Women's Liberation, Black Liberation, etc.

martyr. A witness to the faith who is put to death.

mendicant. Begging; a characteristic of early Franciscan and Dominican Orders in their desire to embrace a life of voluntary poverty.

Montanism. Following Montanus, a movement that had very strict ascetical standards, the expectation of the imminent return of Christ, and the practice of charismatic phenomena, especially prophecy.

mysticism. A type of spirituality arising from an intense experience of the presence of God, which may or may not include union with God. As commonly used, it may include any supernatural phenomena such as visions and voices, but Christian mystics warned against centering attention on these.

Neo-Platonism. A later form of Plato's teaching developed by Plotinus and others, with a more mystical and religious emphasis than Plato's original philosophy.

Nicea. The Council of Nicea in 325 was the first Ecumenical Council, called by Emperor Constantine to settle doctrinal disputes between divided Christians. Among other things, the council agreed to a statement that the Son was of the same Being as the Father. This later became the basis for the statement we know as the Nicene Creed, a fundamental development in the doctrine of the Trinity.

Oriental Orthodox. Churches in Asia and Africa that did not accept the definitions of Chalcedon and came to be separated from the Eastern Orthodox churches; for example the Ethiopian Church.

pantheism. The view that all things are God and God is all things. The distinction between Creator and creation is eliminated.

panentheism. The view that God is in all things and all things are in God.

paradox. A striking truth that is expressed in seemingly contradictory statements.

Pelagianism. Following Pelagius, a view that people are capable and responsible for working out their own salvation instead of needing to rely solely on God's grace for salvation. This view was opposed by Augustine and later by the Protestant churches.

Philokalia. "The love of beauty"; title of Eastern spiritual writings first collected by Basil in the fourth century and later by others in the eighteenth century.

Pietism. A renewal movement in seventeenth-century Lutheran and Reformed churches that emphasized Bible study, conversion, home prayer meetings, institutions to help the needy, friendship across denominational lines, and world mission. The movement later was seen as legalistic, separatist, and sentimental; the word is commonly used to refer to this latter type of spirituality.

Quietism. A movement in seventeenth-century Roman Catholocism that was condemned for its alleged indifference to all things, including personal salvation.

rosary. A set of beads with a small crucifix used as a devotional aid by Roman Catholics and others to pray the Hail Mary and Our Father prayers while meditating on the events of Mary's and Jesus' lives.

Trent. A council of the Roman Catholic Church that responded to the Protestant Reformation. It was held in Trent, northern Italy, from 1548 to 1563.

Vatican II. The Second Vatican Council, held in Rome at the Vatican from 1962 to 1965.

Western church. The church of the western Mediterranean, specifically the Roman Catholic Church, and later the Protestant churches that separated from it.

Notes

Chapter 1

1. John Ackerman, *Listening to God: Spiritual Formation in Congregations* (Bethesda, Md.: Alban Institute, 2001).

2. Henry Nouwen, "Foreword," in Gustavo Gutiérrez, *We Drink from Our Own Wells: The Spiritual Journey of a People* (Maryknoll, N.Y.: Orbis, 1984), xx, xxi.

3. Philip Sheldrake, *Spirituality and History: Questions of Interpretation and Method* (New York: Crossroad, 1992).

4. Bradley C. Hanson, ed., *Modern Christian Spirituality: Methodological and Historical Essays*, American Academy of Religion Studies in Religion, no. 62 (Atlanta: Scholars, 1990).

5. Gordon Wakefield, *Westminster Dictionary of Christian Spirituality* (Philadelphia: Westminster, 1983), v.

6. Wakefield, *Westminster Dictionary of Christian Spirituality*, 361–62.

7. Allan H. Sager, *Gospel-Centered Spirituality: An Introduction to Our Spiritual Journey* (Minneapolis: Augsburg, 1990), 36.

8. Cheslyn Jones, Geoffrey Wainwright, and Edward Yarnold, eds., *The Study of Spirituality* (New York: Oxford Univ. Press, 1986), 592–605.

9. Jaroslav Pelikan, *The Vindication of Tradition* (New Haven: Yale, 1984), 65.

10. C. S. Lewis, "Introduction," in *The Incarnation of the Word of God: Being the Treatise of St. Athanasius De Incarnatione Verbi Dei* (New York: Macmillan, 1947), 6–7.

11. Macrina Wiederkehr, O.S.B., *The Song of the Seed: A Monastic Way of Tending the Soul* (San Francisco: Harper, 1995), 20.

12. Chester P. Michael and Marie C. Norrisey, *Prayer and Temperament: Different Prayer Forms for Different Personality Types* (Charlottesville, Va.: Open Door, 1984).

Chapter 2

1. *Lutheran Book of Worship* (Minneapolis: Augsburg, 1978), hymn 551, Henry van Dyke.

2. Richard Foster, *Celebration of Discipline: The Path to Spiritual Growth* (San Francisco: Harper, 1978), 2.

3. Marjorie Thompson, *Soul Feast: An Invitation to the Christian Spiritual Life* (Louisville: Westminster John Knox, 1995).

Chapter 3

1. Julian of Norwich, *All Shall be Well*, trans. Sheila Upjohn (London: Darton, Longman, and Todd, 1992), 44 (Julian's chapter 27).

2. John Donne, *Poems of John Donne*, vol 1, ed. E. K. Chambers (London: Lawrence & Bullen, 1896), 211–12.

"Hymn to God, My God, In My Sickness"
Since I am coming to that Holy room,
    Where, with Thy choir of saints for evermore,
I shall be made Thy music; as I come
    I tune the instrument here at the door,
    And what I must do then, think here before.

3. Many of his parables deal with this subject. Spiritual writers often quote and sometimes misunderstand one of his sayings (reported only in Luke 17:21): "The kingdom of God is within [among] you." Forgetting all other teachings about the kingdom of God, such writers dismiss all of Christian ethics, worship, and theology to claim that Jesus taught a totally inward spirituality. Although the term *entos* in Greek can be translated either as "within" or as "among," my point is that this particular verse is but one statement about that kingdom and that it must be understood in the context of all the other teachings about this subject (for example, Matthew 13, especially verses 47-50). These other teachings and parables make clear that the kingdom is an eschatological reality—that is, that it refers to the consummation of all things while having a reference to the present. Thus the Rule of God is both the ultimate destiny of the world and a present reality in Christ. It has both inward and outward aspects, just as spirituality itself does.

4. Barbara Rossing, *The Rapture Exposed: The Message of Hope in the Book of Revelation* (Boulder, Colo.: Westview, 2004).

5. Henri J. M. Nouwen, *The Return of the Prodigal Son: A Meditation on Fathers, Brothers, and Sons* (New York: Doubleday, 1992).

6. Macrina Wiederkehr, O.S.B., *The Song of the Seed: A Monastic Way of Tending the Soul* (San Francisco: Harper, 1995), 10–20.

Chapter 4

1. James Hamilton Charlesworth, ed., *The Old Testament Pseudepigrapha*, vol. 2 (Garden City, N.Y.: Doubleday, 1985), 726–27.

2. Ibid., 749.

3. Tertullian, *Disciplinary, Moral and Ascetical Works* (New York: Fathers of the Church, 1959), 103.

4. Sebastian Brock, "Introduction," in Saint Ephrem, *Hymns on Paradise* (Crestwood, N.Y.: St. Vladimir's Seminary Press, 1990), 25–32.

5. Ibid., 40.

6. Ibid., 48.

7. Ibid., 73 (quotation from Hymns on Virginity XLVIII 17–18).

8. See, for example, Benedicta Ward, trans., *The Desert Christian: Sayings of the Desert Fathers: The Alphabetical Collection* (New York: Macmillan, 1980); or Thomas Merton, *The Wisdom of the Desert: Sayings from the Desert Fathers of the Fourth Century* (Norfolk, Conn.: New Directions, 1960). Also see Helen Waddell, *The Desert Fathers* (New York: Sheed and Ward, 1942).

9. Ward, trans., *The Desert Christian*, 72.

10. Ibid., 193.

11. ibid., 196.

12. Gregory of Nyssa, "Life of St. Macrina," in *Ascetical Works*, Fathers of the Church, vol. 58 (Washington, D.C.: Catholic Univ. of America Press, 1966), 163–91.

13. Kallistos Ware, "Ways of Prayer and Contemplation: I. Eastern," in Bernard McGinn, John Meyendorff, and Jean Leclercq, eds. *Christian Spirituality: Origins to the Twelfth Century* (New York: Crossroad, 1987), 398.

14. Saint Patrick, *The Works of St. Patrick*, trans. Ludwig Bieler (Westminster, Md.: Newman, 1953), 70–71.

15. Edward C. Sellner, *Mentoring: The Ministry of Spiritual Kinship* (Notre Dame, Ind.: Ave Maria Press, 1990), 61–75.

16. Whitley Stokes, ed., *The Martyrology of Oengus the Culdee* (London: Henry Bradshaw Society, 1905), 65; quoted in Edward C. Sellner, *Stories of the Celtic Soul Friendship: Their Meaning for Today* (New York: Paulist, 2004).

17. Bernard McGinn, *The Foundations of Mysticism*, vol. 1, *The Presence of God: A History of Western Christian Mysticism* (New York: Crossroad, 1991), 265–343.

18. Ibid., xv–xvii.

19. Pseudo-Dionysius, "The Divine Names," in *Pseudo-Dionysius: The Complete Works* (New York: Paulist, 1987), 49–50.

20. Pseudo-Dionysius, "The Mystical Theology," in *Pseudo-Dionysius: The Complete Works* (New York: Paulist, 1987), 135.

21. Macrina Wiederkehr, O.S.B., *The Song of the Seed: A Monastic Way of Tending the Soul* (San Francisco: Harper, 1995), xiii–xiv.

Chapter 5

1. Kallistos Ware, "The Origins of the Jesus Prayer: Diadochus, Gaza, Sinai," in *The Study of Spirituality*, ed. Cheslyn Jones, Geoffrey Wainwright, and Edward Yarnold (New York: Oxford Univ. Press, 1986), 176.

2. Ware, "The Origins of the Jesus Prayer," 184.

3. *Nicene and Post Nicene Fathers*, vol. 14 (Grand Rapids: Eerdmans, 1959), 549.

4. Athanasius, "On the Incarnation of the Word," in *The Christology of the Later Fathers*, ed. E. R. Hardy (Philadelphia: Westminster, 1954), 55–110.

5. Anselm, *Proslogion*, in *The Prayers and Meditations of Saint Anselm*, tr. Benedicta Ward (New York: Penguin, 1973), chap. 1, 244.

6. Ibid., 51

7. Anselm, "Meditation on Human Redemption," in *The Prayers and Meditations of Saint Anselm*, tr. Benedicta Ward (New York: Penguin, 1973), 237.

8. Thomas Merton, *The Last of the Fathers: Saint Bernard of Clairvaux and the Encyclical Letter, Doctor Mellifluus* (New York: Harcourt, Brace, 1954), 93.

9. Bernard of Clairvaux, *On Loving God*, chaps. 8–11.

10. Bernard of Clairvaux, *Sermons on the Song of Songs*, Sermon 69 (London: SCM Press, 1959), 117–18.

11. Ingrid H. Shafer, *Eros and the Womanliness of God: Andrew Greeley's Romances of Renewal* (Chicago: Loyola Univ. Press, 1986).

12. Beverly Roberts Gaventa and Cynthia L. Rigby, eds., *Blessed One: Protestant Perspectives on Mary* (Louisville: Westminster John Knox, 2002); Kathleen Norris, *Meditations on Mary: With Essays by Kathleen Norris and Excerpts from the King James Version of the Bible* (New York: Viking Studio, 1999).

13. Pope John Paul II, "Rosarium Viginis Mariae," http://www.vatican.va/holy_father/john_paul_ii/apost_letters/documents/hf_jp-ii_apl_20021016_rosarium-virginis-mariae_en.html.

14. Note that the misleading film *Stigmata* totally reverses the meaning, making stigmata a dreadful curse instead of a gift of identification with the crucified Jesus.

15. Thomas à Kempis, *The Imitation of Christ* (Baltimore: Penguin Books, 1975), 3:37.

16. Matthew Fox, O.P., *Breakthrough: Meister Eckhart's Creation Spirituality in New Translation* (Garden City, N.Y.: Image Books, 1980), 39.

17. Hildegard of Bingen, *Scivias*, Classics of Western Spirituality Series (New York: Paulist, 1990).

18. Jan van Ruysbroeck, *Spiritual Espousals* 1:36 (London: Faber and Faber, 1952), 82.

19. Julian of Norwich, *Showings* (New York: Paulist, 1978), Long Text, 52–63.

20. Ibid., 342.

Chapter 6

1. *The Book of Concord:The Confessions of the Evangelical Lutheran Church*, ed. Robert Kolb and Timothy J. Wengert (Minneapolis: Fortress Press, 2000), 355-56.

2. Bengt R. Hoffman, *Luther and the Mystics: A Re-examination of Luther's Spiritual Experience and His Relation to the Mystics* (Minneapolis: Augsburg, 1976); Hoffman, *Theology of the Heart: The Role of Mysticism in the Theology of Martin Luther*, ed. Pearl Willemssen Hoffman (Minneapolis: Kirk House, 1998).

3. Martin Luther, "The Freedom of a Christian," in *Martin Luther's Basic Theological Writings*, ed. Timothy F. Lull (Minneapolis: Fortress, 1989), 596.

4. Walter Trobisch, "Martin Luther's Quiet Time," in *Complete Works of Walter Trobisch* (Downers Grove, Ill.: InterVarsity, 1987), 703–14.

5. Ibid., 444–45.

6. Sermon on Job, OC 34, col. 316; Commentary on Isaiah 42:14, OC 36, col. 69.

7. Paul V. Marshall, "The Anglican Tradition," in *Protestant Spiritual Traditions*, ed. Frank C. Senn (New York: Paulist, 1986), 133.

8. *The Book of Common Prayer: And Administration of the Sacraments and Other Rites and Ceremonies of the Church* (New York: Church Hymnal Corp., 1979), 323.

9. Ibid., 69.

10. *The Collected Works of St. John of the Cross*, trans. Kieran Kavanaugh and Otilio Rodriguez (Washington, D.C.: ICS Publications, Institute of Carmelite Studies, 1979), 711–12.

11. John Ackerman, *Listening to God: Spiritual Formation in Congregations* (Bethesda, Md.: Alban Institute, 2001), "handout 2" (no page number).

Chapter 7

1. Darrell Jodock, *The Church's Bible: Its Contemporary Authority* (Minneapolis: Fortress, 1989), 16–19.

2. Jaroslav Pelikan, *Bach among the Theologians* (Philadelphia: Fortress, 1986), 57–58.

3. Ibid., 140.

4. Ibid., 139.

5. Wilbert R. Shenk, *Henry Venn—Missionary Statesman* (Maryknoll, N.Y.: Orbis, 1983).

6. John Wesley, *The Journals of John Wesley: A Selection*, ed. Elisabeth Jay (New York: Oxford Univ. Press, 1987), 34–35.

7. *Lutheran Book of Worship* (Minneapolis: Augsburg, 1978), Hymns 559, 60, 171, 252, 315.

8. Jonathan Edwards, *Religious Affections*, ed. John E. Smith (New Haven: Yale Univ. Press, 1959), 2.

9. Edwards, *Religious Affections*, 197, 240, 253, 266, 291, 311, 340, 344, 357, 365, 376, 383.

10. de Sales, Saint Francis, *Francis de Sales, Jane de Chantal: Letters of Spiritual Direction*, trans. Peronne Marie Thibert (New York: Paulist, 1988).

11. Wendy M. Wright, *Sacred Heart: Gateway to God* (Maryknoll, N.Y.: Orbis, 2001).

12. Thomas Merton, "Reflections on the Character and Genius of Fenelon," in François Fenelon, *Letters of Love and Counsel* (New York: Harcourt, Brace and World, 1964), 9–30.

13. François Fenelon, *Letters of Love and Counsel* (New York: Harcourt, Brace and World, 1964), 216–18.

14. Ibid., 289.

15. Anonymous, *The Way of a Pilgrim: and the Pilgrim Continues His Way*, trans. R. M. French (New York: Harper, 1954), 6–9.

16. *St. Thérèse of Lisieux: Essential Writings*, sel. Mary Frohlich (Maryknoll, N.Y.: Orbis, 2003), 28–30.

17. Ibid., 34–36.

18. Ibid., 152.

19. Gustavo Gutiérrez, *Las Casas: In Search of the Poor of Jesus Christ* (Maryknoll, N.Y.: Orbis, 1993).

20. Lamin Sanneh, *Translating the Message: The Missionary Impact on Culture* (Maryknoll, N.Y.: Orbis, 1989).

21. *Lutheran Book of Worship*, hymn 134.

Chapter 8

1. Oswald Chambers, "The Relinquished Life," in *My Utmost for His Highest* (New York: Dodd, Mead, 1935; Oswald Chambers Publication Association, 1963).

2. Eugene Peterson, *Subversive Spirituality* (Grand Rapids: Eerdmans, 1997 [1994]), 15.

3. Eugene Peterson, *Take and Read: Spiritual Reading, An Annotated List* (Grand Rapids: Eerdmans, 1996), 109.

4. Eugene H. Peterson, *The Message: The Bible in Contemporary Language* (Colorado Springs: Navpress, 2002), 2054.

5. Karl Rahner, *The Content of Faith: The Best of Karl Rahner's Theological*

Writings (New York: Crossroad, 1992); Harvey D. Egan, *What Are They Saying about Mysticism?* (New York: Paulist, 1982), 98.

6. Rahner, *The Content of Faith*, 149

7. Ibid., 513.

8. Humphery Carpenter. *The Inklings: C. S. Lewis, J. R. R. Tolkien, Charles Williams, and their Friends* (Boston: Houghton Mifflin, 1979).

9. Ellen M. Leonard, *Creative Tension: The Spiritual Legacy of Friedrich von Hügel* (Scranton, Pa.: Univ. of Scranton Press, 1997).

10. Evelyn Underhill, *The Ways of the Spirit*, ed. Grace Adolphson Brame (New York: Crossroad, 1994).

11. Thomas Merton, *Conjectures of a Guilty Bystander* (Garden City, N.Y.: Doubleday, 1966), 140–41.

12. Thomas Merton, *Life and Holiness* (Garden City, N.Y.: Doubleday Image, 1964 [1963]), 9–10.

13. John Main, *Moment of Christ: The Path of Meditation* (London: Darton, Longman, and Todd, 1984).

14. Lauren Artress, *Walking a Sacred Path: Rediscovering the Labyrinth as a Spiritual Tool* (New York: Riverhead, 1995).

15. Richard J. Foster, *Celebration of Discipline: The Path to Spiritual Growth* (San Francisco: Harper, 1978; rev. ed., 1988).

16. Ibid., 8.

17. Morton Kelsey, *The Other Side of Silence: Meditation for the Twenty-first Century*, rev. ed. (New York: Paulist, 1997), 13–14.

18. Dennis C. Morreim, *Changed Lives: The Story of Alcoholics Anonymous* (Minneapolis: Augsburg, 1992).

19. Ernest Kurtz, *Not-God: A History of Alcoholics Anonymous* (Center City, Minn.: Hazeldon, 1979).

20. *Alcoholics Anonymous*, 3rd ed. (New York: A. A. World Services), 59–60.

21. Dennis C. Morreim, *The Road to Recovery: Bridges between the Bible and the Twelve Steps* (Minneapolis: Augsburg, 1990).

22. Reinhold Niebuhr, "Written for a Service in the Congregational Church of Heath, Massachusetts," in John Bartlett, *Familiar Quotations*, 15th ed. (Boston: Little, Brown, 1980), 823.

23. Gerald May, *Addiction and Grace* (San Francisco: Harper, 1988).

24. Robert H. Schuller, *Self-Esteem: The New Reformation* (Waco, Tex.: Word, 1982), 19.

25. Ibid., 21.

26. Kenneth Leech, *Experiencing God: Theology as Spirituality* (San Francisco: Harper, 1989 [1985]), 7.

27. Ibid., 23–24.

28. Henri Fesquet, ed., *Wit and Wisdom of Good Pope John*, trans. Salvator Attanasio (New York: P. J. Kenedy, 1964), 110.

29. Ibid., 157.

30. Ibid., 161–62.

31. Kathleen Norris, *Dakota: A Spiritual Geography* (Boston: Houghton Mifflin, 1993).

32. Kathleen Norris, *Amazing Grace: A Vocabulary of Faith* (New York: Riverhead, 1998), 239.

33. Ibid., 57.

34. Jaroslav Pelikan, *Mary through the Centuries: Her Place in the History of Culture* (New Haven: Yale Univ. Press, 1996).

35. Jeanette Rodriguez, "Contemporary Encounters with Guadalupe," *Journal of Hispanic/Latino Theology* 5, no. 1 (August 1997): 48–60.

36. John Paul II, *Crossing the Threshold of Hope*, ed. Vittorio Messori (New York: Knopf, 1994), 212–13 (emphasis added).

37. Dietrich Bonhoeffer, *Letters and Papers from Prison* (New York: Collier, 1972), 369–70.

38. Daniel Berrigan, foreword to *The Long Loneliness: An Autobiography* by Dorothy Day (San Francisco: Harper, 1981 [1952]), xxii.

39. Dorothy Day, *The Long Loneliness: An Autobiography* (San Francisco: Harper, 1981 [1952]), 285–86.

40. Mother Teresa, *A Simple Path*, comp. Lucinda Vardey (New York: Ballentine, 1995); quoted in Eileen Egan, *Such a Vision of the Street: Mother Teresa— The Spirit and the Work* (Garden City, N.Y.: Doubleday, 1985), 357.

41. Mother Teresa, *A Simple Path*, 25.

42. Ibid., 79.

43. Jean Vanier, *Community and Growth*, rev. ed. (New York: Paulist, 1989 [1979]), 11.

44. Martin Luther King Jr., *Strength to Love* (Philadelphia: Fortress, 1981 [1963]), 112–14.

45. Joan Chittister, *Gospel Days: Reflections for Every Day of the Year* (Maryknoll, N.Y.: Orbis, 1999), February 20.

46. Joan Chittister, *Heart of Flesh: A Feminist Spirituality for Women and Men* (Grand Rapids: Eerdmans, 1998), 3–4.

47. Ibid., 5.

48. Joan Chittister, *Illuminated Life: Monastic Wisdom for Seekers of Light* (Maryknoll, N.Y.: Orbis, 2000), 13–14.

49. Rosemary Radford Ruether, *Sexism and God-Talk: Toward a Feminist Theology* (Boston: Beacon, 1983), 20.

50. Sam Keen, *Fire in the Belly: On Being a Man* (New York: Bantam, 1991), 195–96.

51. Brian Wren, *What Language Shall I Borrow? God-Talk in Worship: A Male Response to Feminist Theology* (New York: Crossroad, 1989).

52. David C. James, *What Are They Saying about Masculine Spirituality?* (New York: Paulist, 1996), 51–52.

53. John Paul II, *Crossing the Threshold of Hope*, 89–90 (emphasis added).

54. Bede Griffiths, *A Human Search: Bede Griffiths Reflects on His Life—An Oral History*, ed. John Swindells (Liguori, Mo.: Triumph Books, 1997), 22.

55. Ibid., 30.

56. Bede Griffiths, *The Golden String* (New York: P. J. Kenedy, 1954).

57. Ibid., 84–85.

58. Ibid., 558.

59. Anthony de Mello, S.J. *The Prayer of the Frog: A Book of Story Meditations*, vol. 1 (Anand, India: Gujarat Shitya Prakash, 1988), xviii.

60. Carlos G. Valles, S.J., *Unencumbered by Baggage: Father Anthony de Mello—A Prophet for Our Times* (Anand, India: Gujarat Sahitya Prakash, 1987), 27.

61. Ibid., 43.

62. Pierre Teilhard de Chardin, *Hymn of the Universe* (London: Collins Fontana Books, 1970), 64ff.

63. Pierre Teilhard de Chardin, *The Divine Milieu: An Essay for the Interior Life* (New York: Harper and Row, 1960), 15.

64. Matthew Fox, *Confessions: The Making of a Post-Denominational Priest* (San Francisco: Harper, 1996.)

65. Matthew Fox, *On Becoming A Musical Mystical Bear: Spirituality American Style* (New York: Paulist, 1976 [1972]), xv.

66. Rosemary Radford Ruether, *Gaia and God: An Ecofeminist Theology of Earth Healing* (San Francisco: Harper, 1992), 3.

67. Ibid., 4.

68. Charles Cummings, *Eco-Spirituality: Toward a Reverent Life* (New York: Paulist, 1991).

69. *Lutheran Book of Worship* (Minneapolis: Augsburg, 1978), 67–68.

Chapter 9

1. William A. Dyrness, *Learning about Theology from the Third World* (Grand Rapids: Zondervan, 1990).

2. David B. Barrett et al., eds., *World Christian Encyclopedia: A Comparative Survey of Churches and Religions in the Modern World*, 2nd ed. (New York: Oxford Univ. Press, 2001), 1:4.

3. Ibid., 1:3, 12.

4. Ibid., 1:3, 12.

5. Ibid., 1:782.

6. Diana L. Eck, *A New Religious America: How a "Christian Country" Has Become the World's Most Religiously Diverse Nation* (San Francisco: HarperSanFrancisco, 2001); Amanda Porterfield, *The Transformation of American Religion: The Story of a Late-Twentieth-Century Awakening* (New York: Oxford Univ. Press, 2001).

7. www.research.att.com/~jrex/faves/quotes/society.html.

8. Gustavo Gutiérrez, *We Drink from Our Own Wells* (Maryknoll, N.Y.: Orbis, 1984).

9. Jon Sobrino, *Spirituality of Liberation: Toward Political Holiness* (Maryknoll, N.Y.: Orbis, 1988).

10. Ernesto Cardenal, *The Gospel in Solentiname*, trans. Donald D. Walsh (Maryknoll, N.Y.: Orbis, 1976).

11. Cardenal, *The Gospel in Solentiname*, 46–49.

12. Barrett, et al., eds., *World Christian Encyclopedia*, 1:4.

13. Harvey Cox, *Fire from Heaven: The Rise of Pentecostal Spirituality and the Reshaping of Religion in the Twenty-first Century* (Reading, Mass.: Addison-Wesley, 1995), 161–64.

14. Hollenweger, Walter J., *Pentecost between Black and White: Five Case Studies on Pentecost and Politics* (Belfast: Christian Journals, 1974).

15. Bukole Wa Ilunga, *Paths of Liberation: A Third World Spirituality* (Maryknoll, N.Y.: Orbis, 1985), 36.

16. Charles Villa-Vicentio, *Trapped in Apartheid* (Grand Rapids: Eerdmans, 1989).

17. John de Gruchy, ed., *Cry Justice! Payers, Meditations and Readings from South Africa* (Maryknoll, N.Y.: Orbis, 1986).

18. de Gruchy, *Cry Justice!* 64–66.

19. Desmond Mpilo Tutu, *No Future without Forgiveness* (New York: Doubleday, 2000).

20. Gordon Mackay Haliburton, *The Prophet Harris: A Study of an African Prophet and His Mass-movement in the Ivory Coast and the Gold Coast 1913–1915* (New York: Oxford Univ. Press, 1973).

21. David B. Barrett, *Schism and Renewal in Africa: An Analysis of Six Thousand Contemporary Religious Movements* (Nairobi: Oxford Univ. Press, 1968).

22. Munib Younan, *Witnessing for Peace: In Jerusalem and the World* (Minneapolis: Fortress, 2003).

23. Kosuke Koyama, *Waterbuffalo Theology* (Maryknoll, N.Y.: Orbis, 1974).

24. Kosuke Koyama, *Three Mile an Hour God* (Maryknoll, N.Y.: Orbis, 1979).

25. Kazoh Kitamori, *Theology of the Pain of God* (Richmond, Va.: John Knox, 1958), 79.

26. Brett R. Dewey, "Suffering the Patient Victory of God: Shusaku Endo and the Lessons of a Japanese Catholic," *Quodlibet Journal* 6, no. 1 (January–March 2004), http://www.Quodlibet.net.

27. Toyohiko Kagawa, *Song of the Slums* (London: SCM Press, 1935), 21; quoted in Jesse M. Trout, *Kagawa, Japanese Prophet* (New York: Association Press, 1959), 25.

28. Toyohiko Kagawa, *Brotherhood Economics* (London: SCM Press, 1937); quoted in Jesse M. Trout, *Kagawa, Japanese Prophet* (New York: Association Press, 1959), 63.

29. Toyohiko Kagawa, *Love, the Law of Life* (London: SCM Press, 1930); quoted in Jesse M. Trout, *Kagawa, Japanese Prophet* (New York: Association Press, 1959), 28.

30. G. Thompson Brown, *Christianity in the People's Republic of China* (Atlanta: John Knox, 1983), 200.

31. Vengal Chakkarai, "The Historical Jesus and the Christ of Experience," in *Readings in Indian Christian Theology*, vol. 1, ed. R. S. Sugirtharajah and Cecil Hargreaves (London: SPCK, 1993), 82.

32. S. J. Samartha, "A Hindu Christian Funeral," in *Readings in Indian Christian Theology*, vol. 1, ed. R. S. Sugirtharajah and Cecil Hargreaves (London: SPCK, 1993), 160.

Chapter 10

1. *Lutheran Book of Worship*, hymn 390.

Index of Names

Index of Subjects